Praise for *The Story of God, the Story of Us*

"Join me in a journey in which faith and reason are made delectable through story. It is a book to be read and read, alone and with others who thirst for the truth in love."

REVEREND DR. JOHN SMITH, president, God's Squad CMC, and founder, Concern Australia

"'Why another book about the Bible?' We don't need 'just another book' . . . but we need this one. Sean enables us to enter the 'Grand Story' by using 'story' and dialogue as effective communication. His style and language make his message easily accessible, enabling us to experience the great movements of the Story, and that's a redemptive dynamic. An added dimension for me is that I know the author, and he lives the Story. *The Story of God, the Story of Us* makes the Story real for the reader."

MAXIE DUNNAM, chancellor, Asbury Theological Seminary

"I love it when someone tells a story that we can get lost in, a story that sparks our imagination and connects the dots. Sean Gladding is a great storyteller who draws us into a story of which we have heard bits and pieces. As the story unfolds we realize it is our story—yours and mine—and we are a part of something much bigger than ourselves. And the story is not over, and it's not just a story after all . . ."

STEVEN G. W. MOORE, executive director, The M. J. Murdock Charitable Trust

"In *The Story of God, the Story of Us* Sean Gladding takes the reader on an imaginative and fresh stroll through the Scriptures. Reeling in distant theological and historical abstractions, Sean makes the whole of the Bible intimate and readable. Parlanced in an accessible, down-to-earth renarration of the Scriptures, Sean fuses biblical tradition with captivating story, compelling dialogue and nuanced reflection."

CHRISTOPHER L. HEUERTZ, international director, Word Made Flesh, author of *Simple Spirituality* and coauthor of *Friendship at the Margins*

"Sean invites us to find ourselves in Scripture. He points us back to the Story. It's not a new story; in fact, it is as old as humanity itself. But it is still very much our story, showing us what we already know and feel: that we, like the Israelites, and like all of creation, are in exile, longing for redemption, in search of the promised land. Sean invites us to see that this Story, God's Story, is our story."

TRAVIS REED, founder, The Work of the People (www.theworkofthepeople.com)

"It is only the person who is long in the study of the Scriptures, and in the contemplation of God through them, who may be granted the capacity in the Spirit to experience the Scriptures freshly, with more of the Light shining in the words and the spaces between them. And if that person is Sean Gladding, then he might write in such a way that a reader is startled at how much he or she missed when studying the same biblical passages. In the classic spiritual tradition of the 'application of the senses' way of reading the Scriptures, Gladding shows us how freshly to see, to hear, to taste and to touch each biblical scene."

FR. RICK GANZ, S.J., Marylhurst University, Oregon

Sean Gladding

The Story of God, the Story of us

GETTING LOST AND FOUND IN THE BIBLE

To the Sprys,
may you ever find your
home in the Story~
tell it well!

IVP Books

An imprint of InterVarsity Press
Downers Grove, Illinois

Sean Gladding.

Summit 2013

Boone, NC

InterVarsity Press
P.O. Box 1400, Downers Grove, IL 60515-1426
World Wide Web: www.ivpress.com
E-mail: email@ivpress.com

*InterVarsity Press® is the book-publishing division of InterVarsity Christian Fellowship/USA®, a
movement of students and faculty active on campus at hundreds of universities, colleges and
schools of nursing in the United States of America, and a member movement of the International
Fellowship of Evangelical Students. For information about local and regional activities, write
Public Relations Dept., InterVarsity Christian Fellowship/USA, 6400 Schroeder Rd., P.O. Box
7895, Madison, WI 53707-7895, or visit the IVCF website at <www.intervarsity.org>.*

Design: Cindy Kiple
Images: night sky with stars: Vladimir Piskunov/iStockphoto
chairs in an open field: Peter Baker/Getty Images

ISBN 978-0-8308-3632-1

Printed in the United States of America ∞

Library of Congress Cataloging-in-Publication Data

Gladding, Sean, 1967-
The story of God, the story of us / Sean Gladding.
    p. cm.
Includes bibliographical references.
ISBN 978-0-8308-3632-1 (pbk.: alk. paper)
1. Bible—Criticism, interpretation, etc. I. Title.
BS511.3.G57 2010
220.6—dc22

    2010014328

| P | 18 | 17 | 16 | 15 | 14 | 13 | 12 | 11 | 10 | 9 | 8 | 7 | 6 | 5 | 4 |
| Y | 25 | 24 | 23 | 22 | 21 | 20 | 19 | 18 | 17 | 16 | 15 | 14 | 13 | 12 | 11 |

Dedicated to the two communities within which
The Story of God, the Story of Us took shape:

Mercy Street
at Chapelwood U.M.C.
Houston, Texas

Communality
Lexington, Kentucky

And to Mary Fisher, mentor and friend
who teaches and lives the Story

contents

Preface

With the sheer volume of books about the Bible, why write another one? And one with the admittedly audacious title *The Story of God, the Story of Us?* The simplest answer is that it was a task my best friend gave me in 2000, when I was interning with him in the community he pastored. "I want you to write and teach a Bible study for people who have never read the Bible—something that gives the 'big picture.'"

That internship lasted eight weeks, and so of necessity the study was eight weeks long. Given that short length of time, the focus of the study became the "big story" of Scripture—a concept I had recently been discussing with a professor in graduate school.

For many years I had read and studied the Bible, usually in small chunks here and there (mostly in the New Testament). Seated in church buildings, I had heard and believed theological abstractions about God that made sense in isolation from each other, but rarely was time given to try to tie them together. Perhaps the most blatant example of this was the claim that "God is unchanging" alongside the claim that "the God of the Old Testament is a god of law, whereas the God of the New Testament is a god of grace" (or, as my friend Matt puts it, "The God of the New Testament obviously went through an anger-management program").

We tend to read all sixty-six books of our Bible the same way, with little if any respect for genre or the individual voices of the various writers. We often fail to recognize the other voices that shape our understanding of Scripture—our families, our churches and our culture. We are usually blind to the prejudices we bring with us to the Bible, and the assumptions we make as we read. If you're like me, the temptation is to focus on the texts that seem to support what I already think and believe, and skip over any that challenge my beliefs or how I am living my life.

But what if there is something, other than the binding, that holds these sixty-six individual books together? What if there is a "big story," with a beginning and a middle, and movement toward an end? If there is an overarching "Story of God," then perhaps that could (and maybe should) be the starting point for any study of Scripture, and may help us avoid the temptations and pitfalls we so readily fall into in our reading of Scripture.

The first *Story of God* was written week-to-week and delivered in lecture style. Time spent over coffee after the study revealed that people with no prior experience of reading Scripture, as well as people with considerable experience of Bible study, found much to discuss together. Shortly after that internship I met Rebecca, now my wife, and some time after that we were invited to lead our downtown missional community through the Story. We brainstormed ways to be more creative with the study, which led to the idea of rewriting it as a narrative: instead of lecturing on the Story, simply tell it!

We needed to find a narrative voice, and we settled on hearing the story of the Hebrew Scriptures through those sitting in exile in Babylon in the sixth century B.C.E. We imagined them asking questions about life and God similar to those that many of us ask today. Each week we would light our "fire" (candles in the center of the room) and sit under the "stars" (Christmas lights strung across the ceiling) to hear the Story much like our ancestors did in the past and many of our brothers and sisters around the world still do today.

We have told the Story many times since then, and each time we

learn new ways to tell, hear and interact with it. We expanded it to
twelve weeks to allow us a little more time in the history of Israel up
to the time of Christ. In the original form we had not included the last
book of the Bible (the Revelation), but over time we realized that people have a lot of questions about that most intriguing of books. So we
added a final chapter to include the story we think it is telling.

Over the years we have made *The Story of God* freely available to
anyone who wanted to use it, emailing it as a Word document to whoever asked. The Story has been told in homes, churches, coffee shops,
pubs, laundromats, college campuses and, most recently, on the Appalachian trail. It has been told on five continents. We have loved
hearing people's experiences of telling the Story with others. We have
often been asked, "Is it ever going to be a book?" I'm glad to finally be
able to say yes.

So—along with Rebecca, who has partnered with me in preparing
and telling the Story for almost a decade—I offer this book to those
who wish to explore the possibility that there is a Story contained
within all the stories, poetry, prophecy and letters that the Bible com-
prises. I do not claim that this is *the* metanarrative of Scripture, only
that this is our understanding of the "grand story" thus far. No doubt
like many of the friends we have made as we have walked through the
Story together, you will find places where you disagree with the telling. Hopefully, like many of our friends, you will also find places that
surprise you, that delight you and, most importantly, that leave you
wanting to read the Scriptures for yourself and with others.

As the Story raises questions for you (as it continues to do for us), I
hope you will allow yourself to sit with the tension for a while before
trying to find answers. We have found that sometimes we have to sit
in the mystery for quite some time before things begin to come together. And sometimes the things that previously came together get
unraveled, and we're back with the mystery again.

I also hope you find some other folk with whom to read it—better
still, with whom to read it aloud. For the vast majority of people
through the ages, Scripture has been something to hear together

rather than to read alone. Reading the Story aloud, with others, helps us overcome the temptation to find in the Bible what we are already looking for, rather than simply following where the Story leads. It also curbs our tendency to interpret it in ways that allow us to continue living the way we currently are, rather than being open to the voice inviting us to be conformed to the likeness of the One whose Story this is.

In some ways Rebecca and I have hesitated to publish *The Story of God, the Story of Us* out of concern that people will miss this valuable experience. However, the book is written in such a way that it can be read either by yourself or in a group, either silently or out loud. Our hope is that you might gather with some other folk—preferably over a meal—assign the various characters (including the narrator's voice) to individuals, maybe light a candle and then read one chapter at a time. Please note: reading *The Story of God, the Story of Us* aloud takes about three times as long as simply reading it—which in and of itself might be a good thing. Footnotes in the text are explanatory and may be read or omitted—whichever best serves the gathered group.

Whether you read the book alone or together, there are two sections at the end of the book I encourage you to make use of. The suggested Scriptures will prepare you to hear the story of each chapter. Please also take time to read the bibliography; I am standing on the shoulders of many others in this telling of the Story, and I hope you will take time to read their books.

In this telling of the Story, I have chosen to use the New American Standard Bible (NASB) translation of the Hebrew Scriptures, not because it is the best translation available but because it is the one I happen to like best. Similarly, I have chosen to use *The Message* for the New Testament as I've really enjoyed hearing the Story in contemporary language. Sometimes we have modified these texts for the purposes of storytelling—for example, we use some Hebrew words instead of the English translation, as we find this helps us hear in new ways what for some of us are familiar stories. The narrative voice for the Old Testament is that of one of the elders of the people of God sitting in exile in Babylon in the sixth century B.C.E. A woman who has been witness to the events unfolding throughout the first century C.E. tells the Story of the New Testament, and her student takes up the Story in the chapter on the Revelation.

Over the last ten years, whenever I read something that deepened my understanding of the Story or expressed an insight in a helpful manner, I grafted it into this narrative. In preparing for publication I have tried to identify where I have done that and give credit to the author. It is quite possible that I have missed a sentence or thought here and there; I would be delighted to correct such oversights in any future editions.

There are several excellent books that offer an overview of the Bible, but thus far we have not been able to find any that tell the "big story" in story form. This is the contribution I hope *The Story of God, the Story of Us* makes to the wealth of other resources available. As you read it alone or with others, our prayer is that you will be drawn into the narrative, and that your life will be shaped by the Story in such a way that you find yourself caught up in the mystery and the wonder that is the life of God's mission in and to our broken world.

Sean (and Rebecca) Gladding

Sleeve Notes

As a teenager, I spent countless hours listening to music in my bedroom. I miss the ritual of choosing a record, carefully removing the vinyl disc from its sleeve, placing it on the turntable and then lowering the needle onto the groove.

An important part of the ritual with any new LP ("long-playing" album) was reading the notes the band included—the producer, the engineers, the road crew and the acknowledgments. Who had influenced them? Who had believed in them? Who were they grateful to? I love sleeve notes.

These are mine.

Mum and Dad
For loving and caring for those on the margins your whole lives—for living the Story long before you knew it, and for teaching the Gladding boys to do the same.

John Hughes
For childhood friendship and for saying thirty years ago, "There's a reason Revelation is at the end, Sean."

Peter Johns
For faithfully wrestling with the Story and helping me do the same.

Roy Murton and Ray Hughes
For teaching me to love the Scriptures.

Mark Heybourne
For copiloting adolescence with me, for the music, and for shades of gray where I saw only black and white.

Greenbelt Festival
For the music, for John Smith and Tony Campolo, and for introducing me to the Story I had not yet heard.

Capernwray Bible School
For one of the best years of my life. And for putting me in a room with Matt Russell.

C.M.A. Norfolk—Jingles, Lin, Joy, Bugs, Janet, Bill . . .
For giving me a tribe when I needed one.

Joy McCall
For love.

Texas Tech Wesley Foundation
For grace.

Dr. Carl Andersen
For letting me into your class and into your family's heart.

Dr. Jim Jackson
For seeing more in me than I ever could, for trusting me and for giving me a job—twice.

Stan and Susan Mathes
For adopting me, feeding me and keeping my Ironhead on the road.

Mary Fisher
For the metanarrative and for keeping your office door open.

Joel B. Green
For teaching me to read from left to right, and for a close reading of the text.

Geoff Maddock, Bill Kenney and Greg Leffel
For being great mates.

Communality
For giving me a place to work out the Story in community, and for twelve years of fidelity in mission.

Mercy Street
For seven beautiful years of messy spirituality.

U2, Martyn Joseph and Bruce Cockburn
For the soundtrack.

Dave Zimmerman
For all the encouragement over the last five years, and for being a gracious editor.

Matt Russell
For being my brother from another mother for a quarter-century.

Rebecca
For choosing me. For Maggie and Seth. And for nine years of telling and seeking to live out the Story together.

The One whose Story this is
For inviting me to find a place in your Story.

1

creation

In which we hear the beginning of the Story and

explore questions of identity and vocation . . .

The old man walks slowly down to the river, as he does every Sabbath at about this time. The week's work is done, and his people are gathering around the fire to break bread together, and to talk. For once the mood is light, and the old man leans back against a tree and closes his eyes. For a moment—just a moment—it is almost possible to imagine he is leaning not against this willow tree but against an olive tree, one of the trees in his beloved garden, on the land which his family farmed for centuries. His mind drifts to another time and another place, and a smile creeps across his face . . .

But then someone plucks a discordant note on a harp, and the mood is immediately broken. Rarely, but rarely do his people sing anymore, and everyone turns to see who has lifted the harp. It is a young man, the protégé of one of the renowned musicians among his people. The old man cannot remember the last time he heard him play, and so he leans forward, curious as to which of the songs of praise* of his people the young man will sing, and why.

But as the young man lifts his voice to the night sky, unfamiliar words leave his lips. It soon becomes clear that this is a new song, a song that gives voice to their deepest feelings, a song that speaks to the ache of their heart for their situation—a song of exile.

"By the rivers of Babylon,
    there we sat down and wept,
    when we remembered Zion."

---

*Throughout *The Story of God, the Story of Us,* "songs of praise" will refer to the psalms.

The young man pauses, and then repeats the line. It is a familiar tune, and as he begins again, a few people join their voices to his. As they sing, some among them begin to shed tears. The young man continues,

> "We hung our unplayed harps upon the willows,
> for there our captors demanded we sing songs for their
>   amusement.
> They tormented us saying, 'Sing us one of the happy songs
>   of Zion.' "

He pauses again, and then looks fiercely at those around him and loudly sings,

> "But how can we sing the LORD's song in a foreign land?"

At this, those around the young man begin to weep freely, and the sound of wailing becomes a chorus for the young man as he continues in a more muted yet determined voice.

> "O Jerusalem, if I ever forget you, may my fingers drop off.
> Should I fail to remember you,
> may my tongue cling to the roof of my mouth,
> if I do not honor you above all else."

The strumming of the harp becomes more strident, almost militant, and the old man, like everyone else, wonders how this song will end . . .

> "O LORD, remember the people of Edom,
> who stood by as Jerusalem was invaded,
> and who called out, 'Burn it, burn it to the ground.' "

The tears on the faces of his audience begin to dry up as the mood turns from one of sorrow to one of anger. And then in a harsh, determined voice, the young man concludes his song:

> "And you Babylonians—depraved people that you are—
> a blessing on the one who pays you back for all you've done to us.

Yes, a blessing on the one who seizes your babies
and smashes their heads on the rocks."

In the silence that follows the last note of the harp, the old man can
feel the sense of impotent rage that is building in his people, a rage
that is always simmering just below the surface. As an elder of his
people, it is to him that they now turn for a word, the word of response that this song demands.

"What say you, old one? When will the LORD repay our oppressors?"

"When will God vindicate the suffering of God's servant Israel?"

"When will God restore the kingdom to us?"

Sitting here in exile, it is hard for them to believe that their God is
the one, true God: if that were so, how could the Babylonians have
defeated them? How could they have been carried off into a foreign
land, far away from their homeland—the land God promised them?
How did they end up here?

Once more the old man is forced to admit to himself that his people
still do not understand—or, they refuse to understand. His people
have forgotten their story. They have forgotten why it is that they find
themselves here in exile in Babylon.

But if they have forgotten, it is his responsibility to remind them, to
tell them their story, the Story of God. And so he moves to the center
of the group, gathers his cloak around him, and begins the narrative
of his people once more, hoping that perhaps this time they will listen, truly listen. He draws himself up and begins to speak.

"Gather round now, my friends, and listen to the story. I know that
it is easy to forget where we have come from, especially when we find
ourselves in difficult circumstances, sitting here in the pain of exile.*
And I know that the world has other stories, other songs. But that is

---

*Exile: A painful word, for a painful experience. Whether it describes the experience
of God's people in captivity in Babylon in the sixth century B.C.E. or the experience
of refugees far from home today; whether the emotional exile those of us feel who are
estranged from our families, or even the experience of those of us who do not feel at
home in our own bodies—exile is indeed a painful place. But as a place that invites
us to ask the question "How *did* we get here?" it can be an invitation to hear the Story
of God, and discover that it is also our story.

why we tell our story, and sing our songs. So hear now again the first words of Torah, the first words of our Scriptures, the first words of the Story: 'In the beginning God created . . .'"

The young musician leaps to his feet and interrupts the elder's recital of Torah. "'In the beginning?!' Who cares about the beginning? What is God doing *now*? The LORD has forsaken us. The LORD has forgotten us. Where is this Almighty God?"

The people are shocked at the young man's disrespect, but several nod their heads in agreement with his sentiment. They too want answers, not stories.

The old man smiles wearily, understanding the frustration the young man is giving vent to. He gestures gently for the young man to be seated, as another's words come to mind.

"Forgotten us? Can a woman forget her nursing child,
and have no compassion on the one she carried in her womb?
Even these may forget, but I will not forget you.
Behold, I have inscribed your name on the palms of my hands.

"I understand," the old man continues, "why you may believe that God has forsaken us. But we are still God's people, and we are part of a Story that did not begin with exile, nor with the Babylonians. We are far from home; indeed, we are a long way east of Eden. But Eden is where the Story begins. I understand that you want answers. But what we have is a Story, which I would have you hear from the beginning."*

Muttering something under his breath, the young man sits down. The people shift position to get comfortable, settling in to listen, as the old man begins the Story once more.

"In the beginning, God created the heavens and the earth. The earth

---

*We usually begin asking questions about God—theology—from a place of felt need; we want answers to our questions, solutions to our problems. But what Scripture offers us is predominantly *stories*—the Story of God. And the Story does not begin with a problem (what some call "the Fall") but with the goodness of creation. It's important for us to begin with God's intentions for creation—including us—before wrestling with all the ways we've messed it up.

was formless, in chaos, and darkness was over the surface of the deep;
and the Spirit of God was moving over the surface of the waters.

"And God spoke: 'Let there be light!' and there was light. And God
saw that the light was good. God separated the light from the darkness,
calling the light 'day' and the darkness 'night.' That was the first day.

"God spoke, and created the seas and the oceans with their crashing breakers and gentle swell. And God created the heavens above,
the sky, with all its wonderful colors. That was the second day.

"God spoke, and created the land and all that grows in it. God created trees, these weeping willows, the olive trees of our beloved homeland. God created cabbages, and carrots, beans and broccoli, papaya
and peppers. God created the flowers of the forest and the field in all
their beauty. And God looked at it all and saw that it was good. That
was the third day.

"God spoke, and created the great lights in the sky, to light up the
day and the night. God also made the stars. And God saw that it was
good. That was the fourth day.

"God spoke, and filled the waters with teeming life and the heavens with birds. God created whales and shrimp, manatees and min-
nows. God created eagles and owls, swans and sparrows. God looked,
and God saw that it was good. And God blessed them. That was the
fifth day.

"God spoke and created the animals: lions and lambs, cats and
cows, ants and elephants.

"Then God spoke, saying, 'Let us make humanity in our image, in
our likeness.' And so God created the first human, *ha-adam*. God created humanity in the image of God, both male and female.

"And God blessed them, and said, 'Be fruitful and multiply, and fill
the earth. Nurture and take responsibility for all my creation.'*

---

*Most Bibles translate the Hebrew here as "rule over" or "take dominion" of creation.
Those words have fairly consistently been enacted as "exploit" God's creation, which
is to work *against* the order and nonviolent harmony of creation of which we read in
this story. Partnership with the Creator God means to take responsibility for, to care
for, to work with the rest of creation, not to exploit it.

"And then God looked out over all that God had made, and saw that it was good: it was very good. That was the sixth day. Thus the heavens and the earth were completed.

"And on the seventh day, God rested, and blessed the Sabbath day, setting it apart as a day of rest for all."

The old man folds his hands in his lap and opens his eyes. "This is how the Story of God begins, and so it is also the beginning of our story.

"Now I know this story is very different from others we have heard. The Babylonians tell us their story of creation, this 'Enuma Elish,' and it is a strange, violent and frightening story. They tell us of the great sea monsters Apsu and Tiamat, the waters of chaos whose offspring were the gods. They tell us that the gods fought amongst themselves, the defeated serving the victors until Marduk, king of the gods, created humans to be the gods' slaves. They tell us that their gods are capricious, untrustworthy, and that humans must do strange, sometimes evil things to please them, to keep the gods from harming them.

"We have little hope and security in the face of such gods. Maybe you have heard other stories about where we come from . . . but those stories are not *our* story. My friends, remember: we were made in the image of God. We are not God's slaves; we are God's *partners* in the work of creation. We are made to be God's friends. And we can trust God. Oh yes, we can trust God. Our God is not like these strange gods, who are far off, to whom the Babylonians build their towers, to whom they scream and dance and cut themselves to try and catch their attention. Our God is a God of order, not chaos. The very story of creation shows us that! Look at the beautiful structure of creation, how each section of three days parallels the other.

On the first day, God created light . . . and on the fourth day, God created the heavenly lights.

On the second day, God created the seas and the sky . . . and on the fifth day, God created the fish and the birds.

On the third day, God created the land and the trees and the plants . . . and on the sixth day, God created animals . . . and God created us in God's image, and blessed us.

"Did you hear it? Can you picture the symmetry? Our God is a God of hospitality, creating a place for a people, a place where all life can flourish. God provides for all creation, as our Story shows. Our God is a God of order; we can trust God to provide for us now as in the beginning.

"I know that it may not seem that way today, for here we are, exiles in a foreign land. Life is hard. We know that. And that is why we must tell each other the Story, and keep telling it, to do exactly what God has continually told us to do: remember . . . remember . . . remember."*

From the listening crowd, a young girl speaks up. "Abba, we believe that God is one, and yet the Story tells us that God said, 'Let *us* make humanity in *our* image.' Why didn't God say, 'in *my* image?' I don't understand."

The old man smiles. This young girl is attentive—hearing what is sometimes easy to miss in familiar words.

"A good question, and one we need to consider when we are talking about what it means to be made in the image of God. As you say, we believe that God is one, as God's people have affirmed from our earliest days in the words of the creed:

Shema Yisra'el, Adonai Eloheinu, Adonai Echad.
Hear O Israel, the LORD is our God, the LORD is one.

"Yet here God speaks as *we*, as *us*. This may sound like the speech of our captors' king, who declares himself 'we' as a way of asserting his superiority—and his dominance. Yet elsewhere in the Story we rarely hear God speak as 'we' or 'us.' So why does God say 'Let *us* make humanity in *our* image'? In the story of creation, we clearly see

---

*As the Story unfolds, we hear God say over and over again to remember the Story—not just in the hard times but, perhaps most importantly, during the good times, when we are most apt to forget who—and whose—we are. It is when we forget the Story that we adopt other stories to live by.

the importance of relationships. We were created to partner with God in the work of creation by caring for it communally, relationally, both male and female together. Perhaps that is why God speaks as 'us': because relationships are so important. Perhaps relationships are so wonderful that God could not help but create in order to share God-self with others. Perhaps. Or perhaps there is some other reason. The Story does not tell us.*

"The story of creation tells us something else about what it means to be human. By the seventh day God had completed the work of creation, and God rested. God blessed the Sabbath day, declaring it holy—a day set apart.

"After creating all that exists, God rests. Now, that does not mean that God spends the seventh day exhausted after the work of creation, like the gods of the Babylonians do in their story. Rather, God spends it at peace, in shalom, knowing that all is well with God's world. And God calls us to the same.

"That is why God's people begin each Sabbath day by saying 'Shabbat shalom,' 'The peace of the Sabbath be with you.' The Sabbath day is an invitation to cease our feverish activity of self-securing, to recognize that life comes to us as sheer gift, and not through our own efforts. It is an invitation to recognize that our lives will not fall apart if we take one day in seven to rest, in defiance of the slave drivers who demand activity from us.

"To take a day of rest is to resist the internal forces that drive us to assert ourselves through our activity. It is to refuse to conform to the restlessness of the culture we find ourselves in, to cease our tireless striving to reshape the world in our own image. We declare that we

---

*Later in the Story we will meet a person whose followers believed him to be the very image of the living God. As these followers inhabited the Story, they began to understand the one God in Israel's *Shema* to exist as a community of three persons: Father, Son and Holy Spirit. The person they followed profoundly shaped this understanding, for although that one is said to have existed in the form of God, he did not consider equality with God something to be grasped, but instead emptied himself, became one of us and took the role of servant. If this person *is* the very image of God, and we are created in that image, then what might that mean for our relationships?

trust in this God who is confident enough to rest. We trust God to provide what we need for life. We trust God to give us shalom, the peace we long for in our lives.

"And God has given the Sabbath day as a gift for *all*, regardless of wealth or position in society, and thus it is a call to end the dehumanizing exploitation of the many who work long hours, for little reward, so that the few might benefit. We neglect the practice of communal Sabbath rest at our peril."

With this the old man stands to stretch, glancing briefly at the young musician to see a thoughtful expression on his face. "Have you ever considered that our observance of the Sabbath is an act of defiance?" A smile spreads across the young man's face. He had indeed been thinking that very thing—and it was a thought that pleased him. "The Babylonians would have us work every day, and they view our taking one day in seven to rest with scorn—a waste of time, unproductive, rebellious even. Yet it is an important way for us to assert and affirm our humanity in the face of captivity—it is indeed a precious gift from God."

The young man's smile fades as swiftly as it had come. "So we observe Sabbath—that's good. But does God observe us? Does God see our suffering? If so, why does God not come down to deliver us? Why does God remain far off in the heavens?"

The old man smiles. "'In the heavens?' You may be interested to hear the rest of the story tonight." Warming his hands by the fire, he continues. "I have told you the story of creation, but do you know that we have a story that some say is even older? It begins like this:

This is the story of creation, of the day the LORD God made earth and heaven . . .

"The story I have already told you focuses on Almighty God, the Creator of all that there is, of *heaven and earth*. But the second creation story focuses on the God who is near, the LORD who made *earth and heaven*. For God is both transcendent and immanent: God is wholly other, yet right here. This is the LORD, the God revealed to Moses in the burning bush. And so the story continues . . .

"The LORD God formed *ha-adam*, the 'soil creature,' out of the dust of the ground—*ha-adamah*—and breathed into his nostrils the breath of life. The LORD God planted a garden in the east, in Eden. Then the LORD God put *ha-adam* in the garden of Eden to cultivate the soil from which he was taken and to tend its produce. And the LORD God commanded *ha-adam* saying, 'You may eat freely from any tree of the garden except for the tree of the knowledge of good and evil. The day you eat from that tree, you will die.'

"Then the LORD God said, 'It is not good for *ha-adam* to be alone; I will make a helper suitable for *ha-adam*.'

"Did you hear that? 'It is not good.' Something in God's creation was *not* good! And that is for the human to be alone. We were indeed created for community, for relationship, and not just with God— which *ha-adam* experienced—but also with each other. This is central to our identity: to be human, to be made in God's image, means 'to not be alone.' How did God take that which was not good—the human alone—and make it good? Like this.

"Out of *ha-adamah* the LORD God formed every beast of the field and every bird of the sky and brought them to *ha-adam* to see. And whatever *ha-adam* called them, that was their name. *Ha-adam* gave names to all the cattle, and to the birds of the sky, and to every beast of the field, but for Adam there was not found an *ezer kenegdo*, a suitable helper. So the LORD God caused a deep sleep to fall upon *ha-adam*: as he slept, God took a rib and created a woman, and brought her to *ha-adam*.

"And *ha-adam* said, 'This is now bone of my bones, and flesh of my flesh. She shall be called *ish-shah* because she was taken out of *ish*.' For this reason *ish* shall leave his father and mother and shall join *ish-shah*, and they shall become one flesh.

"And *ish* and *ish-shah* were naked and unashamed."

As the glow from the fire dims, the old man looks into the faces of the crowd. He knows that what he has to say about this story will not sit well with many of those listening. But it is his responsibility to speak the truth as he understands it, regardless of whether people want to hear it.

"This marriage was the first human community. Marriage is one of the most important themes of our Story. We will hear it again and again, as it is used to describe God's relationship with our people Israel. But we have not done well at remembering this Story. In the beginning men and women were created equal, both made in the image of God. Both male and female were given the work of partnering with God in creation. God blessed them both, and declared their relationship good.

"Even though the woman is the man's helper, an *ezer kenegdo,* that does not imply that she is somehow inferior to the man. Nearly every other time we hear of an *ezer kenegdo* in the Story, it refers to *God,* the helper of Israel. No, we have not remembered our story well regarding the equality *ish* and *ish-shah* shared. And it is as if the author knew that we would not! Did you hear it? 'For this reason *ish* shall leave his father and mother and shall join *ish-shah*.' The first description of marriage is the very *opposite* of how we practice marriage in our culture, where it is the *woman* who leaves her home to join her husband's household."

The old man smiles as he hears the murmurs and whispers working their way through the crowd. These thoughts are controversial, to say the least: the people of God have not traditionally embraced the notion that *ish* and *ish-shah* are created equal and equally bear the image of God. But in exile, on the margins of society, people are sometimes able to hear the Story in different ways. The old man moves to speak again, and the crowd settles back into a now less comfortable silence.

"In the Story, God grants the first humans three gifts that also show us what it means to be human: vocation, permission and prohibition. Their vocation is to partner with God in tending the garden and caring for creation, and to join in God's creative acts by having children. God gives them permission to enjoy the gracious provision of land and food, as well as the gift of a truly free will, capable of making significant choices. And God declares one prohibition: they must not eat from the tree of the knowledge of good and evil.

"The problem is that the prohibition is what we tend to remember most about the God who creates. We pay little attention to our vocation and our freedom. Yet prohibition is only meaningful within the context of freedom; only when we can say 'no' is our 'yes' meaningful. God has given us everything that is necessary for life. But if our freedom to enjoy God's generosity is to be meaningful, we have to have the possibility of disobeying God.

"We will save for another night what happens when *ish* and *ishshah* choose to exercise that freedom by disobeying. For now let us end with that beautiful description of life in the garden: 'The man and the woman were naked and were not ashamed.' The two were entirely vulnerable with each other and with God, friends with God and with each other. The next time we gather, we will hear of the catastrophe that befalls them; for they will go from being naked and unashamed to being afraid of God—their nakedness now somehow shameful—hiding from God behind the very trees God created for them to enjoy. But it is enough for now to remember them as they were in the beginning, enjoying the community with God and each other for which they were made."

The coals of the fire glow gently, giving off light, but little heat. The old man rises to his feet to offer a parting blessing to his people.

"And now it is late. Tomorrow we rest, and—I hope—take time to reflect on the Story." He turns to the young man whose harp dangles loosely from his hand. "We will not soon forget your song, my friend. Our songs have always arisen from our experience, and they are not always the happy songs our captors want us to sing for them. But let us not forget those songs, nor forget our story, lest we become like these Babylonians. Let us put our trust in our God, in whose image we are made, and who will provide for us . . . even here."

2

catastrophe

In which we hear the story of the first humans'
rejection of their identity and vocation, and the
consequences of their sin for all of creation . . .

The old man sits down by the fire as another Sabbath begins. It has been a long week, but the work has been lightened by conversation with his people. They have had many questions about the story of creation since their time together around the fire a week ago.

He looks around the crowd as they settle in by the fire and notices the young man. He is glad to see the harp in the young man's hand, and beckons him over. "My friend, thank you for singing your song last week. Would you be willing to sing us a song of praise again tonight?"

The young man offers him a mischevious grin. "I've been working on another song of exile, if you'd like to hear it."

The old man smiles in return. "Another time, perhaps. I was thinking it would be good to hear one that reminds us of happier days. Maybe one of the songs of ascent."

The smile fades from the young man's face. "Jerusalem lies in ruins. How can I sing a pilgrim song?"

"Please, for me. For our people."

The young man stands, sighs, and begins to tune his harp as the crowd grows quiet. Many of them have been singing his song of protest, relishing its words, as they worked this week. As he plucks the strings tunelessly, tension begins to build; what song will he bring for them tonight?

The old man joins his people in leaning forward to listen as a look of resolve appears on the musician's face. He lifts his voice to the night sky, and begins.

"I will lift up my eyes to the hills;
from where does my help come?"

The old man smiles, relaxes and leans back, not just a little relieved at the young man's choice. The young man pauses, then repeats the first lines of the song of praise, inviting the crowd to join their voices to his. As he continues, he looks at the old man, and a look of understanding passes between them.

"My help comes from the LORD,
Maker of heaven and earth.
God will not allow your foot to slip;
God who keeps you will not slumber.
Behold, God who keeps Israel
will neither slumber nor sleep."

The voices of the crowd swell, as the song evokes memories of pilgrimage to Jerusalem and the joy of the high holy days they have not thought of in a long time. The old man closes his eyes and gives himself to the song, as do many others.

"The LORD is your keeper;
the LORD is your shade on your right hand.
The sun will not smite you by day,
nor the moon by night.
The LORD will protect you from all evil;
God will keep your soul.
The LORD will guard your going out
and your coming in
from this time forth and forever."

As the last notes fade away, the young man glances at the elder of his people, who in turn opens his eyes and inclines his head toward him, grateful for this song of hope. "Thank you, my friend," says the old man, as the singer takes his place in the circle. The old man gazes into the fire for a moment, collecting his thoughts, and then addresses his people.

"When we gathered together last week we heard the beginning of the Story of God. We listened to the days of creation and saw the goodness of our God and of what God has made. We heard that humans are the pinnacle of creation, and that God blessed us, both male and female, *ish* and *ish-shah*. We were created equally to participate in God's continuing work of creation; by caring for and nurturing the world God has given us, and by filling the earth with children who also bear God's image.

"That was our vocation. We also saw that God granted *ish* and *ish-shah* great freedom to enjoy all that God had made, with just one prohibition: they were not to eat any of the fruit from the tree of the knowledge of good and evil. And as the fires burned low last week we left *ish* and *ish-shah* in the garden, enjoying community with this immanent God, this God who draws near, and with each other, being 'naked and unashamed.' Let us return to the garden tonight and discover how the Story of God, the story of us, continues.

"Now the serpent, *ha-nahash*, was more crafty than any beast of the field which the LORD God had made. *Ha-nahash* said to *ish-shah*, 'Did God really say you could not eat fruit from any tree in the garden?' *Ish-shah* said to *ha-nahash*, 'We can eat from every tree, except from the tree in the middle of the garden. God has said, "You shall not eat from it or touch it, lest you die."'

"That's not what God said." The old man looks up to see a young girl covering her mouth, clearly embarrassed. It is the same girl who asked a similarly perceptive question last week.

"Go on," encourages the old man.

"Forgive me," the young girl says, "but God told *ish* not to *eat* the fruit. God did not say it could not be touched." She hesitates for a moment and then asks, "So why does *ish-shah* say that?"

The old man smiles. This child listens well. "A good question. Why does *ish-shah* say that?" The young girl looks at the old man, who now sits in silence. As the eyes of the crowd now turn toward her, color rises to her cheeks, even as her brow wrinkles in thought, as she realizes he is waiting for her response. "Perhaps they are already beginning to doubt the goodness of God. Maybe they thought that if eating it would kill them, they had better not even touch it."

"A good answer," the old man says. He turns back to the crowd. "Obviously they have been to investigate the tree, as *ish-shah* refers to it by its location, 'in the middle of the garden.' Whatever the case, the seed of doubt had been sown, and instead of talking *to* God, *ish-shah* was now talking *about* God.

"*Ha-nahash* had a response for *ish-shah*'s claim. 'You will not die!' the serpent told her. 'For God knows that on the day you eat the fruit, your eyes will be opened and you will be like God, knowing good from evil.'

"'You will be like God.' The subtle serpent taps into our deepest anxiety as humans: the fear that what I have, no matter how good it may be, is not enough. The haunting suspicion that someone else has it better than me. That someone else *is* better than me. So, not only do I not have enough, I am not enough. I am less than.

"When *ish-shah* saw that the tree was good for food, and that it was a delight to the eye and that it was desirable to make a person wise, she took some fruit and ate; and she gave some to *ish* who was with her, and he ate. Then their eyes were opened and they knew that they were naked; and they hurriedly sewed fig leaves together and made themselves loincloths.

"*Catastrophe!* They exercised the freedom that God had given them, and disobeyed God's prohibition. To this point they had lived life naked and unashamed, completely vulnerable with each other and with God. But now that vulnerability was threatening, and they instantly began to try and cover themselves up."

"How could they do it?" someone asked from the crowd. "It was just one tree; they had all the others to eat! Why?"

The old man looked around at the crowd. "Yes, as *ish-shah* rightly said, they could eat from every tree in the garden, except one. How indeed could they take what was prohibited when they were surrounded by so much that was freely given?" He pauses. "Would you or I have acted differently in the face of *ha-nahash*'s manipulation?

What are we capable of doing when we think we do not have enough? When we think we *are* not enough?"

The old man gives a sad smile. "Perhaps it is hard to believe that they would listen to the serpent's temptation. Yet this is not just any old tree, not just the tree in the middle of the garden, as *ish-shah* refers to it. It is the tree of the knowledge of good and evil. The Creator determines those boundaries; God declares what is good, as we heard in the story of creation. But now in response to the serpent's temptation, *ish-shah* grasps for power, engaging in an activity that is God's alone. She makes an ethical determination, deciding for herself, independently of God, what is good for her to do.

"Did you hear it? 'When *ish-shah* saw that the tree was good for food, and a delight to the eye, and was desirable to make one wise, she took some fruit and ate it and she gave some to *ish*, and he ate too.' *Ish-shah*'s moral reasoning was based on what looks good, what tastes good—what 'feels good,' perhaps. Perhaps that is part of her justification for choosing to disobey God.

"When she was tempted, for the first time *ish-shah* considered the possibility that something could be good in and of itself apart from God. *Ish-shah* acted independently of God to make her own decision about what she could and could not do. And so, even before she ate the fruit, she was already trying to grasp for the power that is the Creator God's alone; she had forgotten that she was a creature.

"But the moment she ate, she knew she was. 'And they heard the sound of the LORD God walking in the garden in the cool of the evening, and *ish* and *ish-shah* hid themselves from the presence of God among the trees of the garden. Then the LORD God called and said, "Where are you?"'

"And *ish* said, 'I heard the sound of you walking in the garden, and I was afraid because I was naked; so I hid myself.'

"And God said, 'Who told you that you were naked? Have you eaten from the tree of which I told you not to eat?'

"And *ish* said, '*Ish-shah*, who you gave to me, she gave me the fruit, and I ate it.'

"And God said to *ish-shah,* 'What have you done?'

"And *ish-shah* said, 'The serpent deceived me and I ate.'"

The old man shakes his head, his shoulders bowed, feeling the weight of the catastrophe that is this story. "From the very beginning of our story, when people are caught sinning, instead of taking responsibility for our own actions, we try to blame someone else. Already, community is breaking down. Humans discover that we are capable of doing harm to one another. Self-protection became their first concern, and trust evaporated."

A man calls out from the crowd. "Adam was right; it was the woman's fault. She gave him the fruit!" This statement earns the man a slap to the back of his head from the woman sitting beside him. The sharp sound echoes around the crowd for a moment, followed by collective laughter.

The old man enjoys the moment, grateful for the levity. Once the laughter dies down, he looks to the man who had spoken. "You are not the first to blame *ish-shah* because she gave the fruit to *ish*. For centuries we have made *ish-shah* out to be a seductress, tempting *ish* to sin. But remember, *ish* is standing right there and says nothing when the serpent lies to them. He willingly eats the fruit also.

"Sin is not just something I do. Sin is social; it always impacts the whole community. It impacts the whole universe." The momentary lightness he had been feeling departs, as once more the weight of the catastrophe falls upon the old man. "And so God groaned; the earth groaned; all living things groaned as the harmony of creation was torn apart by the choice those first humans made.

"The impact of their actions touched every part of what it means to be human:

The prohibition—not to eat from this one tree—is violated.

The permission—the provision of land and food, and the gift of free will—is perverted.

The vocation—to partner with God in the care of creation—is neglected.

Community—with God and each other—is shattered.

"From then on they were concerned only with themselves, not the rest of creation. When God asked *ish,* 'Where are you?' did you hear his pitiful response? 'I heard . . . I was afraid . . . I was naked . . . I hid myself.' The intimate community between God and the humans was devastated. *Ish* had become self-absorbed. The humans were no longer naked and unashamed; now they were hiding from God and from each other."

The old man looks into the faces of those nearest him, holding each one's gaze for a moment before continuing. "This is our story. We have all acted as *ish* and *ish-shah* did, independently of God. We do that which we know is wrong, and then we try to justify it, or blame others. 'How could they do it?' we might ask. Perhaps we know all too well the answer to our own question. We are not so different from those first humans."

The old man sees his conviction reflected back in the faces of the people surrounding him—in frowns, in sadness, in eyes unwilling to meet his gaze. But he smiles; there is some good news for those feeling the weight of this story.

"Yet just as God called to them, God calls to us, saying, 'Where are you?' We, like them, may try to hide, to isolate ourselves, to be alone with our sin and our shame, but God is constantly seeking the lost. Perhaps God asks 'Where are you?' not out of anger but in a gracious invitation to once more make ourselves vulnerable—before God, before each other. Perhaps it is an invitation to speak the truth about our sin, an invitation to be found."

The fire is burning low, and someone adds some logs from the pile. The new wood crackles and pops as it catches. The old man takes the opportunity to stand and stretch the tight muscles in his shoulders and back. As he settles down again, the young girl asks another question.

"Abba, God said they would die if they ate the fruit. But they didn't—just as the serpent said. Did God lie to them?"

"Another good question," the old man replies. He is growing fond of this young girl. "I have often wondered if *ish-shah* paused before sinking her teeth into the fruit, wondering if it would be the last thing she would ever do. But after taking a bite, she is still very much alive. You are right; they do not drop dead on the spot. Yet I wonder if something did indeed die as they tasted the fruit.

"Until that moment, *ish* and *ish-shah* had lived as 'one flesh.' In that moment, I wonder if they died as one being and were reborn as two. They remain alive to discover the consequences of refusing to live in God's world on God's terms—consequences which are never just personal.

"To *ish-shah* God said, 'From now on you will have increased pain in childbirth, yet your desire will be for your husband, and he shall rule over you.'

"To *ish* God said, 'Because you listened to *ish-shah*, and ate the fruit that I told you not to, the ground is now cursed because of you; you will have to toil to grow food, weeds will spring up among your crops. You will eat bread only by the sweat of your brow, till you return to the ground, because from the soil, *ha-adamah*, you were taken, and to *ha-adamah* you will return.'

"Now, *ish* named *ish-shah* 'Eve,' because she was the mother of all humanity. And the LORD God made clothes for *ish* and *ish-shah* from animal skins. Then God said, 'Behold, they have become like us, knowing good from evil, and now, if they stay, they may eat from the tree of life and live forever.' And so God cast them out of the garden, to cultivate *ha-adamah* from which *ha-adam* was taken."

The old man looks around him, and a familiar ache seizes his heart. "And so humanity is exiled from paradise—from the garden— and from access to the tree of life." Thousands of years may have passed since, but living east of Eden has not grown any less painful. He continues.

"You may have heard this story referred to as 'the curse,' but it is important to remember that only the serpent and the ground were cursed; the humans were not. God had blessed the humans, and that blessing was not taken away.

"God now declares the consequences of their sin, and the impact that their sin has on all of creation. Here is the grace of God at work:

the consequences to their sin are limited. They do not die. Instead God casts them out of the garden.

"Yes, it is life in exile—life away from the goodness of the garden, life filled with conflict and pain and fear-induced sweat and the distortion of desire. But nonetheless, it is life and not death. This story cannot be reduced to one simply of human disobedience and divine displeasure. It is a story of God's response to the way we live our lives: when what we do deserves death, God insists on life for us.

"From the very beginning of our story, God extends grace to us. Thus once again God does for the humans what they could not do for themselves: whereas the coverings they made for themselves were inadequate, God now clothes them fully. They, and we, cannot deal with shame, but God can, will and does.

"But in providing them with animal skins, for the first time blood is shed in order to cover the sin of humans. We begin to see in this story how our relationships have become so broken. Remember, God created *ish* and *ish-shah* to be equals, yet sadly we know that we have rarely lived that way. When God said to *ish-shah*, 'Your desire shall be for your husband, and he shall rule over you,' God's will for relationships was not being changed.* The power struggle that would ensue between the couple was rather a consequence of their sin.

"Instead of looking to the story of creation to guide us in our relationships, all too often we begin with this story and assume that the consequence of the first couple's sin is the pattern for marriage and communal life.† We exchange the harmony of equality for a power struggle—with men being the winners. I fear in doing so, we all lose."

As the old man anticipated, muttering breaks out, mostly with low,

---

*The only two times these two words—*desire* and *rule over*—are used in the Hebrew Scriptures are here, in God's declaration to *ish-shah,* and in God's warning to Cain in Genesis 4:7.
†If God's declaration—that the husband would rule over his wife—was God's will for relationships and not just the consequence of sin, then this story raises other questions: In order for us to live consistently with all of God's declarations here, would we be wrong to ease our toil and sweat in our working of the ground? Should farmers give up their air-conditioned tractors? Should women refuse painkillers when giving birth?

bass notes. He raises his voice above it. "This is not just a story about husbands and wives. This is a story about humanity. Instead of living in harmony, seeking the common good, we become concerned with power—especially the power to exert our will on one another. And that power, as we know all too painfully well here, uprooted from our homeland, becomes manifest in violence.

"But I am getting ahead of myself. The power struggle begins immediately. The first thing the man does after God finishes speaking is to name his wife 'Eve.' The man's identity is no longer formed primarily by who he is, *ish,* a person made in the image of God, but now by what he does—a tiller of the soil, Adam. So he gives the woman a new name as well. Her identity is no longer formed by who she is—*ish-shah,* a person made in the image of God—but now by what she does: 'Eve,' mother, bearer of children. By naming her, just as he had named the animals, the man exercises power over the woman for the first time.

"In saying 'yes' to the serpent's temptation, both the man and the woman had said 'no' to who they were created to be. It is in this estranged state that Adam and Eve were cast out from the garden, away from the tree of life. God stationed cherubim to guard the place of God's presence, to guard the way to the tree of life, which if they ate from would condemn them to live in this 'no' forever.*

"The man and woman have children, Cain and Abel—another story that shows us the horrendous consequences of talking about God rather than to God. In the story of Cain and Abel we see our deep human anxiety surfacing for a second time, and the massive disruption in all the relationships of the cosmos that followed the disobedience of Adam and Eve. These two brothers voluntarily brought offerings to God from the fruit of their labor. Cain, believing that God regarded his brother Abel as being better than him, became angry, and in his anger and fear of being less than another, Cain murdered his brother."

A profound silence falls over the crowd and is broken only by the

---

*We will encounter the cherubim many times as the Story unfolds.

young girl, who gives voice to the question on many of their minds. "Why didn't God stop him?"

The old man shakes his head sadly, for this is a question he himself has asked many times, in many situations. "Yes, why didn't God stop Cain from doing harm? Why doesn't God stop you or me from doing harm? Many people, much wiser than I, have offered answers to your question . . . to my question." He casts around, as if searching for someone who will give him an answer.

"Now, perhaps God did not intervene in order to honor our free will. Perhaps God did what God could. As Cain's anxiety and anger over the offerings grew, God came to him with encouragement—and a warning: 'Do well and you'll remember that you are accepted. But beware: sin is crouching at your tent flap. Its desire is to have its way with you—but you can and will master it, if you do well.' But it seems Cain listened to a different voice, the voice that told him he was unaccepted, less than. Sin did indeed master him, and he lashed out to kill his brother.

"By removing his perceived competition, his brother, Cain tried to restore his standing before God. Perhaps in an attempt to halt a rapid deterioration of human relationships, God declared that anyone who murdered Cain in revenge would suffer sevenfold vengeance.

"Yet the further east of Eden we go into exile, the worse we become. The next person we meet in the story is Lamech, who also commited murder—not to reinforce his standing with God but rather with his wives. Lamech then declared his own guidelines for vengeance: not sevenfold as God established for Cain, but seventy and sevenfold.

"As the human community grew, so did sin. Community is so powerful that it is possible to perfect evil in it. Ultimately God looked out over humanity, and instead of saying, "It is good," God saw that it was terrible. The wickedness of humanity was great, and every intention and thought people had was only evil continually. The LORD God was grieved, for the earth was corrupted and filled with violence. Indeed, the whole of creation groans with the harm humans have wrought upon it.

"God said, 'I will wipe out humanity whom I have created . . . for I regret that I made them.' God would start over."

"God killed *everybody*?" The young girl, again.

"No," the old man replies. "There was one person who was not caught up in the violence of humanity; one person who walked with God; the anomaly among humanity. God said to Noah, 'The end of all flesh has come before me, for the earth is filled with violence because of humanity; behold, I am about to destroy them.'*

"And so God undid the work of creation. God gave Noah the work of building an ark that would deliver him and his family from the waters of chaos. This is the first time in the Story that God's people are rescued from the sea. God placed Noah and his family on the ark, with mating pairs of all the animals, and then the waters that God had separated on the second day of creation were brought together again in de-creation, and life on earth was destroyed, because of humanity's wickedness.

"Yet God immediately began the process of re-creation, once more separating the waters and declaring to Noah, 'I will never again curse the ground on account of people, for the intentions of their hearts are constantly evil. I will never again destroy every living thing.' God saw that even this catastrophic flood had not solved the problem of humanity's wickedness, and so once more God met us where we were and began a new way to save us from ourselves, and to mend the cosmos that had been broken by our sin. God blessed Noah and his family, and repeated the command given to the first humans: be fruitful and multiply and cover the earth.

"But humanity could not return to our original state in the garden; we remained in exile. And so even with this repeated command, our relationship with creation had profoundly changed. God told Noah,

---

*God's declaration to Noah should give us pause. Sin, evil and corruption are summarized in one word—*violence*—because of which God sends the catastrophic flood. Violence should horrify us, yet we readily embrace violence as an appropriate way to resolve conflict, to protect self- and national interests, and even as entertainment, as a cursory glance at popular movies and video games reveals.

'The fear of you and the terror of you shall be on every beast of the earth and on every bird of the sky; with everything that creeps along the ground, and all the fish of the sea—into your hand they are given: they shall be food for you.' Instead of our living in harmony with creation, now creation lives in fear of us. We extended the violence we did to each other to the rest of creation.

"God spoke to Noah and to his children, saying, 'Behold, I establish my covenant with you and with your descendants, and with every living creature that comes out of the ark. This is my covenant with you: all flesh shall never again be cut off by the waters of the flood, neither will there be another flood to destroy the earth. And this is the sign of the covenant: I set my rainbow in the clouds, so that when it rains, you will see the rainbow, and I will remember my covenant with you and every living creature, and never again will the rain become a flood to destroy all life.

"This promise to Noah is God's first covenant with humanity. But Noah's descendants, perhaps like *ish-shah,* doubted the goodness of God. Perhaps they thought God would send another flood, even though God had promised not to. As they journeyed east, they arrived at the plain of Shinar, and there they said, 'Come let us make bricks and build for ourselves a city, and a tower whose top will reach into heaven, and let us make a name for ourselves, lest we be scattered over the face of the whole earth.'*

"And so, in direct disobedience of God's command to populate the earth, afraid of the vulnerability that would come with scattering, they stayed in one place and tried to reach into heaven to make a name for themselves. Our underlying anxiety—that we are less than—manifested itself again.

"God came down to thwart their plans by confusing their lan-

---

*The Tower of Babel symbolizes the very core of human nature: the pride and independence that spring from our deep-seated fears. Instead of trusting the promises of God to protect and provide for us, we insist on relying on our own resources, on our physical, economic and military strength. We will see this attitude, and the catastrophic consequences it brings, displayed throughout our Story.

guage: instead of making a name for themselves, now they could not even understand each other. God scattered them from there over the face of the earth, abandoning the city and the tower whose name was Babel, because there the LORD confused their language."

"Babel?! That was Babylon?!?" The young musician leaps to his feet.

"Yes," the old man replies. "This city's story began a long, long time ago."

The young man looks around the crowd. "Oh, that God would come down again, and destroy this place."

The old man groans, shifts his weight and pushes himself to his feet. "Perhaps this is a good place to end for now. I hope you will take time to think about the story as you enjoy your Sabbath rest tomorrow. We began the story tonight with the first humans enjoying the goodness and harmony of creation, living in God's world, a world that is very good. We end in a world that is marked by violence—separation, suspicion, distrust, fear, alienation and self-interest—a world that we are, sadly, very familiar with. This catastrophe began when God's creatures decided that the human self should be central in a God-originated, God-centered, God-sustained and God-determined world. We would do well to think more on that."

Looking around at his people, he draws the story to its conclusion. "With the scattering of the people begins the story of the nations, the story of our many families and tribes with our many languages. In the midst of the utter depravity of humanity, in the face of their rebellion—their rejection of God's concern and provision for them—God begins a plan to meet the nations where they are, by calling one family from all the families of the earth in order to bring God's blessing to them all. Thus we come to Abraham, whose story we will hear when we gather again."

The old man looks at his people, says "Shabbat shalom" and turns away from the fire. He smiles at the young girl and looks for the musician. Catching his eye, the elder walks across to the young man. "Would you allow me to lean on you, and escort my weary bones home?" The young man smiles, extends his arm, and the two leave together.

3

covenant

In which we hear the story of the family through whom God would begin to redeem and heal all of creation . . .

As the old man makes his way down to the river, he reviews the vignette he has composed for the beginning of tonight's story. Hearing someone running up behind him, he turns to see the young musician approaching, harp in hand. "Shabbat shalom, old one."

"Shabbat shalom, my young friend. I thank you again for the song of praise you led us in singing last week."

The young man smiles. The old man touches his arm. "May I make a request for tonight?"

"You may certainly make a request," he replies with a grin.

The old man continues to walk, leading the young man by the elbow. "I would have you sing the beginning of a song that tells our story."

The young man thinks for a moment. "Ah," he suddenly understands. "So we will hear of Abraham tonight?"

"Yes, tonight we tell the story of Abraham, our father." They walk in companionable silence, as the young man tunes his harp and brings the words of the song to mind.

The fires are ablaze when the old man and the young musician arrive at the river, and as they make their way through the crowd, the old man notes that many more of his people are present tonight. Word has spread of their gathering—and of the Story. As he takes his now customary place, the young girl approaches, offering a drink from her waterskin. Smiling, he welcomes the gesture before sitting down.

The musician plucks a few notes on the harp, and the people settle down. Parents draw their children close, enfolding the youngest within their cloaks. The harpist looks at the old man, who nods, and he begins the song of praise.

"Oh give thanks to the LORD,
call upon God's name.
Make known God's deeds among the peoples."

As he continues, the people join their voices with his.

"Sing to God, sing praises to God;
speak of all God's wonders.
Remember the wonders which God has done,
God's miracles and the judgments God pronounced.
O descendants of Abraham, God's servant,
Children of Jacob, God's chosen ones.
God is the LORD our God,
God's judgments are in all the earth."

The old man closes his eyes and lifts his voice with his people as they sing together the story he will tell them tonight.

"God has remembered God's covenant forever,
The word which God commanded to a thousand generations.
The covenant which God made with Abraham,
and God's oath to Isaac.
God confirmed it to Jacob as a decree,
To Israel, as an everlasting covenant."

There is scattered applause as the young man sits down. He sighs deeply: it is good to sing the songs of Zion for and with his people. Perhaps he has been wrong; maybe they should sing the LORD's song in exile. Maybe especially in exile, so they remember who—and whose—they are. But then he is overwhelmed by the thought of Jerusalem in rubble, his family's olive groves uprooted and life in this strange land so far away from home, and he fiercely wipes away the tears that come to his eyes. Has God remembered the covenant, as the gathered people have just sung? He looks around at this people in exile, eager expressions on their faces as they wait to hear the old man's story, and his anger smolders once more. Then he turns and discovers the old man looking at him with concern. He stares down at his feet, and a few moments later the old man picks up the story.

"Picture this scene with me. We are in a desolate place. Ahead of us lies a mountain, its craggy peak sharply depicted against the setting sun. As we draw closer, we see two figures, climbing slowly toward the top. One is bent over with age; the other is bent over from the load of wood he carries. They are not talking: they are too tired.

"As they approach the top, the young lad shifts his load and looks around. The wind whistles eerily around them as the light begins to fade. The boy turns to the old man. 'Father, I have carried the wood for the burnt offering, but where is the lamb?'

"His father looks at him with more than a hint of sadness in his eyes. 'God will provide the lamb for the burnt offering . . . my son.' So they walk on together, until they reach the summit.

"The boy unloads the wood while his father wearily builds an altar from the stones lying around. Having placed the wood on the altar, the boy silently turns to his father, who abruptly ties him up and places him on top of the wood. The old man picks up a knife, lifting it high over his head. He looks first to the heavens, and then to his son, and begins to thrust downward . . ."

The old man opens his eyes to find his people leaning in, eager to hear the story. Many of the parents among them are holding their children tightly. He sees sadness in their faces, shock in some. And he sees children with confused expressions. Some look frightened.

But this is their story, and has not God told parents to teach their children the Story in all its beauty and ugliness—both the parts we enjoy and the parts we would rather not think about? He smiles gently at one tear-stained face and continues.

"The last time we gathered, we heard the catastrophic consequences that befell the cosmos following the sin of the first humans. Every relationship was disrupted—that between God and humans, between men and women, and between humanity and the rest of creation. Confronted with the enormous problem of humanity's pervasive wickedness, God's response was the great flood, through which God preserved Noah, a righteous man, and his family. But even a catastrophic deluge did not change the heart of humanity.

"So to save us from ourselves and to mend the broken cosmos, God continues the work of new creation in a new way, choosing one family from all the families of the earth. God made a covenant with that family, the family of Abraham, the old man about to plunge his knife into his only son. Tonight we tell his story.

"These are the generations of Terah. Terah became the father of Abram—whose name means 'exalted father'—and of Nahor and Haran; and Haran became the father of Lot. Now Haran died in the land of his birth, Ur of the Chaldeans. Abram and Nahor took wives for themselves. The name of Abram's wife was Sarai. And Sarai was barren; she had no children. Terah took Abram his son, and Lot his grandson, and they went out together from Ur in the Chaldeans in order to enter the land of Canaan. They went as far as Haran and settled there.

"After many years in Haran, the Lord came to Abram and said, 'Go forth from your country, and from your relatives, and from your father's house, to the land which I will show you; and I will make you a great nation, and I will bless you and make your name great; and so you shall be a blessing; and I will bless those who bless you, and the one who curses you I will curse. And in you all the families of earth shall be blessed.'"

The old man pauses to look around the crowd. "This is a pivotal moment in the Story of God. The Lord said, 'Go!' From the very beginning of our story, God's mission is in view: God will not leave the creation alone to suffer the consequences of sin but instead calls Abram, through whom the story of re-creation will continue.

"We are a sent people. God's command to Abram is to 'go!' Yet this is a command with a promise, a summons with assurance. God told Abram to leave his three sources of security: his country, his relatives and his father's house. Yet God promised to replace all three: 'Abram, leave your homeland; I promise to give you a new land to live in. Leave your family; I promise to give you a new one. Leave your source of blessing (your father); for I promise to bless you myself. And *I* will make your name great."*

"God's promises to Abram are what we all crave. Tower builders try to achieve them on their own, disobeying God's call to go forth. Abram was called to go, and God's strategy to continue re-creation rested in the hands and feet of this one man.

"Now Abram went forth as the LORD had spoken to him. Abram was seventy-five years old when he left Haran with Sarai his wife and Lot his nephew, and all the possessions that they had accumulated. They set out for the land of Canaan, believing in the blessing of God and believing that somehow, through his family, all the families of the earth would be blessed.

"But there is a problem. Did you hear it? Sarai was barren; she had no children.

"God promised Abram a huge family, a great nation, but he and his wife seemed to be physically incapable of having children. Throughout the Story, barrenness plays a prominent role, and as the Story unfolds, we will see it time and time again. Barrenness symbolizes the power-lessness of humanity, yet in our limitedness God acts to give life.

"When they arrived in Canaan, the LORD appeared to Abram and said, 'To your descendants I will give this land.' So Abram built an altar to the LORD who had appeared to him there. And Abram jour-neyed on, continuing toward the Negev. But there was a famine in the land; so Abram went down to Egypt.

"While he was in Egypt, Abram did something that reflects the at-titudes we have already seen in the Story: the desire for self-preserva-tion and self-promotion, and the willingness to harm others out of fear. Sarai was beautiful, and Abram was afraid that an Egyptian would see her and want her for himself—and would kill Abram to get

---

*Throughout the Story, God calls God's people to go—to the orphan, the widow and the stranger; to the broken, the suffering and the marginalized; to the hurt, the lost and the seeking. It has never been God's intention for God's people to huddle together for safety or convenience, as our ancestors did with the tower of Babel. They tried to achieve much with their building: security, prosperity and prominence—trying to "make a name for themselves." We may still be building such "towers" today.

her. Perhaps he was so anxious for the name God had promised him that he chose to protect it—and himself—at Sarai's expense. He persuaded Sarai to pretend she was his sister, and Pharaoh took her into his household.

"But the LORD struck Pharaoh and his household with great plagues because of Sarai, and thus Pharaoh uncovered the deception. Instead of being a blessing for others, Abram's first encounter with another people was to be a curse! Pharaoh had Abram and his family escorted out of Egypt."

A woman's voice calls out, "I can't believe Abraham would do something like that." Another responds, "I can't believe *Sarah* would!" A ripple of laughter rolls through the crowd, gradually receding as a quiet voice emerges from the crowd.

"I thought Abraham was a man of great faith. A man who feared God—that's what we've been told. This story makes it sounds like he was just afraid."

Again it is the young girl. The old man smiles at the innocence—and the perception—of the young. "You are right, on both counts. Abraham was a man of great faith, a man who believed God, a man who feared God. But he was also like us, a man with ordinary fear. And that fear led him to put Sarah in harm's way on more than this one occasion. Abraham's trust in God developed over years, as we will hear as we continue his story.

"Abram returned to Canaan and settled among a warlike people. One night the word of the LORD came to him in a vision and said, 'Do not fear, Abram, I am a shield to you, and your reward will be great.' And Abram replied, 'O LORD God, what will you give me, since I have no children, and so I have had to make my servant Eliezer my heir.'"

The old man pauses for a moment. "In case God missed the point, Abram continued, 'Since you have not given me any children, a person born in my household is my heir.'

"So God said to him, 'This man will not be your heir. You will have a son, and he will be your heir.' And God took Abram outside the tent, and said, 'Look toward the heavens, and count the stars, if you can.

So shall your descendants be.' Despite all evidence to the contrary, Abram believed in the LORD, and God declared him righteous because of his faith.

"God continued, 'I am the LORD who brought you out of Ur of the Chaldeans, to give you this land to possess.' And Abram, perhaps this time seeking reassurance, said, 'O LORD God, how will I know that you will do this?'

"God said, 'Bring me a heifer, a goat, a ram, a turtledove and a pigeon.' And Abram brought them, cut the animals in two, and laid each half opposite the other. When the sun was—"

The young girl speaks up again. "How is that supposed to reassure Abram? I think I'd have preferred some baby clothes or something.."

The old man waits for the laughter to subside. "I know. God's method of reassuring Abram does seem a little strange! Yet it makes sense, given what we know about the customs of some of the peoples living in that region at the time.

"Remember, God comes to meet us where we are. Abram's neighbors made covenants—binding agreements in trade and family life—by doing exactly what God told Abram to do. They would take an animal, kill it and cut the carcass in two. Then they walked between the two halves, which said to the other person, 'If I break the agreement, may I die like this animal.'

"This is what God did with Abram. God used a cultural form Abram would have been familiar with as the basis for God's covenant with him. God did not require Abram to meet any conditions; it would be God's responsibility alone to bring the promises to pass."

The girl seems temporarily satisfied, the old man notes, and so he continues with the Story. "When the sun was going down, Abram fell into a deep sleep, and God said to him, 'Know that your descendants will be strangers in a land that is not theirs, where they will be enslaved and oppressed for four hundred years. But I will also judge the nation who enslaves them, and afterward they will come out, and after the fourth generation they will return here.'"

At these words, the crowd stirs. They know well what it means to be strangers in a land that is not their own. The young musician calls out, "Will God judge the nation that has oppressed *us,* as God did to those who oppressed our ancestors?" The crowd, suddenly restless, looks to the old man for an answer to the question that is never far from their hearts and minds. He stands to his feet, and another's words once more come to mind.

"Listen to me." The old man recites, "O Jacob—Israel, whom I have called. I am God, I am the first: I am also the last. Surely my hand founded the earth, and my right hand spread out the heavens; when I call them, they stand together. Assemble, all of you, and listen! The LORD shall carry out God's good pleasure on Babylon, and God's arm shall be against the Chaldeans . . ."

The musician leaps to his feet. "But when will God do this? Why must we wait so long for God to act?"

For the first time an edge comes to the old man's voice. "I am not finished. Please sit down."

For a moment the young man stands frozen, surprised by the elder's tone of voice. Then, mumbling an apology, he sits down, and the old man continues.

"Thus says the LORD, your Redeemer, the Holy One of Israel; I am the LORD your God who teaches you what is best for you, who leads you in the way you should go." The old man pauses to gaze into the faces of those around him, willing them to listen and understand. "If only you had paid attention to my commandments. Then your well-being would have been like a river, and your righteousness like the waves of the sea. Your descendants would have been like the sand . . . their name would never be cut off or destroyed from my presence."

A deep silence falls over the crowd, and few can meet the old man's gaze. It is one thing to want God to deliver you from difficult circumstances, quite another to take responsibility for why you are in those circumstances in the first place.

The old man's features soften, and he sits down. He looks around at his people and smiles. "Now, where was I? Oh yes, the covenant!"

The people take a collective deep breath, then relax as the old man continues.

"Now when the sun had set, it was very dark, and suddenly a flaming torch appeared and passed between the pieces of the animals. And on that day the LORD made a covenant with Abram, saying, 'To your descendants I have given this land.'

"The covenant was ratified through the shedding of blood. In making the covenant in this way, God was saying to Abram, 'May I die if I do not keep my covenant with you.'"

The old man anticipates a question, and looks toward the young girl. He is not disappointed. "But abba, surely God cannot die?" she asks.

"You speak truly, young one. Do we not sing in so many of our songs, 'Praise be to the LORD, the God of Israel, from everlasting to everlasting'?"

Her brow wrinkles in thought. "Then why does God make the covenant with Abraham in this way? Why say, 'May I die' if you cannot?"

The old man has asked this same question himself, and so he offers the only answer he has. "I do not know. It is a mystery to me."

Her mouth drops open, and the old man laughs. "Does it surprise you that I do not have an answer to every question you ask?" The crowd laughs as well, delighting in the expression on the young girl's face.

"Now, although Abram believed God's promise, after ten years he and his wife Sarai were still childless. Sarai thought that it was taking God too long to fulfill the covenant promise, so she told Abram to sleep with her servant Hagar and claim that child as theirs. So Abram did—"

"I bet he did!" a woman calls out, to more general laughter.

"—and Ishmael was born," the old man continues. "Yet this was not God's plan. As always happens in the Story, whenever we try to 'help God out,' invariably we make things worse, as we shall see.

"A long thirteen years after God made the covenant with him, God came to Abram and said, 'Behold, my covenant is with you, and you shall be the father of many nations. No longer will your name be Abram; from this day forward your name will be Abraham, "father of many," for I will make you the father of many nations.

"'And I will establish my covenant between me and you and your descendants, and it will last forever, and I will be your God. As for Sarai your wife, you shall no longer call her name Sarai, but Sarah shall be her name. And I will bless her and give you a son by her, and she will be the mother of nations.'

"Abram laughed to himself because Sarah and he were so old, and said, 'Oh God, why can't Ishmael be the one?'

"But God said, 'No, Sarah your wife will bear you a son, and you will call his name Isaac, and I will establish my covenant with him. And as for Ishmael, I have heard you; I will bless him, and will make of him a great nation. But my covenant I will establish with Isaac, whom Sarah will bear to you at this season next year.'

"The sign of the covenant God made between Abraham and his descendants was circumcision. When God departed, Abraham, Ishmael and every male in Abraham's household were circumcised, as God had said.

"Now the LORD appeared again to Abraham by the oaks of Mamre while Abraham was sitting in the entrance to his tent. He looked up, and three men were standing opposite him. When he saw them, he ran from the tent to meet them, and bowed to the ground before them. Sarah prepared a meal for them, and they ate together. Then they said to him, 'Where is Sarah your wife?' Abraham said, 'In the tent.' And he said, 'I will surely return to you at this time next year; and behold, Sarah your wife shall have a son.' And Sarah, listening at the tent doorway, laughed to herself.

"Then the LORD did for Sarah as God had promised, and she bore a son to Abraham in his old age. He called him Isaac, which means 'laughter.' Abraham circumcised Isaac when he was eight days old, as God had commanded him. And the lad grew up into a handsome, strong young man."

"What about Ishmael?" the young girl asks. "Did he and Isaac get along?" She glances at her little brother sitting next to her, who promptly punches her in the arm.

Smiling sadly, the old man says, "No, they never really had the chance to get along. Sarah wanted the promises of God all for her son, Isaac, and so she told Abraham to send Ishmael and his mother away."

"That's not fair!" exclaims the young girl.

Her father lays his hand on her arm, apparently uncomfortable with her statement. "*Isaac* is the chosen one, not Ishmael. And you are descended from Isaac, my daughter—you are part of God's chosen people. Ishmael has no place in our story."

The old man looks at the father for a long moment, and then turns his face to the young girl. "You are right, little one. It was not fair. And it deeply distressed Abraham to think about sending Ishmael away. But God promised to provide for Ishmael, and told Abraham that Ishmael too would become a nation. So Abraham sent Ishmael away. And God was indeed with the lad, and his descendants did become a great people."

The old man stands to stretch his aching muscles, before reaching the climax of the evening's story. "Now it came about after these things that God tested Abraham.

"God chose Abraham to be the one through whom the task of re-creation—of mending the broken universe—would continue, and God entered into a unilateral covenant with him. But God did not know if Abraham would be faithful to this call, and so God tested him.

"We know what follows is a test, for the writer of Torah tells us. But Abraham does not. For Abraham, what follows is deadly serious. God called out, 'Abraham!' and Abraham replied, 'Here I am.'

"'Take now your son. Your only son. The son whom you love, Isaac.* I want you to go to the land of Moriah, and offer Isaac there as a burnt offering on the mountain.'"

The young girl leaps to her feet. "What?! That can't be right! Kill

---

*This story of a father sacrificing his son is the first time the word *love* appears in Scripture.

Isaac? How can God ask Abraham to kill the son he has waited for so long? And isn't Isaac the one with whom all the promises of the covenant rest?"

The old man looks into her eyes, now brimming with tears, with sadness and understanding. She asks almost pleadingly, "Are you sure about this? Is this really how the story ends?"

"Yes, I am sure about this." Then he smiles. "But this is not how the story ends." He beckons her to sit, and looks around the crowd as he continues.

"God has already tested Abraham once, with the call to go, the call to leave his *past* behind—asking the son to relinquish his father. And Abraham proved faithful. But now God is calling him to give up his *future*—asking the father to relinquish his son. And just as in the original call, God gives no reason for the demand. But unlike the previous six encounters Abraham has had with God, this time there is no promise accompanying the command. If Abraham is faithful this time and offers Isaac as a sacrifice, then how can God be faithful and keep the covenant?"

"Exactly," says the musician, looking at the young girl before continuing. "Surely Abraham argues with God; this makes no sense at all."

The old man smiles. "Let me tell you what Abraham did. Abraham rose early in the morning, saddled his donkey, took two of his young men with him, and Isaac his son; he split wood for the burnt offering, and arose and went to the place that God had told him.

"On the third day, he saw the mountain ahead, and said to the young men, 'Stay here with the donkey. The lad and I will go yonder, and we will worship God, and return to you.' He laid the wood on Isaac, and took a knife from the saddlebags. And together they started to climb the mountain.

"So here we are, back where we began tonight. Can we begin to imagine the depths of the pain of the father as he laid the wood on the back of his son, his only son, the wood that would be his son's place of death, his place of sacrifice? What was Abraham thinking as he trudged up the mountain with his beloved son, in silence?

"After a while Isaac broke the silence, asking the question that any intelligent young man would under the circumstances. He called out, 'Father!' And Abraham responded to his call, 'Here I am, my son.'

"'I see the wood and the fire, but where is the lamb for the burnt offering?'

"Abraham gazed into his son's eyes, trying to disguise his anguish, and said, 'God himself will provide the lamb for the burnt offering, my son.' *God will have to answer your question, my son, for I cannot.*

"Or perhaps he gazed into the eyes of his son, his beloved son, his only son, and said it this way: 'God himself will provide the lamb for the burnt offering . . .' and then, looking away, '. . . my son.'

A murmur or two can be heard in the crowd, as people hear familiar words in a new way. The old man continues. "So Abraham prepared to kill his son, the son of the covenant. Yet just as he started to swing the knife down, a voice from heaven called out, 'Abraham! Abraham!'

"And he stopped and said, 'Here I am.'

"'Do not harm the lad; for now I know that you fear God, since you have not withheld your son, your only son, the son whom you love, from me.' And Abraham raised his eyes, and saw a ram caught in a thicket by its horns. And he took the ram, and offered him up in the place of his son. And Abraham called that place *Yahweh yireh*, 'The LORD will provide.'

"Then the voice called from heaven again, and said, 'I swear by myself, declares the LORD, because you have done this thing, and have not withheld your son, your only son, indeed I will greatly bless you, and I will greatly multiply your descendants, so they will be like the stars of the heavens, and like the sand of the seashore. And through your descendants, all the nations of the earth shall be blessed, because you have obeyed me.'*

---

*It is only now, after Abraham has done what God asked, that God repeats the promise: "I will bless you, and through your descendants, all the nations of the earth shall be blessed, because you have obeyed me." God's plan for re-creation depends upon Abraham's obedience. Only when Abraham lives up to his role as a willing partner

"Thus God tested Abraham, and Abraham proved faithful. Yet the place of his testing is not called 'Abraham will be faithful.' No, it is called 'God will provide.' For this story ultimately is about the faithfulness of God. The God who makes covenant with Abraham can be trusted, even if God cannot be understood at times. For God both tests and provides."

The old man turns to the young girl. "You asked a question earlier about Abraham's fear. Abraham did many things out of fear, things that harmed others. But because he was willing to obey God and sacrifice his son, God says to Abraham, 'Now I know you fear me.' This fear that God acknowledges is not ordinary fear. It is the very opposite of ordinary fear. It is trust—trust in the God who will provide. Trust is the antidote to fear.

"However, many of us do not want a God like this." The old man takes time to look around the circle of faces before continuing. "Some of us are complacent, and want a God who only provides without testing.

"Some of us are bitter, wanting only a God who tests us, while refusing God's generous provision.

"And some of us are cynical, wanting neither: we do not wish to answer to God, nor rely on God.

"Abraham believes and embraces both, and that is the substance of his faith.

"Abraham's faithfulness did not come easily, nor without anguish, yet God still praised him for it. You and I are on that same journey, and we also can grow into our faithfulness as we learn to trust God and each other more within the context of the community God has placed us in."

The old man sees heads nodding among the adults. Many of the children have fallen asleep. He feels the weariness of the end of a week's labor. It is time to bring the story to an end for this night.

"The story continues through Isaac and his son Jacob. God renews the covenant with each of them, and again miraculously gives them

---

with God does God swear—for the first time—that God's plan for re-creation will move forward.

children even though their wives are barren. They receive the same promises from God: that of land, descendants and God's blessing. And God adds a new promise to the covenant—God's presence with them, something unheard of. So both Isaac and Jacob renew the covenant with God, for they are indeed blessed to be a blessing to the nations. Yes," he looks at the young musician, "even to Babylon."

Before the young man can protest, his elder says, "Remember the words of Jeremiah, sent in his letter from Jerusalem: 'Seek the welfare of the city where I have sent you into exile, and pray to the LORD on its behalf; for in its welfare lies your welfare.'

"Yet Abraham's story also reminds us that God is the one who promises and will provide—good news to those who despair and shattering news to those of us who trust in our pride. You and I face the same decision as Abraham: Do we grimly strive after control over lives that are effectively uncontrollable, or do we surrender our lives to the God who promises, trusting God to provide all our needs?

"It is important to remember that Abraham does not live to see the completion of God's promises. When he dies, he and Sarah have only the one son, Isaac, and only one small plot of land in Canaan. Next time we gather we will hear how God goes about beginning to fulfill the covenant, how God continues the work of re-creation through a people."

The old man moves to dismiss the people for the night, but he is interrupted with the first strains of a song: "Oh give thanks to the LORD, call upon God's name; Make known God's deeds among the people." It is the young man, who wrestles with God in song. The people join in:

"Sing to God, sing praises to God;
     Speak of all God's wonders.
Glory in God's holy name;
     Let the heart of those who seek the LORD be glad.
Seek the LORD and God's strength;
     Seek God's face continually.

Remember God's wonders which God has done,
    God's marvels and the judgments uttered by God's mouth,
O seed of Abraham, God's servant,
    O sons of Jacob, God's chosen ones!
This is the LORD our God;
    God's judgments are in all the earth.
God has remembered God's covenant forever,
    The word which God commanded to a thousand
        generations,
The covenant which God made with Abraham,
    And God's oath to Isaac."

The singing echoes into the night, and the old man's heart is lifted with this poetic reminder that even when we are faithless, God remains faithful.

4

community (part one)

EXODUS

In which we hear the story of the event that began

to shape the people of God's understanding of who

God is and what God is doing . . .

When the old man arrives at the riverside, his people are waiting for him. "Have you eaten, father?" Someone passes him bread and wine. He eats, looking into the faces of those nearest him, and they look back expectantly. They have come to look forward to these evenings at the end of the workweek—not just for the rest which the Sabbath provides but because they love to hear the stories of their people.

They love to hear some of the stories, at least. But as the old man is all too painfully aware, the Story must not simply be heard; it must be understood—and most importantly, the Story must come to shape the lives of its hearers. In the language of his people, "to know" something requires more than simply having information; one does not truly know something until one does it. And that has always been the problem for his people: in failing to live the Story faithfully, they soon forget it. Is that not why God continually told them, "Remember that you were once slaves in Egypt"?

With that thought in mind, the old man puts down the wineskin and looks for the young girl and her family. They are sitting on the other side of the fire, sharing a meal with their neighbors. He catches the young girl's eye and beckons her over. As she tugs her father's sleeve and points toward the old man, he repeats the gesture, this time including her little brother in the invitation. Their father says something to them, and then the old man is pleased to see them jump up and run around to join him.

Smiling broadly, they sit at his feet, and are soon joined by other children. The old man welcomes them all and then stands. The crowd slowly grows quiet, until all that can be heard is the crackle of the flames and the wind whispering in the willows. He looks down at the children, and then sits to address them.

"Tonight we will hear a most wonderful story, a story you have heard every year during the Feast of Passover. It is a story that tells us who—and whose—we are." Tousling the hair of the young girl's brother he says, "And just as you hear the story every year with your family, tonight we will see the story through the eyes of one family. So, find a comfortable spot, and we will begin." He closes his eyes and brings to mind the vignette he has crafted for this evening.

"Picture this scene. The sun is slowly setting, a huge fiery orb on the horizon. A mother and father stand in the doorway of their home, their young daughter between them. The little girl cradles a lamb in her arms—her favorite, a beautiful, spotless, snowy-white lamb. She looks up at her parents with large, limpid eyes. 'Is it time, abba?'

"The father rests his hand on her head and gazes out across the landscape that he has known all his life, the only land he has known, a land that is good for pasture for his flocks, the land that his ancestor Joseph was given by a pharaoh who treated his people well. But that pharaoh lived four centuries ago; this pharaoh is cruel. This land of Goshen is no longer a land of peace but a land of slavery, a land of harsh bondage and backbreaking labor.

"The father gazes out across the land, no longer seeing this vista. Instead, in his mind's eye, he sees a land flowing with milk and honey, the land promised to his forefathers: Abraham, Isaac, Jacob. He wonders if he will ever see it, whether his family will one day raise their flocks there.

"A gentle tugging on his cloak brings him back to the present. 'Abba, is it time?' He gazes down at his daughter with eyes filled with love and sadness, yet a small gleam of hope begins to sparkle as he thinks of all that has happened in the past few weeks. 'Yes, Mahlah, it is time.'

"As the sun dips below the horizon, casting a blood-red hue over the valley, the father places his arms around his wife and daughter, takes one last look around him, looks down at the spotless lamb, and then leads his family into the house, before darkness falls across the land . . .”

The old man opens his eyes to see the eager expressions on the faces of his young audience. “These people are the descendants of Abraham, whose story we heard last week. Abraham’s great-grandson Joseph brought the family of Jacob, whom God renamed Israel, down into Egypt during a time of great famine. There they settled, the guests of a grateful pharaoh. For four centuries the people of Israel lived in Goshen in Egypt, and, just as God had promised Abraham, they were fruitful and multiplied and became a great nation. But a new dynasty of pharaohs arose who viewed the people of Israel not as a blessing but as a threat to national security. So they enslaved them, forcing them to build the great storage cities of Pithom and Raamses.

“Yet despite their affliction, the people continued to grow, and so in an attempt to control the enslaved population, the pharaoh ordered the death of all Hebrew baby boys. Now, a daughter of the tribe of Levi tried to hide her beautiful baby boy from the Egyptians, but when she could do so no longer, she made a tiny ark from bulrushes and placed the boy in it, and then placed it among the reeds of the river Nile. When the daughter of the pharaoh came down to the river to bathe, she heard the cries of the baby and ordered a slave to pull the basket from the Nile. She then took the baby home, to be raised in the pharaoh’s palace.”

The old man pauses. “Can anyone tell me the name of this special baby?” Every hand is immediately raised. He looks around the group, his gaze coming to rest on the young girl’s brother. “Tell me, little one, who is this baby?”

“Moses,” he replies.

“That’s right. She named him Moses, which means ‘one who draws out,’ because she drew him out of the water. This Hebrew baby boy was spared even as many others were killed by a king whose power was threatened. God would one day take this baby, Moses, and raise him up to lead God's people, drawing them out of slavery.*

"For forty years Moses lived in the pharaoh's palace yet he never forgot his identity as one of the people of Israel. One day he came across an Egyptian beating a Hebrew slave. After looking this way and that, he decided to take matters into his own hands, killing the Egyptian and hiding his body in the sand.

"The pharaoh heard of the murder, and so Moses had to flee for his life, to the land of Midian. He married one of the daughters of the priest of Midian, and spent the next forty years shepherding the flocks of his father-in-law, Jethro.

"Now the pharaoh died, and the children of Israel cried out because of their bondage, and their cry for help was heard by God. God remembered the covenant with Abraham, Isaac and Jacob." Leaning forward to gently touch the heads of the children within reach, some who squirm and giggle at his touch, he looks up at the crowd to say, "God looked upon the children of Israel, and God took notice of their plight.

"One day, while Moses was pasturing Jethro's flocks, he came to Horeb, the mountain of God, where he saw a bush spontaneously burst into flames. This happened all the time in the fierce heat of the desert, so he thought little of it. Yet when he noticed that it kept burning, he turned aside to take a closer look.

"When the LORD God saw that he turned aside to look, God called to him from the midst of the bush, and said, 'Moses, Moses.'

"Moses said, 'Here I am.'

"'Do not come any closer,' God replied. 'Take off your sandals, for the place on which you are standing is holy ground. I am the God of your father, the God of Abraham, the God of Isaac and the God of Jacob.'

"Moses hid his face, for he was afraid to look at God. And the LORD said, 'I have seen the affliction of my people who are in Egypt, and have paid heed to their cry because of the slave drivers, for I am aware of their suffering. So I have come down to deliver them from the

---

*Much later in the Story of God we will hear a very similar story of another baby Hebrew boy who will survive the murderous intentions of a threatened king and go on to draw people out of bondage.

power of the Egyptians, and to bring them up from that land, to a land flowing with milk and honey.'"

The old man pauses to take a drink, then continues, feeling the deep sense of awe this story always provokes in him. "God *came down*. Once again we are reminded by our story that we do not worship a God who is distant and far off but a God who draws near, a God who hears our cries, a God who cares about us. A God who comes down to deliver us from the power of those things that keep us in bondage.

"So God said to Moses, 'Come now, and I will send you to the pharaoh, so that you may bring my people, the children of Israel, out of Egypt. And I will be with you, and this shall be the sign to you that it is I who have sent you: when you have brought the people out of Egypt, you shall worship God at this mountain.'*

"Moses said, 'If I go to the children of Israel and say to them, "The God of your fathers has sent me to you," they may ask me, "What is God's name?" What shall I say to them?'

"And God said to Moses, 'I AM WHO I AM. Thus you shall say to the children of Israel, "YHWH (the LORD) has sent me to you. This is God's name forever, YHWH." Gather the elders of Israel together and tell them that the God of their ancestors Abraham, Isaac and Jacob is about to bring them out of the slavery of Egypt into a land flowing with milk and honey. And then you and the elders will go to the pharaoh and will say to him, "The LORD, the God of the Hebrews has met with us, and we must go into the desert to worship the LORD." But he will not permit you to go, unless he is forced to. So I will stretch out my hand and strike Egypt with all my miracles, and then he will let you go.'

"Moses left the land of Midian and began his journey back to Egypt. On the way, God met with him again, saying, 'When you arrive in Egypt see that you perform before the pharaoh all the wonders which I have put in your power; but I will harden pharaoh's heart so that he will not let the people go.'

---

*Mount Horeb is another name for Mount Sinai.

The old man sees the young girl open her mouth to speak but then close it again. "Do you have a question, my young friend?"

She hesitates for a moment. "Yes, abba. I don't understand this part of the story. If God wants the pharaoh to let the people go, why does God harden the pharaoh's heart so he won't let them go?" Heads nod in agreement; others in the crowd are wondering the same thing.

"That is a question many have asked," the old man replies. "The wonders God says Moses will perform are the ten plagues God sent upon Egypt, which were sent to reveal God's power over all the gods of Egypt. Some say God hardened the pharaoh's heart in order for the pharaoh, and all the Egyptians, to see that the gods they served were powerless before the LORD God of Israel.

"Indeed, the LORD told Moses to go to the pharaoh and say, 'For this reason I have allowed you to remain, in order to show you my power, and in order to proclaim my name through all the earth.'"

The young girl's brow wrinkles; she is apparently unconvinced by this answer. The old man smiles—he too wishes every question had a satisfactory answer, but his years have taught him that all too often they do not. He lifts his gaze to the crowd. "Others say it was so that *Israel* would see that the gods of the Egyptians were powerless—and so would learn to trust in the LORD alone." He pauses to let these words sink in before picking up the story again.'"'"

"God continued his instructions to Moses, 'After you have performed these wonders, go to the pharaoh and say, "Thus says the LORD, 'Israel is my son, my first-born.* And I said to you, "Let my son go that he may serve me"; but you have refused to let him go. Behold I will kill your son, your first-born.'"'"

The young girl's brow wrinkles even deeper at these words, but she does not say anything as the old man continues. "Moses arrived in Egypt, and he and his brother Aaron assembled the elders of Israel.

---

*While this story is concerned with the descendants of Abraham, God's covenant with Abraham was for this one people to bless all peoples. In speaking of Israel as "God's first-born" perhaps we see implicitly that God's intention is to have a larger family than this one people.

Aaron spoke all the words which the LORD had spoken to Moses, and performed the signs God had told him to offer the elders. And the people believed; and when they heard that the LORD was concerned about the people of Israel, and that God had seen their suffering, then they bowed low and worshiped.

"Moses and Aaron went to the pharaoh and said, 'The LORD, the God of the Hebrews, sent me to you, saying, "Let my people go, that they may serve me in the wilderness."' But the pharaoh said, 'Who is the LORD that I should obey his voice to let Israel go? I do not know the LORD: I will not let Israel go.' Shortly afterward, the pharaoh commanded the taskmasters to make the people of Israel work even harder, by not supplying them with the raw materials for building.

"The elders of Israel complained bitterly to Moses about their harsh treatment, and Moses in turn complained to God. God replied, saying, 'I am the LORD, and I appeared to Abraham, Isaac and Jacob as God Almighty, but by my name, YHWH, the LORD, I did not make myself known to them. I established my covenant with them to give them the land of Canaan. I have heard the cries of the children of Israel, and have remembered my covenant. Say, therefore, to the children of Israel, "I am the LORD, and I will bring you out from under your burdens, and will deliver you from bondage. I will redeem you with an outstretched hand, then I will take you for my people, and I will be your God; and you shall know that I am the LORD your God."'"

The old man pauses to take another drink, and as he does so the harpist calls out from the crowd. "God keeps telling Moses that God is going to deliver them from bondage. When are we going to hear God actually do it? As you say, every year we hear the story of God's people liberated from slavery. Yet here we are, God's people, still in exile. Nothing has changed. When is God going to deliver us?"

The elder puts down his waterskin and turns to address the young man. "Yes, God promises to save God's people from slavery. But this salvation is not just *from* something, it is also *to* something: to service to the LORD, the God of Abraham, the God of the covenant.

"Remember, we serve God by being faithful to the covenant, by living in ways that embody who God is to all the peoples around us, inviting them into relationship with the LORD. Sitting here in exile as we are, perhaps we would do well to ask questions not only of God but of ourselves as well."

The old man turns back to the crowd. "And so we come to the ten plagues God sent against Egypt. Plagues of frogs, lice, flies, locusts—creatures that cause discomfort in normal times, let alone when a land is filled with them. But these plagues were not simply to inconvenience or distress the Egyptians. Each of the ten plagues that God sends is related directly to an Egyptian god.

"The first plague, where God turns the waters of the Nile into blood, was an act against one of the most important gods of Egypt, the river Nile itself. From the Nile they drew the water that enabled them to grow their crops, the very source of their life and wealth. The ninth plague, the plague of darkness, was an act against the sun goddess Ra. And the ultimate proof of God's power over the gods of Egypt was saved for last.

"The Egyptians, the dynasty of the pharaohs—the sons of Ra—depended on the survival of the son more than the pharaoh himself. For the firstborn son of the pharaoh was the sign of the god Ra's ongoing presence with them. God's judgment on the firstborn of Egypt declared that the gods behind the pharaoh's brutal and oppressive rule were powerless and would be allowed to tyrannize humanity no longer. This final plague is a pivotal moment in the Story of God. After this plague, God told Moses, the pharaoh would let God's people go.

"So Moses went to the pharaoh and said, 'Thus says the LORD, "About midnight I will go out into the midst of Egypt, and all the firstborn in the land of Egypt will die, from the firstborn of pharaoh who sits on the throne, even to the firstborn of the slave girl, and the firstborn of your cattle. There shall be a great cry in the land of Egypt such as there has not been before and such as shall never be again. But the children of Israel will not be touched, that you may understand how the LORD makes a distinction between Egypt and Israel."'"

"Then the LORD said to Moses, 'Speak to all the people of Israel, saying, "Take a lamb, a spotless lamb from your flocks, one for each household, and then at twilight, every family must kill the lamb. Take some of the blood, and put it on the two doorposts, and on the lintel of the houses in which they eat it. Eat the lamb that same night, roasted with fire, with unleavened bread and bitter herbs. And prepare yourselves to leave, wearing your cloaks, with your sandals on your feet, and your staff in your hand. This meal is the LORD's Passover.

"'"For I will go through the land of Egypt on that night, and will strike down all the firstborn in the land of Egypt, and against all the gods of Egypt I will execute judgment—for I am the LORD. And the blood shall be a sign for you on the houses where you live; and when I see the blood I will pass over you, and no plague will befall you to destroy you when I strike the land of Egypt. And this day will be a memorial to you, and you shall celebrate it as a feast to the LORD, throughout all generations you are always to celebrate it."'"

The old man looks around the circle of young faces. "And so here we are, back where we began tonight. I wonder what Mahlah was feeling when her father took the lamb from her arms?"

There is silence for a few moments, and then the young girl responds with a question. "Did she know what her father was going to do?" She pauses, suddenly realizing the implications of the Passover for the people of Egypt. With the hint of a tremor in her voice, she continues. "Did she know what God was going to do?"

Before the old man can respond, her young brother declares, "I wouldn't have let him take my lamb. I would have got one of the scrawny ones." A few people laugh, but the young girl does not. She is looking intently at the old man, waiting for an answer.

The old man looks at the brother and sister and says, "Let's hear what happened to Mahlah and her family, shall we? Mahlah watches as her father takes the spotless lamb and prepares to kill it. 'Abba,' she cries, 'what are you doing?'

"'Mahlah, my love, this lamb is the finest of all our flocks. I know he is your favorite, but this is what the LORD requires from us. Your sacrifice tonight will be our salvation.'

"Perhaps Mahlah is not convinced. 'Why must the lamb die, abba? I love him—it's not fair!'

"'Oh Mahlah,' her father replies, 'I know you do. But unless we obey God, and put the blood of the lamb around the doorway, we will lose something far more precious . . .' The man looks down at his daughter and tousles her hair. 'Now, go get your cloak and your sandals, while I prepare the meal.'"

The old man looks into the faces of the children. They have heard the story of the exodus each year at Passover, but tonight it is almost as if they are there in Egypt with their ancestors.

"When Mahlah returns she watches silently as her mother kneads the unleavened bread, and her father takes a bunch of the hyssop bush that grows outside their house, dips it in a basin that contains the blood of the lamb, and splashes it over the lintel of the doorway and on the two doorposts. He turns, looks at the lamb that is roasting over the cooking fire, and then says to his family, 'We must all stay inside, for death is abroad in the land. The blood of the lamb that has been shed will save us this night.'

"And so the family ate the meal and prayed together, as did all the other families of Israel. And at midnight the LORD went throughout the land of Egypt and struck all the firstborn, from the firstborn of the pharaoh who sat on the throne to the firstborn of the captive in his dungeons and all the firstborn of the cattle. But in the land of Goshen, the LORD passed over every house with the blood of the lamb on the doorway.

"And there was a great cry in the land of Egypt, for there was no home where there was not someone dead. Then the pharaoh called for Moses and Aaron in the middle of the night, and said, 'Rise up, get out from among my people, both you and the children of Israel, and go serve the LORD as you have said. Take your flocks and your herds, as you requested, and go—but first, bless me.'

"And so it was that at the end of four hundred and thirty years, all the people of Israel, the hosts of the LORD, went out from the land of

Egypt." The old man stands, and his voice rings with the ancient proclamation, "And this night is to be observed by all the children of Israel throughout all generations, for the LORD brought them out of the land of Egypt, liberating them from slavery.

"The people had seen the way in which the LORD had struck down each of the Egyptian gods, and now had liberated them from slavery. They were finally on the way to the land promised in the covenant God had made with Abraham, Isaac and Jacob. The Egyptians urged them to leave, in fact, fearing even worse things would happen if they stayed. Before the last plague struck, the Israelites had asked the Egyptians for silver and gold, which they had gladly given them. The Israelites carried these things with them as they took their unleavened dough, wrapped their cloaks about them and left their place of bondage to begin their new life. And thus they plundered the Egyptians."

The young harpist leaps to his feet. "Maybe that's what we need to do then! We should ask the Babylonians for treasure and then wait to see if God kills their firstborn before returning to the Promised Land. A new exodus!" He looks around expectantly, waiting for the crowd to cheer his words. But the mood is very different tonight. He turns back to the old man, who is kneeling painfully before the young girl.

Her face is streaked with tears. She looks into his face and utters a single word: "Why?"

"Why did God kill all the firstborn of Egypt, not just the pharaoh's son?" he asks.

"Yes. Why so many? Servants, captives in the pharaoh's prison . . . even the cattle."

"Why not?" calls out the young musician. "They were all Egyptians; they all benefited from our people's slavery. Would that God had killed them all—and the Babylonians too."

The people look to the old man, who sighs deeply, for he has sympathy for both questions. The young man feels the pain of his people's exile deeply; the young girl feels the pain of all humanity. He gently wipes the tears from her face, then stands to his feet once more.

"The young man is right. We do need a new exodus." There is a murmur of surprise at these words. "But not just for our people. For *all* people. The problem is not that our people are in exile in Babylon; the problem is that all of creation is in exile—east of Eden, far removed from the goodness of the garden. Babylon is just the latest expression of what lies at the heart of the problem: humanity's fear, our need to make a name for ourselves, the violence we do to each other and to all of creation in order to secure a future for ourselves, instead of trusting the God of creation to provide. We need a new exodus from sin. An exodus that not only frees the oppressed from being oppressed, but that also frees the oppressors from being oppressors."

His words echo into the night, until a small voice breaks the silence. "How many lambs will that take, abba?"

He looks down to see the little boy, now holding his sister's hand. The old man smiles wearily and says, "I do not know, son. I do not know." He looks at the young girl. "And I know I have not answered your question, daughter. As the Story unfolds, I fear you will have occasion to ask it again. But it is getting late, and I have to finish the story. May we return to your question another time?"

The young girl nods, trying to take in all the old man has said. He turns back to the crowd.

"And so the people left their life of slavery and began their journey into a new life of freedom. God kept the covenant with the children of Abraham, Isaac and Jacob, including the promise of God's presence with them. God led them into the wilderness, going before them in a pillar of cloud by day, and a pillar of fire by night.

"But the pharaoh had a change of heart. 'What is this that we have done, that we have let Israel go from serving us?' And he led the chariot division of Egypt's military, together with the army and the cavalry units, to chase the children of Israel and bring them back to slavery.

"As the clouds of dust from the horses and chariots swept toward them, the people of Israel were terrified and cried out to the LORD. They challenged Moses, saying, 'Was it because there were no graves for us in Egypt that you have brought us out to die in the wilderness?'

"How quickly they forgot what God had shown them through the plagues. How quick they were to doubt God's care and protection of them." He pauses, then says softly, "How quickly we do also.

"Then Moses said, 'Do not be afraid! Stand by and see the salvation, the liberation of the LORD which God will do for you today; for the Egyptians, whom you have seen today, you will never see them again, forever. The LORD will fight for you, while you keep silent.'

"Moses stood on the shore of the Red Sea, the waves lapping at his feet. He lifted up his staff, and stretched it out over the sea, and the LORD swept the sea back by a strong east wind, creating a path of dry land, with walls of water piled high on both sides. And he led the people through the Red Sea.

"When the pharaoh saw this, he led his chariots into the sea. But the LORD brought confusion to the pharaoh's armies, causing their chariot wheels to swerve, and God made them drive with difficulty. And the Egyptians cried out, 'Let us flee from Israel, for the LORD is fighting for them against us.'

"After the last of the children of Israel had walked onto the far shore, Moses stretched out his hand over the sea once more, and the sea returned to its normal state. The waters came crashing down and covered the chariots and the horsemen, and pharaoh's entire army was destroyed.

"Thus the LORD saved Israel that day from the hand of the Egyptians, and Israel saw the Egyptians dead on the seashore. Once more, God delivered God's people from the danger of the sea. And when Israel saw the great power that the LORD had used against the Egyptians, the people feared the LORD, and they believed in the LORD and in God's servant Moses."

The old man is tired. It has been a long night. He stretches his aching back, then turns to remind his people once more: "This story lies at the heart of the identity of our people. It must be told more than just during the Feast of Passover. For has not God reminded us again and again, 'I am the LORD your God who brought you out of Egypt, out of slavery'?

"In the story of the exodus we see the liberation of God. God heard the cries of the people in bondage, and came down to save them. God delivered them from the tyranny of the Egyptians, and led them out of Egypt to begin their journey to the Promised Land.*

"This is our story. God's intention remains to liberate us from 'Egypt,' from the things that keep us in bondage. God continually wishes to lead us out of those things that keep us distant from God and from each other, those things that lead us even further into exile. Our God is a God of liberation, a God who passes over us, sparing us from death, through the shed blood of a spotless lamb.

"But God not only wanted to get God's people out of Egypt, God also wanted to get Egypt out of them—its stories, rooted in fear and greed, power and prestige, idolatry and ideology. We also have been deeply shaped by the stories of Egypt, the stories of Babylon, the stories of empire. That is why we must keep telling the Story of God to each other, to remind ourselves who we are and to help us resist the power and attraction of those other stories, and break the hold they have over us.

"My friends, we live with the hope that one day God will deliver us from exile here in Babylon, that one day we will return to the land God gave our ancestors, that one day God will restore the kingdom to Israel. But the story of the exodus is also a cautionary tale. Pharaoh's oppressive power was legitimized by the priests and maintained by the military. When the oppressed cry out, God declares, 'I will hear.' We must not become like the pharaoh, because God acts *against* people like the pharaoh.

"Indeed, Torah—the Law of God's people, given by God to shape our identity so that we reflect God's character—makes special provision for the marginalized and the oppressed, the most vulnerable of society.

"We will hear that story the next time we gather." The old man

---

*The story of the exodus is central to the Story of God and to the story of us. It was in the exodus event that God came near to the children of Israel, revealing God's name to them and making them God's people. We are drawn into the people of God as we experience the same liberation that God brought the children of Israel—liberation from the bondage of sin, and all the oppression that sin brings. God's mission is one of liberation, and God's people are called to partner with God in bringing liberation to all those who live in bondage.

scans the crowd, seeking out the young musician, and with a gesture invites him to stand. He does so, somewhat nervously.

"My young friend, may I make a request?"

The young man smiles, visibly relieved. "You may certainly make a request, old one."

The old man smiles in return. "Would you lead us in the song of the exodus that Moses and the newly liberated people of Israel sang, there on the far shores of the Red Sea?"

The young man reaches down for his harp, checks the tuning, and then begins.

"The LORD is my strength and my song,
and God has become my salvation.
This is our God, whom we will praise.

Who is like you among the gods, O LORD?
Who is like you, majestic in holiness,
awesome in praises, working wonders?

Terror and dread fall upon our enemies,
by the greatness of your arm, they are motionless as stone,
until your people pass over,
until the people pass over whom you have purchased with
    blood.

You will bring them and plant them in the mountain of your
    covenant, the place O LORD which you have made for
    your dwelling,
the sanctuary O LORD which you have established.
The LORD shall reign forever and ever."

The old man looks down to see two big brown eyes looking up at him. It is the young girl. She gets to her feet and, after a moment's indecision, hugs the old man briefly before grabbing her brother's hand and running to rejoin her family. The old man watches them walk off, singing the song of exodus together, and he feels hope rising in his heart.

5

community (part Two)

SINAI

In which we hear the story of the covenant through which God continued to shape the identity and mission of God's people . . .

When the old man arrives at the riverside, the fires are already banked high, and the crowd is larger than on the previous Sabbath. "Tell us more stories of Moses, father!" The old man smiles. Yes, Moses, the Lawgiver of his people, the one through whom his people received the gift of Torah,* by which they know God's character and by which the lives of God's people are to be shaped. But it is one thing to hear Torah, another to live Torah. And as the old man looks around him, he feels the ache of exile once more; he knows exactly why his people are here in Babylon.

As he takes his seat, the young musician comes to sit beside him. "Shabbat shalom, old one."

"The peace of the Sabbath be with you also, my young friend. Have you chosen a song for this evening?"

"Yes, father," the young man replies. "There are many songs of praise about Torah. They are all beautiful." He looks down for a moment, then gazes intently into the old man's eyes. "But I found it hard to choose one."

"Why is that?"

"Can you not imagine why?" the young man replies. The lines around the old man's eyes crease deeply as he smiles. Perhaps the young man has been thinking about more than the music. "I think I can," he offers. "But I would like to hear you explain it."

The singer collects his thoughts. "As I was learning the songs of

---

*Torah means "teaching" or "instruction" in Hebrew. It is sometimes called "the Law" or "the Books of Moses." It is the first five books of the Bible, which are also known as "the Pentateuch."

praise from my teacher, he often talked about leading the crowds in singing them in the Temple—seeing people moved by the beauty of both the words and the music in the beauty of the Temple. In such moments, he told me, he felt a great love for our people. And he felt truly close to our God." He pauses. "I confess I sometimes imagined myself doing just that, caught up in love of God, in love of Torah, right there in the Temple . . ."

"But?" the old man offers.

"But," the young man continues, "I wonder if our people's love for Torah ended when the songs of praise did. I wonder if Torah was something that was easy to love in the Temple but not after returning home. I know the songs of praise, but I wonder if I, like them, have ever truly known Torah."

The old man looks into the troubled face of the young man and places his hand on his arm. "That's what comes of listening to the Story."

The young man smiles ruefully. "I know, old one, I know."

"Yet despite questioning yourself, you have still chosen a song for us tonight?"

The young man leans forward, suddenly animated. "Yes, I have. Because I want to love Torah. I want to know Torah. And maybe now, here in exile, with the Temple in ruins, perhaps as I sing these songs it will be different."

The old man's smile broadens. "Well spoken, my young friend. I hope that becomes true for all of us. So, which song of praise have you chosen?"

"I have chosen a stanza from our longest song." He pauses. "And I have rewritten it." The old man lifts an eyebrow, but the singer continues. "I thought that maybe if the people heard the song in a new way, it might help others ask the same questions I have found myself asking."

The old man inclines his head, inviting the young man to stand and sing. As he picks up his harp and rises to his feet, he turns around to say one last thing, his smile fading as he does, and a line of anger appearing between his eyes. "But do not think I have forgotten what the Babylonians have done to us."

With that he turns to the crowd, who have settled down, and he begins to sing. The old man sighs deeply and says to himself, "Small steps . . ."

"Let your love, GOD, shape my life
    with salvation, exactly as you promised;
Then I'll be able to stand up to mockery
    because I trusted your Word.
Don't ever deprive me of truth, not ever—
    your commandments are what I depend on.
Oh, I'll guard with my life what you've revealed to me,
    guard it now, guard it ever;
And I'll stride freely through wide open spaces
    as I look for your truth and your wisdom;
Then I'll tell the world what I find,
    speak out boldly in public, unembarrassed.
I cherish your commandments—oh, how I love them!—
    relishing every fragment of your counsel."

As the young musician takes his seat once more, the people turn to their neighbors in surprise. They recognized the song after a few lines, but changing the words seems . . . bold? Presumptuous? As the old man gets to his feet, they wait to see how he will respond to what the young man has done.

"'I cherish your commandments—oh, how I love them!—relishing every fragment of your counsel.' New words for an old song." He turns to the harpist. "Thank you, my young friend. Your song prepares us for the story we will hear tonight: the giving of Torah to our people at Mount Sinai." With these affirming words the people relax and settle in for the story.

The old man turns back to the crowd. "Hear now of the years our ancestors spent in the wilderness of Sinai, and of the covenant we made with God there, as we continue the story of Moses. Picture this scene . . .

"Moses leaned wearily on his staff and rose to speak to his people one last time. He gazed with undimmed eyes at a sea of upturned faces, much younger faces than his own. For forty long years he had led them, for forty long years he had watched them bury their parents and grandparents, until there was only this generation left. For forty years they had been wandering in this unrelenting wilderness, waiting for the day when they would enter the land God had promised to Abraham, Isaac and Jacob, the land that would become their first real home.

"That day had finally arrived. Moses sighed and turned to look in the direction of the Promised Land, a land flowing with milk and honey. He could not see it; the mountains blocked his view. With a heavy heart he was once again reminded that he would never set foot in it. For forty long years he had led his people on this journey, but now, as God had told him, his journey would end here. It was almost too much to bear, almost unfair, but he knew he had only himself to blame.

"As his gaze returned to the people once more, and as he prepared to speak the final words the LORD God had given him for his people, his heart sank. The words he would speak were words of both blessing and warning, but they were also prophecies. For this stiff-necked people would break the covenant they had made with their God not once but over and over again, and so before they even entered the Promised Land, Moses saw that the day would come when they would be taken from the land. As he gathered his strength to speak, a solitary tear trickled down his wrinkled, weather-beaten face . . ."

The old man looks out over a sea of faces. He knows this is not how his people might have expected the story to begin tonight, but it is the story he believes they need to hear. "This is our story. As we sit here in exile we know that Moses' fears have been realized."

At these words, loud muttering breaks out. No, this is not what the people came to hear tonight. But he continues, as he must. "We have broken our covenant with God. Like our ancestors, we have failed to be faithful to the LORD God. And as always, it is because we have forgotten our story. Perhaps it is because those charged with telling the Story faithfully have failed to do so." He hangs his head for a moment, and the people grow quiet. Looking up once more he says, "So tonight, let us listen again, as we continue the Story of God, the story of us.

"As the fires burned low last week, we left that ragamuffin group of slaves on the shores of the Red Sea, having just witnessed the miraculous deliverance God had given them from their Egyptian oppressors. Tonight we will hear how God takes those slaves and transforms their identity to create a nation: the children of Israel, the people of God.

"The story does not start well. Having witnessed the mighty acts of God in Egypt, and at the Red Sea, it seems the people soon forgot them when they were in the wilderness, the land between Egypt and the Promised Land. They continually complained about the lack of food and water, even after God miraculously provided for them. Every morning God gave them 'manna,' a kind of bread they had never seen before. Every morning they collected the food God provided, some gathering much, others gathering little, but no one went hungry."

"Why not?" It is the young girl's brother. She looks at him, her mouth agape in surprise. "What?" he says. "Are you the only one allowed to ask questions?"

The old man laughs and addresses the young girl. "It would seem that your curiosity is contagious!" Then he turns to the boy. "Some say no one went hungry because the people pooled all they gathered and distributed it equally." He looks up at the crowd. "Remember, God's resources are not to be hoarded, as those who tried to do so learned, when the manna they did not eat or share went bad.

"Even though the people continually complained in the early days of their newfound freedom, God was faithful to the covenant with Abraham, Isaac and Jacob. In the third month after God brought them out of Egypt, they came to the Sinai desert and camped there, in front of the mountain, just as God had promised Moses.

"Moses went up the mountain, and the LORD called to him, saying, 'Thus you shall say to the children of Israel, "You have seen what I did to the Egyptians, and how I bore you on eagles' wings and brought you to myself. Now then, if you will indeed obey my voice and keep my covenant, then you shall be my own possession among all the peoples, for all the earth is mine; and you shall be to me a kingdom of priests and a holy nation.'"

"When Moses spoke these words to the people, they replied as one, 'All that the LORD has spoken we will do!' The people knew what kings and priests were, having seen them in Egypt, but there were none among this group of slaves." The old man pauses before continuing. "God was telling them the role they—and we—are to play in God's world: being priests of a holy God in the midst of broken and corrupt humanity, mediators of God's covenant. God's people exist for the sake of the world, not for our own sake. Our ancestors' identity as God's people would be formed by their faithfulness in obeying the mission God lay before them."

The young boy has another question. "So how did slaves become priests?" His sister follows with, "And a nation? I mean, they didn't have a king, or even a country."

"By entering into the covenant that God had made with Abraham, Isaac and Jacob," the old man responds. "But six centuries had passed since Abraham's day, and life and culture had changed. So, once again, God met the people where they were, and took a cultural form the people were familiar with, and co-opted it for the covenant God would make with them.

"With the rise of the age of empires, powerful nations entered into treaty relationships with their weaker neighbors. The more powerful party in such treaties, known as the 'suzerain,' offered protection and security in return for the exclusive loyalty and devotion of the weaker party, the 'vassal.' The suzerain was under obligation to care for the vassal; the vassal was under obligation to be loyal to the suzerain.

"Often the language of such treaties was the language of love. Thus, 'love' of the suzerain was loyalty to him; to betray the suzerain was to 'hate' him. The beginning of such treaties, the 'historical prologue,' would detail what the suzerain had done for the vassal. This would be followed by the conditions of the treaty: what the vassal promised to do for the suzerain in response to what the suzerain had done for him. If the conditions were kept, then 'blessings'—the benefits of having a powerful protector—would result. If the conditions were not kept, 'curses' would follow. These were often described in terms of the gods bringing plagues upon the disloyal vassal, which usually meant that the suzerain would send his military against the vassal."

"Have we been cursed then?" the little boy blurts out.

The old man lets the question hang in the air for a moment. "That is a good question, little one." More silence, and then the old man continues. "Witnesses—the gods of the two kings making covenant—were called upon to seal the treaty, which was then carved into two copies on stone tablets. After the appropriate oaths and sacrifices were made, each king received one of the tablets and deposited it in the Temple of the god by whom he had sworn his oath. Finally, a provision was made for the covenant treaty to be read periodically before the vassal king and his people."

The old man pauses to take a drink from his water skin. "This is what happened at Mount Sinai. In a formal ceremony, the people of Israel gathered before their suzerain, the LORD God, and heard the terms of the covenant treaty God offered them. They are some of the most familiar words we know. They begin with the historical prologue: 'I am the Lord your God, who brought you out of the land of Egypt, out of the house of slavery.'

"They continue with the conditions: 'You shall have no other gods before me. You shall not make for yourself an idol. . . . You shall not worship them or serve them; for I, the LORD your God, am a jealous God, visiting the sin of the fathers on the children, on the third and fourth generations of those who hate me, but showing *hesed*, lovingkindness, to thousands, to those who love me and keep my commandments.'

"Thus begins the Ten Words*: the covenant our people made with the LORD God. What is the point of these specific conditions? Our ancestors had lived among the multitude of Egypt's gods for centu-

---

*The "Ten Words" are also known as the "Decalogue" or the "Ten Commandments."

ries, and so to help them understand that they were to worship the LORD alone, God uses language they could understand; the language of politics. No other suzerains! We are to pledge our allegiance to the LORD alone.

"Within the Ten Words is a restatement of the importance of keeping Sabbath. For a group of slaves, the Sabbath would be a weekly reminder that they were no longer in Egypt—as well as a warning not to become like the Egyptians. For the Sabbath was also to be for the servants and livestock that would come with the prosperity of their new life.

"Within Torah, Sabbath rest was also extended to the land—one year in seven the land was to be allowed to lie fallow and rest. And Moses gave God's dire warning for failing to give the land its Sabbath rest. 'I will scatter you among the nations, so that the land will enjoy the rest it did not receive while you were living in it.'" The old man pauses to allow these words to sink in.

"What about the blessings and the curses you were talking about?" The young boy again. The old man turns to him and replies, "These can be found in Torah.* They are many and long, but they boil down to this: 'All these blessings shall come upon you if you will keep the commandments of the LORD your God and walk in God's ways. But if you will not obey the LORD your God . . .'"—the old man pauses—". . . you will be torn from the land."

The people shift uncomfortably in the silence that follows the old man's words. He continues, "The covenant concluded with Moses calling heaven and earth to bear witness to it. The giving of Torah at Mount Sinai is how God transformed us from a group of powerless slaves into a kingdom of priests and a holy nation, a people for God's own possession. The Ten Words are more than a collection of rules; they are practices that God gave the people to shape their new life of freedom together—practices that would protect them from themselves, from the fear and anxiety that pervades humanity and from

---

*The blessings and curses of the suzerain-vassal covenant are listed in Deuteronomy 28.

the darkest impulses that had been shaped in them from being enslaved. These practices would nurture within them a deep sense of the common good, would transform them from a group of slaves into a holy nation—people made in the image of God who would reveal the character of God to the peoples around them.

"God's character is primarily revealed through God's *hesed* love for us. For God, loving us means keeping God's promises to us. *Hesed* is covenant loyalty, translated as lovingkindness, mercy, love and compassion. We keep Torah in *response* to God's favor—not in an attempt to *earn* it.

"Torah shows us what faithfulness to the covenant looks like. Torah creates the community of the people of God. It tells us how to live together. Torah is not intended to keep other people out; rather, Torah creates boundaries for maintaining our identity as God's people. As we live faithfully to the law of the covenant, we call others into such relationship with the Creator God, and thus fulfill our mission to be a blessing to all the peoples of the earth.

"You may have heard negative things about Torah—after all, no one likes being told what to do." He catches the little boy's eye and winks. "But God's Torah is grace for God's people, the grace to live life as God intended.

"Torah actually limited some of the harsh practices of the day. 'An eye for an eye, and a tooth for a tooth,' set strict limits on vengeance taking. Remember Cain? Remember Lamech? Before Torah, the practice had been, 'Injure me, and I'll kill you if I can.' Thus Torah brings order and harmony.

"Torah also gave provisions for the people to restore their relationship with God when they sinned. When we read the provisions of Torah's sacrificial system, we notice something central to the way God relates to us: when what we do should lead to death, God offers life to us. Under Torah, whatever is associated with death is unclean; whatever is associated with life is clean.

From the crowd someone calls out, "So that's why we can't eat vultures. And I thought it was because they tasted bad!" The old man enjoys the laughter that follows and then continues. "Yes, my friend, that is why our people do not eat vultures. Or buzzards. That is why we do not touch the carcasses of dead animals. All these practices are to instill a reverence for life in us.

"We also see this reverence for life in the way Torah makes special provision to protect the vulnerable. God is deeply concerned with the plight of the marginalized in society, whom Torah primarily identifies as 'the orphan, the widow and the stranger.' This group shows up time and time again throughout our scriptures as those who need to be taken care of by the people of God. How we treat the most vulnerable among us reveals how faithful we are to the covenant we have made with God, and whether we are participating in the mission of God or not.

"Now, after the conditions of the covenant treaty were given to the people, after Moses had spoken all the words of the LORD, the people answered with one voice saying, 'All the words which the LORD has spoken we will do!'

"And Moses wrote down all the words of the LORD. Then he arose early in the morning and built an altar at the foot of the mountain, with twelve pillars for the twelve tribes of Israel. They sacrificed young bulls, and Moses took half the blood and sprinkled it on the altar.

"Then he took the book of the covenant and read it in the hearing of the people; and they said, 'All that the LORD has spoken we will do; we will be obedient!' So Moses took the blood and sprinkled it on the people and said, 'Behold the blood of the covenant, which the LORD has made with you in accordance with these words.' Just as we saw in the covenant God made with Abraham, once more we see that ratifying the covenant involves the shedding of blood.

"Then Moses went up on the mountain for forty days and forty nights, to receive the tablets of stone on which God would write down the covenant treaty. Included in this covenant were the instructions for the building of the tabernacle, the meeting place in which God would come to live in the midst of God's people, something unheard of among the surrounding nations. Torah also gave directions for the people as to how to remain pure in the midst of the corrupt nations around them—to be a holy nation, as God is holy."

The young girl has a question. "You said the people broke covenant with God—was that many years after they made the covenant?"

The old man shakes his head sadly. "No. The first time was just days later. When the people saw that Moses delayed in coming down from the mountain, they assembled before his brother Aaron and said to him, 'Make us a god who will go before us, because we do not know what has become of Moses, the man who led us out of Egypt.'

"They may have come out of Egypt, but they had not left Egypt behind. How swiftly they forgot the covenant they had just made with God! Instead of trusting God, whom they could not see but whose miraculous works they had seen, they returned to the practices of Egypt. Aaron made a golden calf, an idol they had seen the Egyptians worship, a god they had seen unmasked as powerless by the plagues the LORD God had visited on Egypt—but nonetheless a god they could see. Already they were disobeying the covenant; already they were being disloyal and unfaithful to the God who had delivered them from slavery. God had promised *hesed* love, faithful love, a love that keeps its promises. In return God had asked for loyalty, for the faithfulness of covenant love. But instead, God's people betrayed God.

"Aaron placed the golden calf before the people, and they said, 'This is your god, O Israel, who brought you up from the land of Egypt.' When Aaron heard them say this, he built an altar before it and said, 'Tomorrow shall be a feast day to the LORD.' Aaron tried to identify this idol with the LORD, and in doing so he acted against the second of the Ten Words.

"Then the LORD spoke to Moses, 'Go down at once, for your people, whom you brought out of the land of Egypt, have corrupted themselves, quickly turning away from the way which I commanded them. I have seen this idol they have made, I have seen this people, and behold, they are an obstinate people. Now then, let me alone, that my anger may burn against them, and that I may destroy them; and I will make of you a great nation.'"

The young girl calls out again. "Would God really destroy God's people?"

"What do you think, young one?" the old man answers.

She hesitates, chewing her lip, deep in thought. "I don't know. I don't think so. After all, God didn't destroy them. So why did God say that?"

The old man thinks for a moment. "I wonder if God was perhaps testing Moses. God offered Moses the chance to claim the covenant of Abraham for himself—for God to make of Moses a great nation, to make his name great. And apparently all Moses had to do was step aside and watch."

A deep silence falls over the crowd, broken after a moment by the voice of the young girl's brother. "So, what did Moses do?" The old man smiles, and continues.

"Moses pleaded with the LORD his God, and said, 'O LORD, why does your anger burn against your people, whom you have brought out of the land of Egypt with great power and with a mighty hand? Why should the Egyptians be able to say, "God brought them out of Egypt just so God could destroy them"? Turn from your burning anger and change your mind about doing harm to your people. Remember Abraham, Isaac and Israel, your servants to whom you swore, by yourself, to make them a great nation, and to give them a land that their descendants would inherit forever.'"

The old man turns toward the young girl. "Moses interceded for the people, pleading with God to spare them, and reminded God of the covenant. Moses had taken to heart this covenant he and his people had made with God. His identity had been formed; he understood his role as one of God's people: to act as a priest, as a mediator between a sinful people and a holy God. Instead of claiming the special rights for himself that God offered him, he stood in solidarity with his people and begged God's forgiveness for them."

The old man turns back to the crowd. "And God did as Moses had asked. God's mind changed! God had determined to harm the people, but God relented.

"Then Moses went down from the mountain with the two tablets of the covenant in his hand, tablets that were God's work and whose writing was God's. Moses took both copies of the treaty and walked into the feast the people were having before the golden calf, which was turning into a drunken orgy.

"Moses' anger burned, and he threw down the tablets and shattered them at the foot of the mountain, vividly symbolizing how the people had broken the covenant. He took the calf and ground it into dust, throwing it into the water, and made the people drink, to taste the bitterness of their sin.

"Moses returned to the mountain to plead with God to spare the people from destruction. And God spoke to Moses, saying, 'Depart from here, you and the people you brought out of Egypt, and go to the land which I swore to Abraham, Isaac and Jacob, a land flowing with milk and honey. But I will not go in your midst, because you are an obstinate people, and I would destroy you.'

"And once more Moses interceded on behalf of the people, saying, 'If your presence does not go with us, do not lead us away from here. For how can it be known then that your people have found favor in your sight? Is it not by your going with us, so that we may be distinguished from all the other people on the face of the earth?'

"And the LORD said, 'My presence shall go with you, and I will give you rest. Now, cut out for yourself two stone tablets like the former ones, and I will write on the tablets the words that were on the former tablets which you shattered.' God remained faithful to the covenant, even as God's people did not.

"And God once more gave Moses the conditions of the covenant, and then said, 'Write down these words, for in accordance with these words I have made covenant with you and with Israel.' So Moses was there with the LORD forty days and forty nights; he did not eat bread nor drink water. And he wrote on the tablets the words of the covenant."

"So Moses passed the test," the young girl states.

The old man replies, "If it was a test, then, yes, Moses was faithful to the covenant." Turning to the crowd, he continues. "Moses was not alone in being tested. At his call for someone to enact God's judgment on the people for breaking covenant, men from the tribe of Levi responded, killing three thousand of their kinsmen that day—the tragic cost of their idolatry." The old man's shoulders sag as he relates this painful story. "Yet this act of judgment brought repentance. Following the radical disobedience of the people with the golden calf, they next showed radical obedience to God in their building of the tabernacle, the tent of meeting, the place where God's presence would rest in their midst. God called the people to bring offerings with which the craftsmen among them would build the tabernacle. They responded so enthusiastically that Moses had to order them to stop giving!

"The building of the tabernacle is the climax of tonight's story, although it is not the end of it. Once the people had made covenant with God and obeyed God fully in building the tabernacle, God came to dwell in the very midst of the people. All anyone had to do was stand in the entrance of their tent and look toward the tabernacle—there they would see a cloud above it during the day, and a pillar of fire by night, the sign of God's presence with them, the glory of the LORD in their midst. This was something no other people had ever experienced.

"The instructions God gave for building the tabernacle included those for making the ark of the covenant, which would house the stone tablets of the covenant and be kept within the tabernacle in the Holy of Holies. The ark was the throne of God, Israel's suzerain, Israel's king, and it was there that God would meet with the high priests of our people, speaking from above the mercy seat between the two cherubim made of pure gold."

"Cherubim?" the young girl asks. "Like the cherubim God placed at the entrance to the Garden of Eden?"

"Yes . . . and no," the old man replies. "Those cherubim were there to prevent Adam and Eve from reentering God's presence, the Garden, in their estranged state. These cherubim, and those embroidered on the veil that separated the Holy of Holies from the rest of the tabernacle, were there to guard the way to the presence of God. But even though guarded by cherubim and set apart through the sacrificial system and the priests, God had once again come to dwell in the midst of humanity.

"And so the people began their journey toward the Promised Land. But once again, they soon tired of God's daily provision of manna. The troublemakers among them complained, saying, 'Who will give us meat to eat? We remember the fish, which we used to eat free in Egypt, the cucumbers and the melons and the leeks, the onions and garlic, but now our appetite is gone. There is nothing to eat except this manna.'

"The people disdained God's gracious provision and longed for the food they had known in slavery. How like us! How often we practice 'euphoric recall'—remembering only the good parts of our years in bondage to sin while ignoring the misery of those years, disdaining God's gracious deliverance and provision for us now. This pattern would become entrenched in their lives, revealing the lack of trust they placed in God and in the covenant God made with them.

"Moses assembled the people and gave them God's response to their complaints. 'Tomorrow you shall eat meat. You have wept, saying, "We were well off in Egypt." Well, the LORD will give you meat, so much so that you'll be up to your necks in it and it will make you sick; because you have rejected the LORD who is among you, and have wept before God, saying, "Why did we ever leave Egypt?"' And so the LORD brought a huge flock of quail to feed them.

"This was not the last time the people would doubt God's care for them. Moses sent spies into the Promised Land to bring a report back as to what they could expect when they entered it. Ten of the twelve spies brought a report back that giants lived in the land, and the people wept once more, saying, 'If only we had died in Egypt. Or even died in this wilderness. Why is the LORD taking us into this land only for us to die by the sword? Let us appoint another leader and return to Egypt.'

"And God grew angry, saying to Moses, 'How long will this people refuse to believe in me, despite all the signs I have done in their midst? I will destroy them, and I will make you into a nation mightier than they.' And once more, Moses reminded God of the covenant and of God's character, and begged God to forgive the people according to God's *hesed*, God's lovingkindness.

"Moses' intercession saved the people, but this latest instance of their putting God to the test had drastic consequences. For refusing to believe that God would go before them to give them the land promised to Abraham, God declared that they would wander in the wilderness for forty years—one year for every day the spies had been in Canaan—until their entire generation died. Their children would enter the Promised Land, but they would not."

The old man looks out across the crowd. "And so, here we are, back where we began tonight. Moses stood before this new generation, on the eve of their setting foot in the Promised Land for the first time. As he did so, he brushed the back of his hand across his eyes, knowing that he would never set foot in the land himself, for even Moses had disobeyed God, in one foolish moment of pride in which he tried to take God's glory for himself.

"For the last time Moses stood to speak God's word to God's people. His words echo down through the centuries to us. 'And now, O Israel, listen to the law which I am teaching you to perform, in order that you may live and go in and take possession of the land which the LORD, the God of your fathers is giving you. So keep them and do them, for thus the people who witness how you live will say, "Surely this great nation is a wise and understanding people." For what great nation is there that has a god so near it as is the LORD our God whenever we call on the LORD?

"'For the LORD has taken you and brought you out of Egypt, to be a people for God's own possession. You have seen the signs and the wonders which the LORD has done for you, that you might know that the LORD is God; there is no other besides the LORD. O Israel, be careful to live according to God's law, that it may be well with you, and that you may become a great nation, just as the LORD, the God of your ancestors, has promised you, in a land flowing with milk and honey. Hear O Israel! The LORD is our God, the LORD is one! And you shall love the LORD your God with all your heart, and with all your soul, and with all your might.

"'And these words, which I am commanding you today, shall be on your heart and you shall teach them diligently to your children. For you are a holy people to the LORD your God; the LORD your God has chosen you to be a people for God's own possession out of all the peoples who are on the face of the earth. Know that the LORD your God is God, the faithful God, who keeps God's covenant and God's *hesed* to a thousandth generation with those who love God and keep God's commandments.

"'And now, Israel, what does the LORD require from you, but to fear the LORD your God, to walk in all God's ways and love God, and to serve the LORD your God with all your heart and with all your soul and to keep the LORD's commandments? And all the blessings of the covenant shall come upon you if you will obey the LORD your God. But it shall come about, if you will not obey the LORD your God, then your enemies will defeat you, and the LORD will bring a nation against you from afar, and you shall be torn from the land which you are about to enter.

"'I call heaven and earth to witness against you today, that I have set before you life and death, the blessing and the curse. So choose life in order that you may live, you and your descendents, by loving the LORD your God, by obeying God's voice, and by holding fast to God, so that you might live in the land which the LORD promised to your fathers, to Abraham, to Isaac and Jacob.'

"Thus our ancestors made covenant with the LORD their God. And that covenant was written in stone, in the words of Torah. Keeping Torah is not to earn God's favor; it is our response to the favor God has already shown us. We are to be holy, as the LORD our God is holy. As they kept the commandments, their identity would be shaped, and the way they lived their life together would reveal the character of God to all those around them. It would demonstrate the richness of human community, with a deep sense of the common good."

"So did their children keep the commandments?" the little boy asks.

The old man's shoulders sag, as he feels the weight of the answer to the boy's question. "No, they did not. Israel failed to keep the covenant. Moses saw that this would happen, and so, even before they entered the land God had promised in the covenant with Abraham, Moses told the people, 'The LORD your God will raise up for you a prophet like me from among you and you shall listen to him when he appears.'"

The little boy thinks for a moment, and then his eyes grow large. "Are you the prophet like Moses?"

Surprise renders the old man speechless for a moment, before he laughs out loud. "Me, little one? Oh no. We are still waiting for the one Moses said would come."

The old man rises to his feet and invites the crowd to join him. As they stand he says, "There is much to think on in the story we have heard tonight. I hope you will find time to do so during your Sabbath rest tomorrow. We have heard of the curse of being torn from the Promised Land—the curse of exile. Let us end tonight with a blessing, God's blessing, the blessing that the priests have spoken over our people since Aaron himself was high priest."

The old man looks into the faces of his people, and feels God's *hesed* love for them. His voice catches as he begins the ancient words:

"The LORD bless you, and keep you.
The LORD make God's face shine upon you,
    and be gracious to you;
The LORD turn God's face toward you,
    and give you shalom."

6

conquest

In which we hear the story of God's fidelity to

provide God's people with a land, and the people's

infidelity once in it . . .

*T*he old man gathers his cloak around him. The night is a little cool. The people are quieter tonight; they did not like the way the story ended the last time they gathered. As well they should not, he reflects.

But he knows they will enjoy tonight's telling of the Story. He will be narrating the victories God gave the people as they entered the Promised Land. But there is still much to be learned from their ancestors' experiences, so he chooses the opening scene carefully. The old man closes his eyes, composes his thoughts and then begins.

"As the man approached the small group assembled under the shade of a huge palm tree, he found himself sweating. He was not sure if it was caused by the heat of the noonday sun, or if this was the sweat of fear. The commander in chief of the divisions of Naphtali and Zebulun of the army of Israel, he had been summoned to the counsel meeting of his people's leader.

"His was an all but ceremonial position, as his people had lived under the yoke of Jabin, king of Canaan, for twenty years. They had been crushed by his ruthless general, Sisera, commander of the king's iron chariots, before which no army could stand. Why was he being summoned now? Why did the judge of his people want to see him? He feared that there could be only one reason: the judge was about to order him to march against Sisera.

"As he approached the gathering, stories of previous wars came to mind. Three times the children of Israel had been oppressed before, and three times the LORD their God had raised up a judge to deliver them. But this judge, before whom he was about to appear, was different. Those other judges had been ordinary men raised up for a specific task. This judge was actually the ruler of God's people. This judge sat under the shade of this palm tree and dispensed justice. This judge was God's prophet, the mediator of the divine word—the very mouth-piece of God.

"As he drew near, the crowd parted to let him pass. Trying to keep his knees from trembling, he knelt before the leader of his people. And his heart sank as he heard these words.

"'Barak, son of Abinoam, the LORD, the God of Israel, has commanded you to lead your divisions to Mount Tabor. There you will face Sisera and his armored brigade, and the LORD will give him into your hand. Thus will Israel be delivered from the oppression of Jabin.'

"Barak raised his gaze to his ruler, and his fear got the best of him. 'I will go and do as you say, but only if you go with me.'

"And Deborah, the prophet of God and the judge of her people, said, 'Very well—but you have already lost the honor that would have been yours. For the LORD will give Sisera into the hands of a woman.'"

"Deborah?" The old man opens his eyes and looks toward the young girl, who continues, "But I thought all the judges of our people were men. Gideon, Samson—great heroes like that."

The old man smiles. "Our people have many stories, many heroes. And some stories we tell more than others." He smiles at her, and turns to the crowd.

"The last time we gathered, we heard the story of the covenant that the people of Israel made with the LORD their God at Mount Sinai which transformed them from a ragamuffin group of slaves into a nation. And we heard how God came to dwell in the midst of God's people in the tabernacle.

"But we also heard how quickly the people forgot all that God had done for them, and complained about God's gracious protection and provision for all their needs. So of all the adults God brought out of Egypt, only two men, Joshua and Caleb, entered the land God had promised their ancestors. Even Moses, the great leader of the people of

Israel, did not enter the land, because of his own act of sinful pride.*

"And so, on the day the children of that sinful generation were to enter the land of Canaan, the Promised Land, Moses spoke these words to them: 'Hear, O Israel! You are crossing over the river Jordan today to go in to dispossess nations greater and mightier than you, a people of giants before whom no one can stand. Know therefore today that it is the LORD your God who is crossing over before you as a consuming fire. God will destroy them and God will subdue them before you, so that you may drive them out and destroy them quickly, just as the LORD has spoken to you. Do not deceive yourselves that God will give you the land because of your righteousness, for you are a stubborn people. No, it is because of the evil things that the peoples of Canaan do, and in order for God to keep the promise God swore to your ancestors, Abraham, Isaac and Jacob.' Tonight we will hear that story—the story of the conquest of Canaan.

"The LORD God had commissioned Joshua the son of Nun to replace Moses as leader of God's people. Joshua was Moses' assistant and had been present on Mount Sinai when the LORD God gave Torah to Moses. Joshua had been one of the twelve men who had gone across the Jordan to spy out the land of Canaan forty years earlier. His name was originally Hoshea, but Moses renamed him Joshua, or Yeshua, which means, 'The LORD is salvation.'

"After the death of Moses, the LORD spoke to Joshua. 'Arise, cross this Jordan river, you and all this people, into the land which I am giving to them. And every place your foot treads I have given it to you, from the wilderness and Lebanon, to the great river Euphrates, all the land of the Hittites, and as far as the great sea toward the setting of the sun will be your territory.

"'Be strong and courageous, for you shall give this people possession of the land, which I swore to their fathers. Be careful to meditate on Torah, so that you may be careful to do all that is written in it, for then you will be prosperous and will have success. Be strong and cou-

*You can read this story in Numbers 20.

rageous! Do not be afraid, for the LORD your God is with you wherever you go.'

"Now, just as Moses had sent Joshua to spy out the land forty years before, Joshua sent two men to spy out the city of Jericho, the first city they would have to conquer. When they reached the city, they chose to stay in the house of Rahab, a prostitute."

A woman calls out, "Now why doesn't that surprise me?" provoking a peal of laughter. The old man chuckles, and then continues.

"A neighbor reported this to the king of Jericho, who demanded that Rahab turn them over to his soldiers. But she lied to them, saying that the spies had already left. She told the two spies, 'I know that the LORD has given you the land, and we are terrified of you, and all the inhabitants of the land are afraid of you. For when we heard that the LORD your God parted the seas for you and defeated great armies for you, we were terrified, for the LORD your God is God in heaven above and on earth below. Now, when you take the city, promise to spare my family, just as I have spared you today.' And the spies promised her they would."

"Wait a minute," the young musician calls out. "You said last time that our ancestors wandered in the wilderness for forty years because they were scared of the Canaanites. The spies said the people were giants. And all the time, the Canaanites were terrified of our people?"

"Yes," the old man replies. "For forty years the people of Jericho had been living in terror of the day when the people of Israel would arrive. And the generation that doubted that the LORD could defeat the Canaanites died in the wilderness—all except Joshua and Caleb." He turns back to the crowd. "The spies returned to Joshua and made their report, saying, 'Surely the LORD has given all the land into our hands, for the inhabitants are terrified of us.'

"And so Joshua gathered the people, and they packed up their camp and prepared to enter the Promised Land. The priests carried the ark of the covenant—where God's glory resided—out of the tabernacle and came to the Jordan river. The people followed, and as the priests walked down into the water, God piled up the waters of the river on either side of them. The people of Israel crossed into the land of Canaan on the dry land in the middle of the river. Just as they had entered the Sinai desert through God's miraculously drying up the Red Sea, they now left it in the same way, through the river Jordan.

"Now when the kings of the land heard what the LORD God had done at the river Jordan, they were terrified of the children of Israel. The nation of Israel camped at Gilgal, the place where God had brought them across the river, and there they celebrated the Feast of Passover. And on the very next day, they ate some of the produce of the land for the first time, and the LORD ceased to give them manna any more, for they no longer needed it.

"As Joshua walked up a hill that overlooked Jericho, he was confronted by an armed man. Joshua asked, 'Are you for us, or for our adversaries?' The man said, 'I am captain of the host of the LORD.' Joshua fell on his face before him and said, 'What has my lord to say to his servant?' And the captain of the LORD's host said to him, 'Remove your sandals, for the place where you are standing is holy ground.' God came to Joshua at the very beginning of the conquest of the land of Canaan to remind him that it was God who would defeat Israel's enemies.

"Jericho was tightly secured in anticipation of a long siege. The LORD instructed Joshua to have the army of Israel march around the city for six days, led by the priests. On the seventh day they were to march around the city seven times, and then the priests were to blow their shofars, the ram's horn.*

"And the people did as the LORD had spoken, and as the priests blew the shofars, Joshua called out, saying, 'Shout! For the LORD has given you the city. And the city shall be under the ban, and everything in it belongs to the LORD; everyone is to be killed; only Rahab and her family are to be spared, for she hid the spies that we sent.' And so the army of Israel shouted out loud, and the walls of the city crumbled."

"Where was the LORD's host when Jericho fell to the Babylonians?"

---

*A shofar is a wind instrument used in ceremonial and military contexts by the Israelites.

The young musician is once more on his feet. "Where was the LORD's host when Jerusalem was destroyed?" Many murmur in agreement with the young man's question, but for the first time a few people encourage him to be quiet. "Have you not been listening to our story?"

But he will not be persuaded. "I have been taking comfort in the words of Job—he understands our plight. Listen: 'My soul is poured out within me; days of affliction have seized me. At night it pierces my bones within me, and my gnawing pains take no rest. God has cast me into the mire, and I have become like dust and ashes. I cry out to God for help, but God does not answer me; I stand up, God, and you turn your attention against me.'"

Silence follows these words, until the old man asks quietly, "What would you have God do for us?"

The young man replies, his voice flat, "Have you forgotten my song so quickly, old one?"

"No, I have not forgotten. You would have vengeance on our Babylonian captors. You would see the destruction of our enemies." The old man holds the gaze of the musician before saying, "Do you remember these words, which Job also spoke when defending himself? 'Have I rejoiced at the extinction of my enemy, or cheered when evil befell him? No, I have not allowed my mouth to sin, by asking for his life in a curse.'"

The young man remains standing for a few moments before sitting down again. The old man turns from the musician to search the crowd for the young girl. Finding her, he says, "I imagine you have a question also, my young friend."

She tries to blink back the tears that are streaking down her face. The old man marvels at the depth of compassion she displays and waits for her response. It is the one he anticipates. "Why does God tell them to utterly destroy the city, to kill everyone in it? How can a God of *hesed* love order the deaths of thousands?"

"Believe me, I understand your question," the old man replies, "and it is one that has been asked many, many times. People much wiser than I have attempted to answer it. Perhaps their thoughts might help you as you wrestle with this disturbing story." He sighs heavily, whispering to himself, "Perhaps they will not."

"God's mission is to mend a broken universe; God will not abandon creation to the ruin that humanity's sin has brought upon it. And God's plan to mend the universe is to bless the whole world through God's people, the children of Israel. God will establish them in the land promised to them, and there—as they live their lives faithfully to the covenant they made with God at Mount Sinai—they will be a witness to the nations around them of who God is and will welcome others into relationship with the LORD.

"But God understands that God's people are prone to succumb to the temptations that seem to assail us from all sides. If the world is to be blessed through this one people, then it is imperative that they begin their new life as God's people in the land that God has given them with no influence from the people of Canaan, who might tempt them to abandon the covenant they have made with God.

"The people of Canaan, as God had warned Israel earlier, had many evil religious and social practices, epitomized by the practice of child sacrifice. However, the people of Israel may not have understood these practices to be evil, as they were so common throughout the cultures around them. We find such things abhorrent today, but they may not have.

"And God knows that if any of the people of Canaan are allowed to remain in the land God is giving Israel, God's people will indeed fall into their evil ways. The tragedy of the golden calf makes that all too clear. So they understood that the declaration that everything in the city of Jericho was 'under the ban,' or devoted to the LORD, meant that the Canaanites had to be destroyed.

"Just as with their fathers, so it is with their children: if they do not utterly drive out the inhabitants of Canaan, they will soon find that Canaan gets into them. That is why God instructed them at Sinai not to make a covenant with any of the peoples of the land, 'And they shall not live in your land, lest they make you sin against me; for if you serve their gods, they will ensnare you.'

"Well, this is exactly what happened, beginning with the people of Gibeon, who tricked Joshua into making a covenant treaty with them because he did not seek the LORD's counsel about them. Although the people of Israel were successful in battle—because the LORD fought for them—they left small 'enclaves' of Canaanites throughout the land who, with their altars and their sacred high places, seduced the people of Israel away from being faithful to the covenant they made with God. They were a constant source of temptation for God's people, the consequences of which were catastrophic. It should not surprise us that the symbol for many of the Canaanite fertility cults was a serpent."

He looks into the young girl's eyes and says, "That is why God told them to destroy the Canaanites: in judgment of their evil practices, and so that the children of Israel would not adopt those same practices themselves." He holds the young girl's gaze and sees understanding, but not acceptance. With a weary sigh, he turns back to the people.

"In time, the people conquered the whole land, according to all that the LORD had spoken to Moses, and Joshua gave it for an inheritance to all the tribes of Israel. Thus the land had rest from war. Not one of the good promises which the LORD had made to the house of Israel failed; all came to pass. God kept the covenant with God's people.

"This gift of rest, the ability to trust that God would protect them from any future enemies, was to be a sign to the nations of God's presence with them. God was trying to teach our people three important lessons: that the land was a gift of God's covenant grace; that this gift provided living space for every member of God's people; and that the gift of land was conditional on Israel's faithfulness to the LORD God, and their rejection of Canaanite religious and social practices.

"Joshua learned those lessons, and so before he died, he gathered the people together to warn them. And once again, he told them the Story: 'Thus says the LORD, "I took your father Abraham and multiplied his descendants, and gave him Isaac. To Isaac I gave Jacob, and he and his sons went down to Egypt. Then I sent Moses and Aaron, and I plagued Egypt, and afterward I brought you out. And Egypt pursued you, and I brought the sea upon them. Then you crossed the Jordan River and came to Jericho, and I gave them into your hand. I gave you a land on which you had not labored, cities which you had not built, and vineyards and olive groves you did not plant." Now, therefore, fear the LORD and serve the LORD in sincerity and truth; and put away the gods which your fathers served in Egypt, and serve the LORD. And if it is disagreeable in your sight to serve the LORD, choose for yourselves today whom you will serve, whether the gods of Egypt, or the gods of Canaan; but as for me and my house, we will serve the LORD.'

"And the people answered, 'Far be it from us that we should forsake the LORD to serve other gods; for the LORD our God is the One who brought us and our fathers out of Egypt from bondage, and drove out these peoples before us and gave us this land. We also will serve the LORD, for the LORD is our God, and we will obey God's voice.' Thus the people renewed the covenant with God."

The old man pauses to take a drink from his water skin. "But then it all started to go horribly wrong. The people, in their pride, did not drive out all the peoples who were living in the Promised Land, choosing instead to enjoy the comforts of the land they had acquired, and intermarry with these peoples. Their children, who had not seen what God had done, did not know the LORD. This new generation did evil in the sight of the LORD and served the gods of the Canaanites, the baals, and they broke covenant with God. And God was angry with them, and allowed their enemies to defeat them. But then the LORD raised up leaders for them who delivered them from their oppressors. This period of our people's history may be called the cycle of the judges.

"The central problem of the people of Israel was that they forgot God's great acts on their behalf. They stopped telling their story. They forgot their identity and abandoned the LORD their God for the gods of the Canaanites. This was the evil that they continually did in the sight of the LORD.

"So, the LORD would send a nation to oppress them. Then the people would cry out to the LORD for deliverance. The LORD would raise up a judge to deliver them. Their oppressor would be defeated. And then the people would have rest.

"But then they would forsake the LORD, and go after the gods of the Canaanites once more. And so the LORD would send a nation to oppress them, and the cycle would begin again.

"Our ancestors continually went through this cycle. Yet even as they were faithless, God was faithful. When the Philistines and Ammonites, two of the peoples of Canaan, once more rose up against the children of Israel, the people of Israel cried out to the LORD, saying, 'We have sinned against you, for we have forsaken our God and served the baals.' And the LORD said to the children of Israel, 'Go and cry out to the gods which you have chosen; let them deliver you in your time of distress.' And the children of Israel said to the LORD, 'We have sinned; do whatever you want with us, but please deliver us!' So they put away the foreign gods from among them, and served the LORD; and God could bear the misery of God's people no longer. And once more, God raised up a judge to deliver God's people.

"The first of the judges were Othniel, Ehud and Shamgar. Some of the names of later judges may be more familiar to us: Gideon, Samson and the last of the judges, Samuel." He turns to look at the young girl. "But possibly the most intriguing of the judges is Deborah. She is the only judge in our story who was actually holding the office when God raised her up to deliver God's people. As judge of Israel she arbitrated disputes and decided legal cases. These decisions were thought to be divinely revealed, and thus Deborah remembered and formed a body of wisdom and precedent that had divine authority. She was the prophet of God.

"Deborah commanded Barak to go into battle, and he deferred to her leadership in the area of his own expertise, warfare. Her authority was derived from her role as judge, the mediator of God's word. The word we heard her speak to Barak when we began the story tonight came to pass. Barak led his divisions into what should have been a one-sided battle against the all-powerful chariots of Sisera, but once more the LORD gave the people of Israel miraculous victory in battle. Sisera himself escaped, and hid in the tent of his chief metalworker, Heber the Kenite, a man who had abandoned his commitment to his own people, and to the LORD. And there his wife Ya'el killed Sisera, fulfilling the prophecy of Deborah.

"Although she is often overlooked in our telling of the Story, of all those listed in the book of Israel's judges, Deborah, a woman, was the only one who held the role and office of judge throughout her life. Perhaps it would be wise for us to remember this as we think about issues of the leadership of God's people."

He turns to the young girl and suddenly sees an image of her, grayhaired and sun-wrinkled, leading her people through the Story with the authority that wisdom brings. A smile spreads across his face; the young girl tilts her head, trying to read his thoughts, as he gets to his feet. "As the time of the judges drew to a close, the story ends with these words: 'In those days there was no king in Israel, and everyone did what was right in their own eyes.' The LORD had kept his covenant promises to Abraham, Isaac and Jacob—those of a people, a place and God's presence with them. They conquered the land of Canaan, but remained a loose-knit alliance of the twelve individual tribes, vulnerable to attack from outside enemies and those peoples whom they allowed to remain within the land.

"The next time we gather we will hear the story of the first kings of our people, the time when our people and our land knew a peace, a shalom, that we have never known since. Until then, may you and I remember the words of Joshua ben Nun, and choose, as he did, to serve the LORD—even here in Babylon."

The old man stays to warm himself by the fire before the walk home. As his people begin to leave, he hears the harpist's voice above the crowd. The old man strains to hear which song of praise he has chosen, but he quickly realizes this is a much older song: the song of Deborah.

"Awake, awake Deborah;
 awake, awake, sing a song!
Arise, Barak, and take away your captives,
O son of Abinoam.

The kings came and fought,
they fought the kings of Canaan.
The stars fought from heaven,
from their courses they fought against Sisera.

Most blessed of women is Ya'el,
most blessed is she of women in the tent.
She reached out her hand for the tent peg,
and her right hand for the workmen's hammer.

Then she struck Sisera,
she smashed his head;
between her feet he lay,
between her feet, he bowed, he fell;
where he bowed, there he fell, dead."

The cheers of the crowd echo into the night sky, and the old man winces at this celebration of an enemy's demise. But then he shrugs, for is this song not part of the story of his people? He savors the warmth of the fire a moment longer before turning to walk home.

7

crown

In which we hear the story of the first three kings

of Israel . . .

The old man slowly walks down to the riverside once more. He has given a great deal of thought this week to the telling of tonight's story. The people have been excited all day; they know that they will hear of the glory days of Israel's history. They are ready to be caught up in the stories of Saul and David and Solomon, the first kings of their people—to be reminded of the time when nations paid tribute to their king, not the king of Babylon. The old man frowns and mutters under his breath, "Ah, but did everyone in Israel share in the glory of those days? Even as God blessed the king, did everyone share in that blessing?"

The touch of a hand on his arm interrupts his thoughts. He had not heard the young musician approach. "Shabbat shalom, old one."

"Shabbat shalom, my young friend."

The young man smiles and asks, "Then we are still friends? Even after my outburst last week?"

The old man returns the smile, and places his arm through the young man's as he continues to walk. "Of course. It is always good to ask questions." He stops and turns to face the young man. "Especially if we are open to hearing whatever answers may come—including answers we may not like, or no answer at all."

Seeing the confused expression on the young man's face, the old man laughs. "And in my experience, whatever answers do come often just lead to more questions. So yes, we are still friends." His voice takes on a serious tone as they walk. "What encourages me is that you keep coming back to hear the Story. And that you bring your questions to the Story."

The young man has brought his harp. "So," the old man asks, "what new song do you have for us tonight? Or have you rewritten another old one?"

The young man laughs and says, "I don't think our people would permit me that pleasure tonight. All week long they have pestered me to sing their favorite songs of David. If I sang them all, we would still be there when the sun rises tomorrow!"

Chuckling, the old man asks, "So what will you do?"

The young man absentmindedly plucks the strings of his harp and says, "With your permission, I would like to sing two of David's songs—one before you begin the story, and one when you finish."

The old man nods his head in consent as they approach the crowd gathered around the fire. The people greet the storyteller and the poet as they make their way to the now well-worn spot where the old man has taken his place these past weeks. The young man tunes his harp and stands. An expectant hush falls across the crowd, and as he begins the song he looks into their smiling faces. What song of David is more beloved than this one? They lift their voices with the harpist's and sing together.

"The LORD is my shepherd,
    I shall not want.
God makes me lie down in green pastures;
    God leads me beside the still waters.
God restores my soul;
    God guides me in the paths of righteousness
    for the sake of God's Name.

Even though I walk through the valley
    of the shadow of death,
I will fear no evil.
For you are with me;
    Your rod and your staff, they comfort me.

You prepare a table before me
    in the presence of my enemies;

You anoint my head with oil;
> my cup overflows.
> Surely goodness and *hesed* will follow me
> all the days of my life,
> And I will dwell in the house of the LORD
> forever."

A stillness follows the song, and the gentle lapping of waves on the riverbank is as soothing as the familiar words. The old man collects his thoughts as he prepares to begin the Story once more.

As he does so, the ever-present ache of exile rises above the comforting sounds of the river, as the image of the house of the LORD in ruins breaks the peace the song had brought. Tonight he will tell his people the story of the great kings of Israel, and of the building of the Temple. But he will begin with the call to remember—"Remember that you were once slaves in Egypt"—because even kings forget sometimes.

Despite the warmth of the fire, he feels a chill. He wraps his cloak around him and looks into the eager faces of his people, then closes his eyes. "Picture this scene . . .

"The man struggled to his feet and adjusted his grip on the rope. He looked back at the long line of men doing the same. Then the order came. 'Pull!' He leaned in to the task. As he dug his feet in and heaved, the enormous block of stone behind him groaned and began to inch forward.

"For weeks he had been pulling on this rope. For weeks he had been spending himself in backbreaking labor. He had tried to convince himself that his task was a noble one, that he should not resent being forced to work on this building project. But he could not; because the cold, hard fact was that he did not have a choice. His king had ordered him to leave his farm and work on the Temple, and so here he was.

"Others around him had already reached the point of resentment, and around the campfire at night they vented their anger. They wondered aloud how this was possible: had they not been told over and over again that God had delivered their ancestors from slavery in

Egypt, that God had delivered them from backbreaking work such as this? So how could it be that the king of Israel was acting like the king of Egypt?

"No, they weren't slaves, but so what? They still had no choice but to work. And they could not call on God for deliverance, because here they were, building a Temple for God to dwell in. If God truly cared for the poor, the marginalized and the oppressed, then why would the house of God be built in this way? As the sun beat down on him, the man once more leaned into his task, and began to wonder himself . . ."

The old man opens his eyes. Some of his people are turning to their neighbors, confused, frowning. This was clearly not the story they had anticipated. He hopes they will understand before the story is finished.

"The last time we gathered, we heard the story of the conquest of the land of Canaan—the land promised to Abraham, Isaac and Jacob—and the fulfillment of the promises God had made to Israel. But as the time of the judges drew to a close, the people of Israel were only a loose network of individual tribes, holding their own territories with a tenuous grasp while continuing to be plagued by the Canaanites they had left in the land contrary to God's instructions. In particular, the Philistines who held five cities on the coast proved to be a constant threat to our ancestors' very existence.

"Tonight we will hear the story of this crucial period in the Story of God: the transition from tribal coalition to monarchy, which saw the rise of the most glorious era of our people's history and the establishment of the Davidic dynasty.

"Our story begins with a woman, Hannah. Every year she and her husband would go to Shiloh, where the ark of the covenant was, in the tabernacle, and there they worshiped the LORD their God. Hannah, like many other women in our story, was barren: she had no children.

"During one visit she was praying before the LORD and begged God for a son, promising that if God granted her petition she would dedicate him to the priesthood. God granted the longing of her heart, and she gave birth to a son, Samuel. Three years later, Hannah took her son to Eli, the latest in the line of priests, at Shiloh, and there she left Samuel to serve the LORD.

"Now Eli was old and wise, and faithful to the LORD. But the sons of Eli were worthless men, representing the toll that Canaanite corruption had taken on the people of Israel. They withheld the offerings from the LORD that the people brought, and they practiced ritual prostitution at the very doorway of the tabernacle. Eli despaired that when he died, his sons would lead the people to break covenant with God. And a man of God came to Eli, and told him that because of the wickedness of his sons, the priesthood would pass to another.

"Word from the LORD was rare in those days. But one night, while Samuel was asleep, the LORD called him, and confirmed what he had already told Eli. Samuel was afraid to tell Eli what the LORD had said, but Eli insisted. So Samuel told him everything, and Eli accepted what the LORD had said. Thus Samuel grew and the LORD was with him, and let none of his words fail to come to pass. And all Israel knew that Samuel was confirmed as a prophet of the LORD.

"Time passed, and once more the Philistines went to war with Israel. After a surprise defeat, the people of God fell back into their old ways, and instead of seeking the LORD's guidance as to what to do, they brought the ark of the covenant from Shiloh and marched behind it into battle, trusting its presence in their midst to win the battle for them.

"Instead, they were routed, their army was decimated, the Philistines took the ark, and the sons of Eli were killed. When the news of what had happened was brought to Eli, he died on the spot. The Philistines oppressed Israel from that day forward. But they returned the ark of the covenant to the people of Israel, for its presence in their midst brought plagues upon them similar to those God had brought against Egypt.

"After twenty long years, Samuel told the people, 'If you return to the LORD with all your heart, remove the foreign gods from among you and direct your hearts to the LORD and serve God alone, then God will deliver you from the Philistines.' So the children of Israel destroyed the Canaanite idols they had adopted, the baals and the Ashteroth, just as Samuel had said.

"The Philistines, seeing that all Israel had gathered together, went out to join battle with them. And the LORD indeed delivered God's people from the Philistines on that day, and Samuel placed a stone to mark the victory, naming it 'Ebenezer,' saying, 'Thus far the LORD has helped us.' And so the Philistines were subdued and did not encroach on the borders of Israel for the rest of the time of Samuel's leadership of God's people.

"When Samuel grew old, however, his sons acted just like Eli's sons, taking bribes and perverting justice. The elders of the people came to Samuel and said, 'You are old, and your sons do not walk in your ways. So we want you to appoint a king for us, like all the other nations.'"

The old man pauses to look around. The people have leaned in at this first mention of a king. They are eager to hear the stories they were expecting. He smiles wryly and continues. "The people's request for a king displeased Samuel, and so he asked God what he should do. God answered, 'Listen to the voice of the people, for they have not rejected you, but they have rejected me from being king over them. Like everything they have done since the day that I brought them up from Egypt, so they are doing to you also.'

"Samuel tried to warn the people of the price they would pay for having a king, but they refused to listen to him, saying, 'No, there shall be a king over us, that we may be like all the other nations, that our king may judge us and go out before us and fight our battles.' And the LORD said to Samuel, 'Listen to their voice, and appoint them a king.'

"To this point God had been dwelling as their king, in their midst, enthroned in the tabernacle between the cherubim of the ark of the covenant. But now the people demanded to become a monarchy, like all the other nations.

"This in itself was not necessarily wrong. In the giving of the Law at Sinai, God had spoken these words to Moses: 'When you enter the land which the LORD God gives you, you will set a king over you whom the LORD your God chooses. This king must be from your people. He shall not build up a herd of horses, nor marry many wives, in case his heart is turned away; nor shall he amass wealth for himself.'

God had laid down conditions for the kings who would reign over Israel. They were not to build up a standing army, nor enter into covenant treaties with other nations through marriage, and they were not to amass wealth. Thus they would continue to rely on God to provide for their needs, and to protect them, which would be a witness to the other nations that God was indeed present in their midst. God's reign would continue through the king.

"It is understandable that the people demanded a king. The Philistine peoples had united and allied themselves with the other Canaanite peoples, and were once more a threat. But instead of asking God to give them victory in battle, they demanded a king to lead them. Instead of embracing their unique role in the world as God's people, our ancestors wanted to be 'like all the other nations.'

"And so, once more, God met them where they were, and gave them their king, the first king of Israel—Saul, a choice and handsome man, more handsome than any other among his people, standing head and shoulders above them all. Samuel came to Saul and poured oil on his head, anointing him king of God's people.

"Saul's first test as king came when the Ammonites besieged Jabesh-gilead. Saul summoned all those who would fight with him, and in his first battle, he utterly defeated the Ammonites, confirming his reign. But Samuel knew Saul would have a difficult time ruling them. They were divided along geographical lines in the Promised Land: ten tribes to the north, and two to the south. The dream of a united kingdom would take many years to be fulfilled.

"When Samuel realized his life was coming to its end, he gathered all Israel to him, saying, 'Here is the king whom you have chosen, the king whom you have asked for. The LORD has set a king over you. Know this: if you will fear the LORD and serve God, and listen to God's voice, and not rebel against God's commands, then both you and the king who reigns over you will follow the LORD your God. But if you will not listen to the LORD, but rebel against God, then the hand of the LORD will be against you, as it was against your fathers.

"'But do not fear, for the LORD will not abandon God's people, on account of God's great name. For the LORD has been pleased to make you God's people. Only fear the LORD and serve God in truth with all your heart, considering what great things God has done for you. But if you still act wickedly, both you and your king will be swept away.'

"But once again, the people did not heed the warning. When the Philistines gathered their forces against Saul, he was afraid, and although Samuel had told him not to enter battle until he arrived to make offerings to the LORD on behalf of the people, Saul became impatient and made the offering himself—the offering which only a priest could make.

"When Samuel realized what Saul had done, he said, 'You have acted foolishly and have broken the commandment of the LORD your God. And so instead of establishing a dynasty through you, the LORD has sought out a man after God's own heart, a man of God's own choosing, and has appointed him over God's people, because you have disobeyed the LORD.' Even though he is the king, God's anointed one, the king is not sovereign over Israel: God is. And so the king must listen to the words of God's prophet.

"Saul never learned this lesson. He proved his inadequacy to rule again during his campaign against the Amalekites. The LORD had put the Amalekites 'under the ban'—dedicated to utter destruction for fighting against God's people in the Sinai desert. But after Saul had defeated them, he allowed their king to live and kept the best of their livestock for himself.

"When Samuel caught him, Saul pretended that he had kept the livestock only to sacrifice them to the LORD. Samuel rebuked him, saying, 'Has the LORD as much delight in burnt offerings and sacrifices as in obeying God's voice? Behold, to obey is better than sacrifice.' Samuel left, and did not see Saul again until the day of his death, and he grieved for what his king had become. God then sent Samuel to anoint a new king, a king that God chose, rather than the people.

He anointed David, a young man, and the Spirit of the Lord fell upon him mightily from that day forward.

"David went to serve King Saul, and ministered to him, and was his armor bearer. And Saul loved him greatly. Once more the Philistines gathered an army against the people of Israel, and their champion, a giant named Goliath, came out daily to challenge and taunt the Israelites. But no one would accept the challenge.

"No one, that is, except David. Saul tried to dissuade David from going out to fight Goliath, saying, 'You are but a youth. This Philistine has been a warrior since his youth.' But David recounted the many times he had fought to protect his father's sheep, concluding, 'The Lord, who delivered me from the maw of the lion and the claw of the bear, will deliver me from the paw of this Philistine.'

"Saul dressed David in armor, but David refused to wear it. Taking the weapon of a shepherd, a slingshot, God's anointed one, David, killed Goliath and led the rout that his first victory over the Philistines became."

The people cheer. This is more like it; these are the stories they have been waiting to hear. They raise their wineskins and toast David. Someone passes the old man a skin, and he takes a long drink, enjoying the moment before continuing.

"At first Saul was pleased, but he became jealous as David's popularity among the people grew. Saul's son, Jonathan, whom Saul had planned would succeed him as king, became great friends with David. Meanwhile, David won many more battles, and Saul began to perceive David as a threat to his rule.

"Saul's jealousy and insecurity led him to attempt to kill David on several occasions. David was eventually forced to flee for his life, but even on the run, people were drawn to him, and he gathered a ragtag band of men around him. Saul tried to hunt him down, turning his attention from his real enemy, the Philistines, to his imagined enemy, David. On two occasions David had an opportunity to kill Saul, but both times he refused, unwilling to harm his king. But Saul was not so merciful. When he discovered that a town had sheltered David, he had the inhabitants killed, including eighty-five of the LORD's priests.

"During this time Samuel died. Once more the Philistines amassed their forces on the Plain of Jezreel, and Saul tried to seek the counsel of the LORD concerning the battle. But the LORD did not answer him. And so, at the lowest point of his rule, Saul visited a medium, to try to contact the now-dead Samuel. The prophet whom Saul had not listened to when he had been alive now appeared to him, telling him that he would lose the battle—and his life.

"And so the Philistines swept down in their chariots on the armies of Israel, killing all before them. Many of Saul's sons, Jonathan included, were killed. Mortally wounded, Saul escaped, and rather than being captured, he fell on his own sword, taking his life and ending his reign on this shameful note."

The crowd's festive mood evaporates as quickly as it had arisen.

"When David heard the news, he mourned the loss of Saul and Jonathan and the thousands who had fallen in battle alongside them. Saul's death left a power vacuum, and his generals tried to seize the throne for whichever of Saul's remaining family they favored. David prayed to the LORD about what he should do, and the LORD sent him south, to Hebron, where he was anointed king by the tribe of Judah.

"The rivals for the throne went to war with each other, until finally all the tribes of Israel came to David at Hebron and said, 'We are your flesh and blood. When Saul was king over us, you were the one who really led us.' So the elders anointed David king over all twelve of the tribes of Israel, and thus the people of God were finally united under one king.

"David understood the tension between the northern and southern tribes, so he chose the city that would become his capital very carefully. The Jebusites had lived in Jerusalem for two and a half centuries unconquered by the Israelites. But seeing that it lay between the north and the south, David led his troops against it and took the city. Thus Jerusalem became his capital, the city of David.

"When the Philistines heard that David had been made king over all Israel, they assembled their entire army against him. And David inquired of the LORD as to how he should do battle with them. The LORD gave David instructions, which David followed exactly, destroying the entire Philistine army, ridding the land of the Philistines for the first time in 150 years and securing peace within his borders." The old man pauses for the renewed toasts and cheers this famous victory draws from the crowd. "Having made Jerusalem the seat of his political power, David now made it the religious capital of the people by bringing the ark of the covenant to Jerusalem. David danced with joy as he led the procession of the ark into the city, in adoration of his God. Once there he offered sacrifices to the LORD and blessed the people.

"David built a palace and enjoyed the rest that the LORD had given him from all his enemies. But something began to nag at him. One day he sent for Nathan, God's prophet, and said, 'I live in this beautiful palace, but the ark of God dwells in a tent. I will build a beautiful house for the LORD's dwelling place.'

"But the LORD told Nathan to tell David, 'I have not dwelt in a house since the day I brought up the children of Israel from Egypt. I have been moving about in this tabernacle. When did I ever say to my people, "Why have you not built me a house?"'"

The old man pauses. As he has thought about the Story this week, questions have arisen for him. He has wondered whether to raise them with his people. Would they understand? But then he smiles to himself. How can he encourage his people to ask their questions if he will not be honest about his own? "I have found myself asking questions about the Temple this week," he says.

The people stir at this interruption to the rhythm of the story—and at the old man's statement. The young girl leans forward; perhaps the old man's questions will explain the story he began the evening with.

"We serve the LORD, maker of heaven and earth. What could we possibly build that could 'house' God? And why would we want to?"

The question hangs in the air for a moment before another is asked, this one by the girl. "But didn't God live in the tabernacle?"

The old man turns to find the face that goes with the voice. "Yes, young one, God came to dwell in the midst of God's people in the tabernacle. But a tabernacle is very different from a temple." He turns back to the crowd. "Tents move around. Temples stay put. In the tabernacle God led the people through the wilderness; when the cloud of God's presence moved, the people packed up the tabernacle and followed. What is lost when we can no longer pull up stakes and move where God leads us? Do we shape a building only to discover it begins to shape us? Do we become more invested in the building than the God the building is for?" He pauses, then speaks in a voice barely above a whisper, as the people strain to hear. "Did we trust in those deceptive words, 'This is the Temple of the LORD, the Temple of the LORD, the Temple of the LORD'?"

The people begin to mutter loudly. This is not what they came to hear. Someone calls out bitterly, "The Temple is gone, old one."

He sighs wearily and says, "I know. I know." His heart aches with the swirl of emotions he feels.

A small voice speaks into the heaviness of the moment. "So why did David want to build a Temple for the LORD?" The young girl's question pulls the old man out of the dark place he had suddenly found himself in. He straightens his back and turns to her to reply. "David's intention may have been to honor God by building a beautiful home, just as the other nations around them built temples for their gods. But as we heard, God had not asked the people to build a temple." He smiles, grateful to find his way back into the story. "But perhaps once again, God meets God's people where they are.

"The LORD told Nathan to say to David, 'When your days are complete, and you lie down with your fathers, I will raise up your descendant after you, and I will establish his kingdom. He shall build a house for my name, and I will establish the throne of his kingdom forever. My *hesed*, my lovingkindness, shall not depart from him, as I took it away from Saul. And your house and your kingdom shall endure before me forever; your throne shall be established forever.'

"And so God renewed the covenant with David, as God had with the patriarchs before him. God tells David, 'You will not build a house—a temple—for me. But I will build a house—a dynasty—for you.' And this dynasty will last forever."

The young man interrupts him. "But we have no king. Where is this everlasting dynasty now?"

"If we believe that God will be faithful to the covenant God has made with our people," the old man says, "then we must wait for another Son of David, another anointed one, who will lead our people back into covenant faithfulness with God."

"How long must we wait?" replies the young man.

The old man sighs and says, "I do not know, my young friend." He turns back to the crowd and continues. "David's military victories, and the consolidation of his power in Jerusalem, made Israel the most powerful kingdom from Mesopotamia to Egypt. However, with that power perhaps came complacency. During the following spring, the Ammonites invaded from the north and besieged Rabbah. But instead of leading his army into battle, as other kings would have done, David stayed in Jerusalem. And there he broke covenant with God, committing adultery with Bathsheba, the wife of one of his generals, Uriah the Hittite, whom he ordered to be killed in an attempt to conceal his sin.

"At the height of David's power, the prophet Nathan confronted David with his sin—a crucial role the prophets played throughout Israel's history. Unlike all the kings that would follow him, David accepted Nathan's rebuke, repented of his sin and accepted the consequences for what he had done.

"Truly there never was a king like David. During his reign he united the twelve tribes of Israel, and finally after many centuries he completed the conquest of Canaan. He established Jerusalem as the seat of political and religious authority, and made Israel the mightiest nation in the region.

"But, as we have seen before, sin is never personal. It is always social. David's sin led to chaos in the kingdom, and he struggled to keep peaceful relations between the southern tribes—his blood relatives—and the ten northern tribes. His own son Absalom tried to take the throne from him. It would not be until his son Solomon came to the throne that our people Israel would truly enter our golden era.

"As David's time to die drew near, he gave his son Solomon the charge to be faithful to the covenant God had made with them. Solomon had every reason to do so: he had been given the land God had promised and was the king of the strongest nation in the whole region. God had kept covenant; would Solomon?

"During Solomon's reign, Israel enjoyed forty years of undisturbed rest from war. They experienced unparalleled economic and political prosperity, and Solomon became renowned throughout the world as a man of great wisdom. Indeed, he had asked God for that very thing in order to rule his people well, and God had granted his request. Solomon collected and wrote the great body of our people's wisdom, the books of Proverbs, Ecclesiastes and the Song of Solomon. But what he is remembered for most is the building of the Temple in Jerusalem."

The old man takes a drink of water. He has reached the conclusion of tonight's story. "And thus we return to where we began tonight. Solomon engaged in massive building works to centralize his political and religious authority in Jerusalem. He built a great palace for himself. He fortified cities in Hazor, Megiddo and Gezer, strategic locations for national security. He built storage cities and cities to garrison his chariots and horsemen. And he built the wonder that was the Temple itself." The old man looks around the crowd before continuing. "And all with conscripted labor from outlying villages, whose men were forced to work on the king's building projects one month in three. Solomon used his massive resources and wealth to protect his massive resources and wealth."

The young musician turns to him again. "Wait! The Temple was built with forced labor? Solomon forced his own people to work on his building projects?"

"Yes," the old man replies. "The book of Kings makes it clear that Solomon built storage cities, and garrisons for the horses and chariots,* using forced labor—slaves, if you like. And not just from the peoples

---

*These were, ironically, imported from Egypt.

they had conquered, but also from among his own people."

The young man splutters. "Then he was building another Egypt—our people were making bricks in slavery again!"

The old man sighs. "Perhaps now you understand my questions. Solomon was building a temple for the God who sets people free from slavery . . . using slaves." A profound silence falls over the crowd as these words sink in.

"On the day that the Temple was dedicated, the LORD gave Solomon this warning: 'If you or your sons turn away from following me, and do not keep the commandments but go and serve other gods and worship them, then I will cut off Israel from the land which I have given them, and this house, the Temple, I will cast out of my sight; the Temple will become a heap of ruins, and as people pass by it they will ask, "Why has the LORD done this to the land, and to this Temple?" And they will say, "Because they forsook the LORD their God who brought their ancestors out of Egypt, and adopted other gods and worshiped and served them, therefore the LORD has brought this catastrophe on them."'"

An even deeper silence falls over the crowd as the image of the Temple in ruins comes to everyone's mind.

"Tragically, Solomon ignored God's warning. Along with his great building projects, he created a standing army of 1,400 chariots and 12,000 horsemen. He built a merchant fleet, and amassed great wealth for himself. The weight of the tribute he collected each year was 666 talents of gold.* And he married the daughters of kings and nobility throughout the world, entering into covenant relationship with them. All the things that the LORD had commanded kings not to do, Solomon did. And they led him away from serving the LORD, and he did what was evil in the sight of the LORD, building high places to pagan gods for his wives, and sacrificing to them.

"Although Solomon refused to listen to God's voice, for the sake of the promise God made to David, God allowed Solomon to reign over

---

*The number 666 was a cultural indicator that something is evil, wrong and opposed to God.

Israel for forty years. And so we reach the end of what we think of as the golden era of our people Israel's history.

"Let us think for a moment about the great irony of Solomon's reign, and heed its warning. Solomon's great achievements were marked by three things: affluence, oppression and static religion. The covenant God made through Moses had been almost completely reversed under Solomon. Yet Israel was the wonder of the region during his reign; God's people had indeed become like all the other nations.

"So, even though we are here in exile, as far removed from those days as we can possibly be, this story should give us pause. For if we are to be faithful to the covenant, then we must beware of falling into the same three things that marked Solomon's reign:

- an economics of affluence in which we become so well off that both the pain around us and the pain we cause others are not noticed;

- a politics of oppression in which the cries of the marginal are not heard or are silenced;

- a static religion, in which God has no other business than to maintain our standard of living, and whose prophets we try to silence when they speak words we do not want to hear."

With those words, the old man turns to the young musician. "Perhaps you would bring our time together to a close with the other song of David you chose for tonight."

The young man takes up his harp once more, stands and leads his people in a song that suddenly feels deeply poignant.

"Be gracious to me, O God,
    according to your *hesed* love;
according to the greatness of your compassion,
    blot out my transgressions.
Wash me thoroughly from my iniquity,
    and cleanse me from my sin.

For I know my transgressions,
    and my sin is ever before me.

Against you, you only have I sinned,
and done what is evil in your sight.

Create in me a clean heart, O God,
and renew a steadfast spirit within me.
Do not cast me away from your presence,
and do not take your Holy Spirit from me.
Restore to me the joy of your salvation,
and sustain me with a willing spirit.
Then I will teach transgressors your ways,
and sinners will be converted to you.

For you do not delight in sacrifice,
otherwise I would give it.
You are not pleased with burnt offerings.
The sacrifices of God are a broken spirit;
a broken and contrite heart, O God,
you will not despise."

The young man lowers his harp, turns to his elder and offers his hand. The old man reaches up to grasp it and allows the young man to help him to his feet. Once more he places his arm through the young man's. They turn toward home, the crowd parting before them before departing themselves, many deep in thought.

8

conceit

In which we hear the story of the division of the kingdom and the word of the prophets to the people in exile . . .

It is the Sabbath. The sun has set, and as daylight fades the old man makes his way down to the river once more. He walks slowly, feeling the weight of his years and the weight of his people's exile. He understands the importance of Sabbath, God's beautiful gift of rest and freedom from the slavery of activity to which people seem prone to give themselves. This gift of Sabbath, extended to all people—indeed, to all of creation—he has encouraged, cajoled and pleaded with his people to accept and adopt, and he takes delight in the increasing numbers of people who are doing so. But as his joints creak, his back aches and his step slows, he admits to himself that he is mainly grateful not to have to work tomorrow.

The sound of laughter reaches his ears. He looks up to see the light of the fires around which his people sit and break bread together. It is good to hear his people laugh—for many years there has been little joy in their lives. He enjoys the sound of pleasure that sharing a meal produces.

Then he sighs and begins walking again. Tonight he will bring the Story to an end as he relates the story of the kings of Israel and Judah—a story that ends here, in exile in Babylon. And he knows that as he does so, the laughter will soon fade away.

He has told the Story in hopes that his people will understand why it ends with them here in exile. He pauses, and corrects himself. No, the Story does not end in exile. For has not God spoken through God's prophets that one day his people will return to the Promised Land?

But when they do return, what kind of people will they be? That is the question. Will their experience in exile change them? Will they understand why breaking the covenant led to their experience of God's judgment? Will they learn from this experience? Will they return to covenant faithfulness, to believing allegiance in the God of Abraham, Isaac and Jacob? "May it be so," he quietly prays.

He makes his way through the crowd and accepts some bread and fruit, eagerly pressed into his hands by the mother of the young girl who has been a source of encouragement—and hope—for him these weeks. Perhaps her generation will be different. Perhaps.

He takes his seat and enjoys the simple meal, washing the bread down with a drink from the wineskin someone passes him. As he savors the sweetness of the fruit, the young musician sits down next to him. "Shabbat shalom, old one."

"The peace of the Sabbath be with you, my young friend."

The young man hesitates before saying, "The people have asked me for a song tonight. I wanted to ask your permission before singing."

The old man raises an inquisitive eyebrow. "What song are they requesting?"

"The song that inspired me to write the new song I sang those weeks ago."

The old man quietly sings the opening lines of the song he thinks it is. The young man nods. The old man thinks for a moment, considering the choice. "Sing for the people. Let us feel keenly the pain of exile before we hear the Story once more."

The young man stands, and as he does so, the crowd slowly grows quiet. He lifts his harp and begins.

"Why have you rejected us forever, O God?
Why does your anger smolder against the sheep of your
      pasture?
Remember the people you purchased of old,
the tribe of your inheritance whom you redeemed—
Mount Zion where you dwelt.

Turn your steps toward these everlasting ruins;
all this destruction the enemy has brought upon the sanctuary.

Your foes roared in the place where you met with us;
>they set up their standards as signs.

They behaved like men wielding axes
>to cut through a thicket of trees.
They smashed all the carved paneling
>with their axes and hatchets.
They burned your sanctuary to the ground;
>they defiled the dwelling place of your name.
They said in their hearts, 'We will crush them completely!'
>They burned every place where God was worshiped in
>the land.

Why do you hold back your hand, your right hand?
>Take it from the folds of your garment and destroy them!
But you, O God, are my king from of old;
>you bring salvation upon the earth.

Do not hand over the life of your dove to wild beasts;
>do not forget the lives of your afflicted people forever.
Have regard for your covenant,
>because haunts of violence fill the dark places of the land.
Do not let the oppressed retreat in disgrace;
>may the poor and needy praise your name."

As the harpist takes his seat, the old man observes the crowd. Some faces are streaked with tears. Others frown in anger. Still others stare blankly into space. Whatever joy and lightness of spirit they have been feeling dissipates as the dying notes of the song fade into the night.

The old man turns to the musician, expecting him to give voice to the subcurrents of anger and despair that wend their way through the crowd. The young man holds his gaze, but says nothing. For once the old man cannot read the emotion playing on the young man's face.

Turning to the crowd, he finds tears coming unbidden to his own eyes. He may know why his people find themselves in exile. He may know why the Temple lies in ruins. But understanding does not always ease the pain. He wipes the back of his hand across his eyes, and with a silent prayer he continues the story.

"I was a young man when I was brought into exile here in Babylon, during that first deportation of our people these long years past. The song our young harpist has played strikes a chord in my heart even now. When we left our homes, carried off into captivity, I remember turning to take one last look at Jerusalem. I wondered if I would ever see its beauty again; I wondered if any of us would ever worship in the Temple again.

"For years I clung to the hope that the LORD would act on our behalf. If I had been a musician I may have written a song much like our young friend's here. Like so many of our people, I believed that as long as the presence of the LORD remained in the Temple, one day God would act on our behalf and restore the kingdom to us; we would return home." He pauses. "That all changed on the night of Ezekiel's vision."

At these words the older members of the crowd stir. "Yes, some of you remember that night. Those years ago, I sat in the crowd on nights much like this one, asking the elders of our people to tell us the stories of Israel: of Abraham, Isaac and Jacob; of Moses and Joshua; of David and Solomon. Yet when the prophets among our people told us the Story, we were not so quick to listen. We refused to believe that exile in Babylon was God's judgment on our pride, on our conceit, on our failure to keep the covenant. We were God's people, and one day God would vindicate our suffering and bring about a new exodus: deliverance from captivity and a return from exile.

"We believed it. Until that night."

The old man's eyes fill with tears once more, but this time they roll unchecked down his cheeks as he continues. "I was sound asleep when I heard the noise. A cry of such pain, such anguish—I can hear it even now. Rubbing the sleep from my eyes, I got dressed and wandered out of the hut to find the source of the cry.

"There was Ezekiel, stumbling, falling, muttering, 'Gone, gone . . .' We gathered around him, but he did not see us. His eyes were focused on another place. Tears streamed down his face, and he was whimpering. Then, suddenly, he became aware of our faces looking expectantly at him—some mocking, some fearful. He looked at us, first with anger, and then, slowly, with pity.

"I broke the silence. 'What is it, old man? What have you seen?'

"The prophet repeated himself with a whisper, causing us to strain to hear. 'Gone, it's gone.'

"We didn't know what he was talking about. Ezekiel raised his head and looked at us, slowly fixing his eyes on each of our faces. 'Your hope. That's what's gone.'

"I was scared. 'Stop talking in riddles,' I begged. 'What do you mean?' Then he spoke the words that changed everything.

"'I warned you, but you would not listen. Just as the LORD foretold, Jerusalem has been destroyed.'

"A communal gasp escaped us. 'No, it's not true,' someone uttered. 'How do you know?' another asked. There were tears on our faces now.

"'That's not all,' he continued. 'The Temple . . .'

"'What of the Temple?' someone cried.

"'The Temple has been burned.'

"I remember screaming, unwilling to believe what I was hearing. And then, shaking with emotion, with tears streaming down his face, Ezekiel said, 'I saw the glory of the LORD go up from the cherubim to the threshold of the Temple, and the Temple was filled with the cloud, and the court was filled with the brightness of the glory of the LORD . . . then the glory of the LORD departed from the threshold of the Temple and stood over the cherubim . . . then the cherubim lifted up their wings and the glory of the God of Israel hovered over them.'

"He paused before saying, finally, 'And the glory of the LORD went up from the midst of the city.' Ezekiel had seen the presence of the LORD depart. God was no longer in the Temple. We stood there stunned for a moment, and then we began to weep."

The old man looks out into the crowd. "Many of you were among those who were brought here in that last deportation. You confirmed what Ezekiel had seen in his vision. When you did, our hearts broke.

We were crushed under the weight of our emotions: murderous rage, despair, anguish, hopelessness. Yet into that place God's prophets have continued to speak. But do we listen? Can we hear the Story they have told—indeed, the Story that I have been trying to tell?"

The old man pauses for a drink of water. He feels the familiar ache for his people, his longing for them to understand, and for that understanding to lead to repentance. Placing a hand on the shoulder of the young musician sitting beside him, he pushes himself to his feet, and continues. "Tonight I will conclude the story of the kings of Israel, as we bring our story up to this present moment.

"You have heard the stories of the golden era of the history of our people, the reigns of David and Solomon. Under the rule of David, the conquest of the land of promise was completed, and the twelve tribes of Israel were united under one king. Under Solomon, Israel became the most powerful nation from Mesopotamia to Egypt, and people came from far and wide to see the glory of his kingdom.

"Yet in the midst of God's richest blessings, Solomon forsook the covenant he had made with the LORD God and led his people into idolatry, adopting the pagan practices of the many foreign wives he married. Through social oppression, particularly of the ten tribes in the North, through building a standing army and by amassing wealth for himself, Solomon abandoned the covenant. Although he built a house for the LORD, the great Temple in Jerusalem, he did not honor the name of the LORD in the way he lived. He lost sight of the vision of what God's people are called to be.

"As his life drew to a close he reflected on what he had accomplished and concluded, 'Vanity of vanities! All is vanity!' Perhaps he recognized the futility of his life, of the pursuit of wealth and pleasure, the grief that knowledge brings, the uncertainty of political power, and the inescapable fact that we will all one day die. Acknowledging what his life had become, he left this warning to those who would come after him: 'When everything has been said, my conclusion is this: Fear God and keep God's commandments. For God will bring every act to judgment, everything which is hidden, whether it is good or evil.'

"But those who came after him failed to heed his warning. Solomon reigned in Jerusalem over all Israel for forty years. When he died, his son Rehoboam became king. The ten northern tribes sent representatives to the new king with this request: 'Your father, Solomon, forced us to work for him; lighten the hard service your father put us to, and we will serve you.' Rehoboam's elders in Judah advised him to grant their petition, but the young men he had grown up with offered different counsel. Rehoboam chose the advice of his young friends over the elders of Judah and told the ten northern tribes, 'Whereas my father loaded you with a heavy yoke, I will add to it; my father disciplined you with whips, but I will discipline you with scorpions.'"

The young musician speaks up. "So Rehoboam became even more like the kings of Egypt than his father Solomon was?"

The old man shakes his head. "Perhaps he thought he would. Maybe he was hoping to make even more of a name for himself than his father had. But that is not what happened. When Rehoboam sent Adoram, who was over all the forced labor, to bring back workers, the ten tribes rose up against him and stoned him to death, beginning the rebellion that would divide the kingdom in two once more: the ten tribes of Israel to the north, leaving the tribe of Judah to the south.

"Jeroboam became king over Israel, and although a civil war looked imminent, God sent a prophet to Rehoboam telling him not to fight with his kinfolk. For once, the king obeyed the word of the LORD. But Rehoboam and the people of Judah did evil in the sight of the LORD. Their sins were worse than their fathers' had been. They participated in all the evil practices of the nations, which the LORD had driven out before them. And in the fifth year of Rehoboam's reign, the king of Egypt came up against Jerusalem and looted the Temple of the treasure that Solomon had amassed.

"After this, there was war between Rehoboam and Jeroboam continually. And when Rehoboam died, his son Abijam became king and walked in all the sins of his father before him.

"Thus begins the endless litany of the reign of the kings of Israel and Judah. Each one seemed to try to outdo his father in terms of the evil practices they adopted from the nations around them. The nation remained split in two, and the unity that David had striven for was shattered forever.

"But God's people were not abandoned to their own devices. God sent prophet after prophet to call the people back to covenant faithfulness, to cease their evil practices and to call on the name of the LORD once more.

"During the reign of King Ahab of Israel, who did more to provoke God than all the kings before him, God sent the prophet Elijah with the word of the LORD. In a dramatic showdown on top of Mount Carmel, Elijah, the prophet of God, challenged 850 of the prophets of Baal and Asherah to prove whom the people should serve: the LORD God, or the pagan gods they had adopted. The LORD God vindicated God's prophet Elijah with a fiery display of God's power, and the people rose up and killed the false prophets.

"But they soon slipped back into their old ways. And king after king after king led the people into breaking covenant with their God."

Someone calls out from the crowd, "What we need is another Elijah! A prophet of God who can defeat the gods of the Babylonians— to show them that our God is the LORD."

Before the old man can respond, the young musician speaks up. "What God did through Elijah was not a demonstration of God's power for the pagans' sake. It was for Israel's sake, to call our ancestors back to faithfulness to the covenant." He looks at the old man but says to the crowd, "We have the Story. Would another Elijah change our hearts?"

At these words the old man raises an eyebrow in surprise, while some in the crowd mutter angrily. He continues.

"The story takes a tragic turn under King Hoshea, who became king over Israel in Samaria. Shalmaneser, king of Assyria, came up against him, and Hoshea paid him tribute, becoming his vassal. But when he tried to throw off the yoke of oppression, instead of turning to the LORD for deliverance, Hoshea sent messengers to the ancient enemy of Israel, the king of Egypt, for help. When Shalmaneser discovered his treachery, he invaded the whole land, captured Samaria and carried the ten tribes of Israel into exile in Assyria, where they were assimilated into Assyrian culture and lost their identity forever. This came to pass because the people did not obey the voice of the LORD their God, succumbing yet again to the temptation of idolatry and breaking covenant with the LORD. They forsook the commandments that Moses had given them, making for themselves two golden calves to worship, even offering their children to the flames in sacrifice. So the LORD removed them from the land, leaving only our people, the tribe of Judah.

"When Israel was carried off into exile, Hezekiah was king over Judah. And he trusted in the LORD God of Israel, doing right in the sight of the LORD, just as his ancestor David had done, keeping the commandments which the LORD had commanded Moses. He removed the high places and cut down the Asherah, which other kings had installed before him. And the LORD was with him, and he rebelled against the king of Assyria and did not serve him.

"But then Sennacherib came to power in Assyria, and he invaded Judah and besieged Jerusalem. Instead of seeking the help of other nations, as the kings before him had done, however, Hezekiah called on the name of the LORD. And the prophet Isaiah came to him and said, 'Because you have prayed to the LORD, God will save the city for God's own sake, and for the sake of God's servant, David.' That night, the angel of the LORD went out and destroyed the Assyrian army, and the land of Judah knew rest once more.

"But before he died, Hezekiah welcomed a delegation from the king of Babylon, who asked for his help to fight the Assyrians. Hezekiah foolishly flaunted the wealth and beauty of the Temple before them. And Isaiah the prophet came to him and said, 'Behold, the days are coming when all that is in your house, and all that your fathers have laid up in store, shall be carried off to Babylon; nothing shall be left. Thus says the LORD.' Instead of being grieved at this, Hezekiah thought, 'at least there will be peace in my days.'

"After Hezekiah's death, his son Manasseh came to power. He fell into the ways of the kings before him, doing evil in the sight of the LORD. And his son Amon, king after him, also did evil in the sight of the LORD."

"Were there no good kings at all?" asks the young girl.

The old man turns to her and replies, "Yes, there was one. During this dark period of the Story, there was a final ray of hope, King Josiah, for he did right in the sight of the LORD and walked in all the ways of his father David. He ordered the Temple, which had fallen into disrepair, to be restored. And while this was being done, the workers found the book of the Law, which had been lost for decades. They brought it to Josiah, and when he read it, he was horrified at how far from God's covenant the people had gone.

"He feared that what had happened to Israel would happen to Judah, and so he sent for a prophet to bring the word of the LORD to the people. That prophet, the woman Huldah, came to King Josiah and said, 'Thus says the LORD God of Israel, "Because your heart was tender and you humbled yourself before the LORD when you heard what I spoke against this place and against its inhabitants that they should become a desolation and a curse, and because you have torn your clothes and wept before me, I truly have heard you. Therefore you will go to your grave in peace and you will not see the evil which I will bring on this place."'

"King Josiah ordered the nation to gather at the Temple, and there, in response to the word of the LORD which came through the prophet Huldah, after hearing the story of what God had done for them, they renewed the covenant with God once more."

The old man shakes his head and turns back to the crowd. "Yet sadly, this revival lasted just one generation. Josiah's sons were as evil as all the other kings before them. God sent prophet after prophet to try and woo God's people back to the LORD. They warned the people, 'You saw the Northern tribes carried off into exile! Don't think it can't happen to you!' But they were continually ignored."

And now the old man pauses, his head bowed. For this is where he enters the Story himself. He looks up and continues in a trembling voice.

"But your fathers, among whom I am numbered, in our conceit thought that we were immune to disaster. After all, we had the Temple in Jerusalem—God's very presence in our midst. How could anything happen to us? But disaster was just around the corner.

"God sent one final prophet to warn us, Jeremiah, the 'weeping prophet.' He grieved for our people not only because he saw the fate that was about to befall us but also because no one would listen to him; no one else could see what was so transparent to him. His hope was that the ache of God for God's people could somehow penetrate the numbness of our conceit.

"He stood in the gate of the Temple and cried out, 'Thus says the Lord, the God of Israel, "Change your ways, and I will let you live in this place!"

"'"Do not trust in deceptive words, saying, 'This is the Temple of the Lord, the Temple of the Lord, the Temple of the Lord.' For only if you amend your ways, if you truly practice justice between a person and their neighbor, if you do not oppress the orphan, the widow and the stranger, and do not shed innocent blood, nor walk after other gods to your ruin, then I will let you dwell in this place, in the land that I gave your fathers, forever.

"'"Behold, you are trusting in deceptive words to no avail. Will you steal, murder and commit adultery, and swear falsely, and offer sacrifices to Baal, and walk after other gods, then come and stand before me in this House, which is called by my name, and say, 'We are delivered!'—that you may then do all these abominations? Has this House, which is called by my name, become a den of thieves in your sight? Behold, I have seen it myself," declares the Lord.'

"Here was our great conceit. We acted against every one of the Ten Words and then dared to come before the Lord in God's Temple to seek God's blessing. Such breathtaking arrogance! Yet even then God would not abandon us. God came to us and gave us the chance to return to covenant faithfulness: to practice justice, to care for the vulnerable, to give up our idolatry."

The old man's shoulders slump forward. "But we did not listen.

And so, as God promised, disaster fell on us, because of our prideful conceit. During King Jehoiachin's reign over Judah, Nebuchadnezzar, king of Babylon, besieged Jerusalem and captured the city. Then he led away into exile all the mighty men of Israel, the craftsmen, the smiths; none remained in the area of Jersualem except the poorest of the rural poor."

Once more the old man wipes away the tears that have fallen freely as he has narrated his own story. "Yet even in exile we failed to keep covenant with God. And neither did those left in Israel."

He looks into the crowd, to see many staring at their feet, unable to meet his gaze. "A decade later, during the reign of King Zedekiah, on the seventh day of the fifth month, which was the nineteenth year of the reign of King Nebuchadnezzar, king of Babylon, the captain of his army came to Jerusalem and burned the Temple to the ground, along with the king's palace and the rest of the city, and they broke down the walls, and the remainder of our people Judah were carried into exile in Babylon.

"And thus we come to the lowest point in our history. For, worst of all, God's presence left the Temple. Our faith was grounded not in the LORD God who made covenant with us but in the Temple, where the LORD dwelt in our midst. We seemed to think that as long as we had God's presence in the Temple, how we lived did not matter. Yet our people's continual breaking of our covenant with God, despite the centuries of patience God had shown God's disobedient people, did indeed lead to judgment—just as the prophets tried to warn us. We were indeed torn from the land and carried off into exile, just as the ten tribes of Israel had been. And so, here we are."

A profound silence falls over the crowd, which no one is willing to break until a small voice asks the question on everyone's lips. Taking the hand of his big sister, the little boy asks, "Abba . . . is this the end of the Story?"

The old man lifts his eyes to find every face in the crowd fixed upon his. He turns to the little boy who looks sad beyond his years. Suddenly the old man straightens his back, throws back his shoulders and, as hope is rekindled in him, loudly proclaims, "No!"

Heads snap up at the old man's cry. People wipe tears from their eyes and lean in, desperate to understand the note of hope they hear sounded in the old man's proclamation.

"Our God is a God of grace. Even in the midst of this deserved disaster, the LORD has promised that God will be faithful to the covenant, even when we are not." The people lean forward, desperate to hear why the old man believes this. "Ezekiel not only had nightmares. He also had beautiful visions. In one, God came to him and said, 'One day I will sprinkle clean water on my people, and you will be clean; I will cleanse you from all your filthiness and from all your idols. Moreover, I will give you a new heart and put a new spirit within you; and I will remove the heart of stone from your flesh, and give you a heart of flesh. And I will put my Spirit within you and cause you to walk in my commandments, and you will be careful to keep the covenant. And you will live in the land that I gave to your forefathers; so you will be my people, and I will be your God.'"

The little boy looks up at his mother from his seat in her lap, his eyes asking, *Is this true?* His mother smiles down at her son, hugs him close and turns her eyes back toward the old man, the faintest of hope now being kindled within her.

"Remember the words of the prophet Isaiah. For he saw the day when the redeemed of the LORD would come with joyful singing back to Zion; and everlasting joy would be on their heads. They would obtain gladness and joy, and sorrow and mourning would flee away. And revisiting the history of God's people—which always begins with the barren, with Sarah, with Rebekah, with Rachel and with Hannah—Isaiah said, 'Shout for joy, O barren one, you who have borne no children. Break forth into joyful shouting and cry aloud, for you will have more children than all mothers. You will spread abroad to the right and to the left, and your descendants will possess nations, and they will resettle the desolate cities.'"

The crowd's mood lifts as they imagine what these words might mean for them. Many are smiling, some turn to hug their neighbors.

The old man sees this and says, "But remember: with the promise came the reminder of what God expects from God's people. For have we not fasted before the LORD and cried out for deliverance from exile? Have we not sung the song tonight asking God to act on our behalf?

"Hear again the word of the LORD to God's people, spoken through the prophet Isaiah. 'The people seek me day by day. They ask me for just decisions. They say, "Why have we fasted, and you do not notice?" Rather than your fasts, sitting in sackcloth and ashes, is this not the fast which I choose? To loosen the bonds of wickedness, to undo the bands of the yoke, and to let the oppressed go free? Is it not to share your bread with the hungry, and to bring the homeless poor into your home; when you see the naked to cover him; and not to ignore the plight of your brothers and sisters?

"'When this is how you live, then you will call, and the LORD will answer. When you remove oppression from your midst, when you stop standing in judgment over others, if you give yourself to the hungry, and care for the afflicted, then your light will rise in darkness, and the LORD will continually guide you, and satisfy your desire in times of dryness, and give strength to your bones.

"'For the LORD gives strength to the weary, power to those who are worn out. Those who wait for the LORD will renew their strength; they will mount up on wings like eagles, they will run and not grow weary, they will walk and not become tired.'

"For all our people's grasping for power in the past, here we are, powerless in exile. Yet Isaiah evokes a picture of the future that gives our people a remarkable gift. He tells anew the old, old Story of God, the story of us. And that is that God is always at work to do a new thing, that God is always doing for us what we cannot do for ourselves. It is not in grasping that we will obtain it but in receiving it as pure gift.

"This is the task of the prophets: to remind God's people of the past, and to tell God's people what lies in the future—not so we can sit back and wait for it to happen but so that we change the way we live today, to live faithfully in light of the promise of that coming day.

The prophet's message is best heard in reverse: the future affecting our now."

"What does that mean for us, old one?" someone calls from the crowd.

"What it has always meant: to keep the covenant we have made with God. As the prophet Micah told us before we were carried into exile, 'God has told you what is good; and what does the LORD require of you but to do justice, to love *hesed*, and to walk humbly with your God.' Do justice. Love covenant fidelity. Put away your conceit."

He pauses, then continues. "And perhaps it is for us to take seriously the words of Jeremiah, written in his letter to us when we were first brought here those many years ago. 'Thus says the LORD of hosts, the God of Israel, to all the exiles whom I have sent into exile from Jerusalem into Babylon, "Build houses and live in them; and plant gardens, and eat their produce. Take wives and become the fathers of sons and daughters, and multiply there and do not decrease."'"

A voice from the crowd interrupts him. "But we have done all that."

The old man continues, "'And seek the welfare of the city where I have sent you into exile, and pray to the LORD on its behalf; for in its welfare is your welfare.'"

"Pray for the Babylonians?" the voice calls out again. "We will pray for our people—but not them. We will bless our people, not theirs."

The old man feels anger rising in him at this declaration, but it soon passes to be replaced by a deep weariness. "Then you still have not heard the Story, my friend. For God has chosen our people from among the many peoples of the world to bless those very same peoples. God's purpose is not to bring you and me out of exile; it is to deliver the entire world from exile—for we are all living east of Eden, in a world full of arrogance, violence, injustice, self-protection, greed and misuse of power. If we are ever to fulfill the covenant the LORD God made with Abraham, to be a blessing to the peoples of the world, then perhaps we are to begin by being a blessing to the people among whom we are living right now."

The crowd grows quiet once more, as the old man's words sink in.

He looks around at his people, his eyes coming to rest on the young girl. Her brow is wrinkled; the old man smiles knowingly and asks, "Do you have a question?"

The young girl replies, "When you were quoting Isaiah's message, you said that those who wait for the LORD would 'mount up on wings of eagles.' That sounds a lot like what the LORD said to our people when God brought them out of Egypt. Then perhaps we *are* waiting for a new exodus."

The old man's face breaks out into a broad smile. "We have a prophet in our midst!" The people laugh, and the young girl blushes. The old man's voice takes on a serious tone as he says, "You are right, my young friend. And you have answered your brother's question. The Story does not end with exile in Babylon; it will continue with a new exodus."

He turns to the crowd. "For just as Jeremiah said, 'Days are coming when it will no longer be said, "As the LORD lives, who brought up the sons of Israel out of the land of Egypt," but, "As the LORD lives, who brought up the sons of Israel from the land of the North where God had exiled them."' This new exodus will not be limited to God's people Israel; the new exodus will be for all people, as Isaiah caught a glimpse of: 'In that day Israel will be the third party with Egypt and Assyria, a blessing in the midst of the earth, whom the LORD of hosts has blessed, saying, "Blessed is Egypt, my people, and Assyria, the work of my hands, and Israel, my inheritance."'

"And the new exodus will not only be for all peoples; it will also be deliverance from all the things that keep people in bondage. It will be deliverance for all of creation, as it groans under the weight of what humanity has done."

"When will this new exodus happen?" someone asks. "When will God bring our people back from exile?"

The old man ponders the question before answering. "If we believe the words of Jeremiah, then the years of our exile will be seventy." At this, people turn to their neighbor to talk excitedly. They have heard this before, but tonight . . . tonight it seems possible that the word of the LORD through Jeremiah may come to pass. The old man calls out above the crowd, "But I am not saying that the return from exile is the new exodus."

The people slowly grow quiet once more. "Then what *are* you saying?" someone asks.

"The vision of a new exodus is so much greater than our people's return from exile. Isaiah saw that God's servant Israel would be a light to the nations, so that God's salvation might reach to the ends of the earth. 'For behold, I create new heavens and a new earth, and the former things shall not be remembered or come to mind.' God's salvation, God's shalom, shall heal the whole of creation, so that once more the wolf and the lamb shall graze together, for the violence that has plagued creation will be no more. The creation will return from exile, so that God will make the wilderness like the Garden of Eden once more. This is the prophet's vision of where God's Story is leading."

Caught up in this expansive vision, the young girl asks, "If that is where the Story of God is leading, then who will lead God's people there?"

"The new exodus will require another prophet like Moses—just as Moses himself saw. And it will require another Solomon—another son of David—a king who will fulfill and not break Torah as Solomon did. A son of David who will not amass wealth for himself, who will not build up military might, who will not oppress the poor.

"For, as the prophet Isaiah saw, 'the people who walk in darkness will see a great light; those who live in a dark land, the light will shine on them. For a child will be born to us, a son will be given to us; and the government will rest on his shoulders; and his name will be called Wonderful Counselor, Mighty God, Eternal Father, Prince of Peace. There will be no end to the increase of his government or of peace, on the throne of David and over his kingdom, to establish it and to uphold it with justice and righteousness from then on and forever. The zeal of the LORD of hosts will accomplish this.'

"This is the One that the prophet Daniel has seen in a vision here in exile: 'I kept looking in the night visions, and behold, with the clouds of heaven, one like a Son of Man was coming. And he came up to the Ancient of Days, and was presented before God. And to him was given dominion, glory and a kingdom, that all the peoples, nations and people of every language might serve him. His kingdom is an everlasting kingdom which will not pass away.'"

A reverent hush falls on the crowd. The old man's face is streaked with tears once more, but these are tears of joy, tears of hope. "When God brings us back to the land God promised to Abraham, Isaac and Jacob—when we go home—this is the King we will be waiting for. Another son of David, bringing shalom. Another Moses, bringing covenant faithfulness, believing allegiance to the LORD our God. A King with an everlasting kingdom."

The old man invites the crowd to stand. He blesses them, saying, "So let us go to serve the LORD our God here in exile, seeking the welfare of our neighbors as we await the day when God will bring us back from exile. And there let us wait for the King who is coming, God's anointed one. Shabbat shalom, my friends."

The old man takes the arm of the young musician and leaves with his people, who depart in near silence, nurturing the flame of hope that has been kindled in them, daring to believe that the Story is not yet over.

Interlude

Babylon, like all empires, eventually fell. Under the conquering king, Cyrus of Persia, my people returned home to Jerusalem. They had been in exile for seventy years, fulfilling the word of the LORD by the mouth of Jeremiah, that the land might have the Sabbath rest our people had failed to give it.

I was the little girl with all those questions. I am now a woman, with children of my own—born in the land God promised to Abraham. I returned with my people, but although we rebuilt our homes when we arrived in Jerusalem, the nations around us prevented us from rebuilding the city's defenses. The walls lay in ruins, the gates gone, burned to ashes.

It was not until Nehemiah came to lead us that the walls and the city were rebuilt. Then under Ezra's leadership, the Temple was rebuilt. It was a shadow of its former self, and those few who remembered Solomon's Temple wept when they saw it.

There is no cloud, no shekinah glory—God's presence is no longer visibly present in the midst of God's people. We have no king. Though in the land, we remain in exile, a new slavery to another foreign overlord. And so we wait for God to return once more to the Temple, for God to forgive our sins. We wait for the new exodus.

We wait.

9

christ

In which we hear the story of the One who embodies

God's love and fidelity, and who opens the way for a

new covenant . . .

The woman looks around at those assembled in the courtyard, the *ekklesia** that meets in her home, and feels deep gratitude for the life that she knows today, the life the Story has brought. Yes, these are difficult and dangerous times, but there is also so much joy—and hope. She feels a great love for those who have broken bread with her, many of whom she would never have known had it not been for the Story.

Against the backdrop of after-dinner conversations around the table, she turns to her guest, a visiting merchant. He does not know the Story . . . yet. Her mind goes back to the day when it all began for her; she knows if she were to close her eyes, she would find herself there as if it were only yesterday. She smiles at him and says, "Let me tell you about the day the Story began for me.

"I was a little girl. It was the first time I had made pilgrimage to Jerusalem, the holy city of my people, for the feast of Passover. I was so excited by all the sights and sounds, the great crowd of people singing the songs of the festival—the songs of ascent—over and over again. As we approached the city, we joined another large group of people coming in from Bethany, in the shadow of the Mount of Olives. They too were singing the song that had become my favorite, and so I joined in, singing from atop my horse.

This is the gate of the LORD;

Ekklesia is a Greek word meaning variously "assembly, congregation, council." It was used to describe social and political gatherings; the early churches used it to describe themselves.

The righteous will enter through it.
I shall give thanks to you, for you have answered me;
   And you have become my salvation.

"And then I saw him—the man my father talked about all the time. He was elevated over the crowd, on a horse like me, it seemed. But then I looked closer. It was not a horse; it was a donkey. The crowd kept singing.

The stone which the builders rejected
   Has become the chief corner stone.
This is the LORD's doing;
   it is marvelous in our eyes.
This is the day which the LORD has made;
   Let us rejoice and be glad in it.

"People were laughing, full of joy as they sang. Some started breaking palm branches from trees and were waving them—I remember looking around anxiously; I knew the Romans had ruled that we were not allowed to display the symbols of our nation anymore—but no one seemed to think that it was a bad thing to do on this day. Some people were laying their branches on the road, while others were laying their cloaks down before the man on the donkey. It looked like the parade when the new Roman general came to Judea. I wondered what it all meant. Then someone continued the song, and we began singing the same line over and over and over:

Blessed is the one who comes in the name of the LORD.
Blessed is the one who comes in the name of the LORD.

"I looked over at some of our religious leaders. They did not appear to be joining in with the crowds. So I looked back at the man, the center of all this excitement, and I asked myself, *Who* are *you?*"

The woman's guest leans forward, caught up in her story. "So?" he asks. "Who was the man?"

"That man was Jesus Christ, the son of David, the son of Abraham."

"His father and grandfather?" the merchant asks.

"No!" An old friend of their host interrupts from the right of the merchant. "They are the two most important figures in our people's history. Our God made covenant with Abraham, promising him a land and a nation. David was the great king of our people. Since exile in Babylon, for centuries we have awaited a son of David to take the throne."

"Then your Jesus is of noble lineage," the merchant says.

The woman answers, "Indeed," reaching behind her to her most treasured possession: a collection of scrolls. "For our people, a person's family tree is very important. Perhaps I could read the genealogy of Jesus for you?" The merchant nods in assent, and she unrolls the scroll and begins to read. "To Abraham was born Isaac; and to Isaac, Israel; and to Jacob, Judah and his brothers . . ." She reads the genealogy of forty-two generations, concluding, ". . . and to Jacob was born Joseph the husband of Mary, by whom was born Jesus, who is called Christ."*

The merchant's brow wrinkles. "Something troubles you?" the woman asks.

"No," he replies, "but it is a most unusual genealogy." Some of the newcomers of the *ekklesia,* overhearing the exchange, nod in agreement. He continues, "The lineage is interrupted four times—with the inclusion of the mothers of some of Jesus' forefathers."

The woman smiles. "An astute observation, my new friend. Yes, this genealogy includes four women in Jesus' heritage."

One of the newcomers says, "But we never list women in our ancestry."

"And if we did, I'd leave those four out!" comments another.

The merchant turns and asks, "Why?"

"Let's just say," the newcomer responds, "their stories are . . . not quite so noble."

The merchant turns back to his host, who offers a further explanation. "Tamar, Rahab, Ruth and Uriah's widow, Bathsheba—the stories of these women are overshadowed by sexual intrigue and tragedy. Certainly we might be surprised to find them here for that reason. But

---

*You can read the genealogy in its entirety in Matthew 1.

their stories are not what make their inclusion so startling. There is something else these women share in common." She looks past her guest to her old friend.

"They are all gentiles," he offers. "They are not children of Abraham."

"Is that important?" asks the merchant.

"It is both surprising and important," she replies, looking around at the diverse group gathered in her home, "as we have come to understand."

The merchant continues. "What of Jesus' parents? Were they of noble status?"

His host laughs. "Not by most people's standards. But the account of Jesus' birth suggests that all is not as it seems with this family. God's messenger Gabriel, one of the heavenly host who serve the LORD, came to a young girl named Mary. She was engaged to be married to a carpenter, an honorable man named Joseph. Gabriel said, 'Mary, you have nothing to fear. God has a surprise for you: you will become pregnant and give birth to a son and call his name Jesus.* He will be great. He will be called the Son of the Most High; the LORD God will give him the throne of his ancestor, David, and he will rule Jacob's house forever—no end, ever, to his kingdom.'

"Mary protested, 'But how? I've never slept with a man.'

"Gabriel said, 'The Holy Spirit will come upon you and the power of the Most High will hover over you; therefore the child you bring to birth will be called Holy, Son of God.'

"When she carried this amazing news to her cousin Elizabeth, Mary burst into a song of praise,

> I'm bursting with God-news; I'm dancing the song of my Savior God. God took one good look at me, and look what happened— I'm the most fortunate woman on earth! God's mercy flows in wave after wave on those in awe of God. God knocked tyrants off their high horses, pulled victims out of the mud. The starving

---

*"Jesus" is the Greek form of the Hebrew name Yeshua, which means "God saves."

poor sat down to a banquet; the callous rich were left out in the cold. God embraced God's chosen child, Israel; God remembered and piled on the mercies, piled them high. It's exactly what God promised, beginning with Abraham, and right up to now.'"

"A beautiful and intriguing song," the merchant comments, before asking, "But this Joseph, did he believe Mary's story?"

"Not at first," the woman replies. "It took a visit from Gabriel to convince him." As the merchant shakes his head, she smiles and says, "I understand—the beginning of Jesus' story is quite . . . unique. When Caesar Augustus called for an empire-wide census to be taken, Joseph took Mary and left Nazareth their home to journey to Bethlehem in Judea, because he was of the house of David. And there, in a backwater of the mighty Roman Empire, Jesus was born. Heralded as Savior and Christ the Lord by angels on the night of his birth, he was nevertheless laid in a borrowed crib, his birth witnessed only by shepherds.

"On his eighth day of life, Mary and her husband, Joseph, took the baby boy to the Temple to be presented to the LORD, as Torah required, and to be circumcised to receive the sign of the covenant. There was a man in Jerusalem named Simeon, who was righteous and devout, and who had been looking for the hope of Israel. The Holy Spirit was upon him and had revealed to him that he would not see death before he had seen the LORD's Christ.

"Simeon came in the Spirit into the Temple; and when the parents brought in the child Jesus, to carry out the custom of Torah, he took the child in his arms and blessed God, and said, 'God, you can now release your servant; release me in peace as you promised. With my own eyes I've seen your salvation; it's now out in the open for everyone to see: a God-revealing light to the gentiles and the glory of your people Israel.'"

"And the LORD, whom you seek, will suddenly come to the Temple . . ." The woman turns to the young man who spoke these words.

"Yes," she says. "The prophet Malachi saw the day when the LORD would return to dwell in the midst of God's people once more. Ezekiel also saw that day and gave a description of the beauty of the Temple to which the LORD would return. King Herod, with the encouragement of the Sadducees, committed vast resources to rebuilding such a temple."

Her old friend interjects, saying to her guest, "The Sadducees are the ruling elite of our people, descendants of the Hasmonean priest-kings."*

"Thank you, my friend," the host continues. "Herod saw the project as a way to win the hearts and minds of the people he ruled; the Sadducees saw it as hastening the day when Israel's light would once again shine brightly. They were—and still are—waiting for the *Shekinah* glory to return to the Temple. Yet when God's glory did indeed return, in the person of this eight-day-old baby, only an old man and an old woman—the prophetess Anna—recognized it.

"Some time later, some distinguished visitors—magi from the East—arrived in Jerusalem and stirred up the city. They came to Herod the king and asked, 'Where is the one born King of the Jews? For we saw his star in the East and have come to worship him.' Herod sent them to Bethlehem on the advice of his counselors, who found in the words of Micah a prophecy pointing to this small town: 'From you One will go forth for me to be ruler in Israel.' Herod sought to destroy this threat to his own rule, sending his soldiers to kill all boys two and under in Bethlehem, the infamous 'slaughter of the innocents.' But Joseph, warned in a dream, took Mary and Jesus down into Egypt, where they remained until Herod died."

The woman's friend murmurs, "A new Moses, bringing a new exodus." But no one catches his words, and the woman continues her story.

"We know little of Jesus' life until John the baptizer appeared in the desert, the messenger whom the prophets Isaiah and Malachi had foretold, the one who was to prepare the way before the Lord—the way back from exile.

"Now, in the fifteenth year of the reign of Tiberius Caesar, when Pontius Pilate was governor of Judea, and Herod was tetrarch of Galilee, and his brother Philip was tetrarch of the region of Iturea and Trachonitis, and Lysanias was tetrarch of Abilene, in the high priest-

---

*The Hasmonean dynasty lasted a century and was the only time Israel ruled itself between exile in Babylon and the time of Christ.

hood of Annas and Caiaphas, the word of God came to John, the son of Zacharias, in the wilderness." The woman pauses, marveling once more at the unlikely nature of those God draws into the Story. She comments, "The word of God did not come to the houses of power or the established systems of religion—to the Temple or even the high priest. Instead it came to John, who was out in the wilderness—the place where God so often meets with God's people.

"John came into the country around the Jordan river, preaching a baptism of life-change leading to the forgiveness of sins, as described in the words of Isaiah the prophet: 'Thunder in the desert! "Prepare God's arrival!"' John's message to those who came out to be baptized by him was straightforward. 'Brood of snakes! What do you think you're doing slithering down here to the river? Do you think a little water on your snakeskins is going to deflect God's judgment? It's your life that must change, not your skin. And don't think you can pull rank by claiming Abraham as father.' John, like the prophets before him, warned the people not to presume on their privilege as descendants of Abraham but instead to be faithful to the covenant Abraham made with God.

"The interest of the people by now was building. They were all beginning to wonder, 'Could this John be the Messiah?' John said to them, 'I'm baptizing you in the river. The main character in this drama, to whom I'm a mere stagehand, will ignite the kingdom life, a fire, the Holy Spirit within you, changing you from the inside out.'

"Jesus came to John, and when John saw him approach, he cried out, 'Behold the Lamb of God, who takes away the sin of the world.' Jesus asked John to baptize him. John at first protested, but Jesus went down into the water and told John that this was part of God's plan—because Jesus was not just identifying with his people in his baptism; he was being anointed King by God's prophet, just as Samuel had anointed David.

"And so John baptized Jesus, and as he came up from the water, while he was praying, the Holy Spirit descended on him in the form of a dove. And a voice came from heaven: 'You are my Son, whom I love; with you I am well pleased.' The Spirit hovered over the waters, as in creation, descending in the form of a dove, the bird that the poor offer as their sacrifice. Perhaps in his baptism Jesus was not only being anointed King: he was being set apart for sacrifice, for self-giving. From the very beginning, the course his life would take was being laid before him."

The merchant interrupts. "What is this Spirit that descends on this Jesus? Whose voice is it that claims Jesus as a Son?"

The woman responds, "Good questions, my friend. This story points to something that has proven difficult for many of us to grasp, given the Shema of my people, which declares that God is one—and yet here are three. Perhaps," she offers, eager to return to the story, "we can discuss this after we've heard the story of our Christ?"

He nods, and she continues. "Jesus, full of the Holy Spirit, left the Jordan and was led by the Spirit into the wild. For forty days and nights he was tested by the devil in the wilderness. He ate nothing during those days, and into that place of utter weakness came the serpent of old, the devil.

"Jesus faced three temptations at the end of those forty days; they were different from each other but the same at heart, offering an easier, softer path than the one that lay before him. In this story we hear echoes of Israel's years of wandering in the wilderness. There Israel, God's firstborn son, put the LORD their God to the test. Would the Son of God remain faithful to the Father where Israel was not?

"The devil said to Jesus, 'If you are the Son of God, tell this stone to become bread.' And Jesus replied, 'It is written, "No one can live by bread alone, but by doing God's will."' God had called Jesus into this fast, and God would call him out of it. Where Jesus resisted temptation, Israel had failed: they demanded manna, instead of trusting God to provide for them, as Jesus did.

"And so the devil led him to Jerusalem, and had him stand on the pinnacle of the Temple, and said to him, 'If you are the Son of God, jump! Is it not written, "God has placed you in the care of angels. They will catch you, so you won't so much as stub your toe on a stone"?'

"Now, if Jesus did this, revealing his identity so publicly in the Temple, the people would have proclaimed him Messiah there and then. But this was not the path his Father had laid out before him, and so he answered, 'It is written, "You shall not put the LORD your God to the test."' Again, Jesus resisted the temptation that Israel failed in—for they had continually put God to the test.

"And so the devil took him to the peak of a huge mountain. He gestured expansively, pointing out all the earth's kingdoms. Then he said, 'All of this can be yours in all its glory. Just go down on your knees and worship me and they're yours.'

"Surely this was the greatest temptation of all: if God's intention was to establish the kingdom of the Son of Man forever, then here was a painless way to do just that. But to do so would involve the great sin of Israel, idolatry: worshiping another and not the LORD. Jesus answered him, 'Be gone, Satan! It is written, "Worship the LORD your God, and only God. Serve God with absolute single-heartedness."' Once more, Jesus responded by quoting from Torah, which had deeply shaped his identity just as it was supposed to have shaped the people of Israel. Where Israel had failed to be obedient, Jesus was faithful. When the devil had finished the temptations, he left. And angels came and ministered to Jesus' needs."

The woman pauses to take a drink before continuing. "From the wilderness, Jesus returned to Galilee where he had grown up. He taught in the synagogues, and his reputation as a rabbi began to grow. He proclaimed the gospel of the kingdom of God, healed every kind of disease and delivered the demon-possessed. He called twelve men to be his students, disciples who would follow him and learn from him."

"Why twelve? Is that the typical size of a rabbi's school?" asks the merchant.

The woman turns to her friend and says, "How would you answer the question?"

He considers his response before saying, "Our people were waiting for the LORD to return to the Temple, to live in their midst once more, just as God had dwelt in the tabernacle and Solomon's Temple—enthroned in the midst of the twelve tribes of Israel. And here is Jesus, calling twelve disciples to follow where he leads." As the implications of this response sink in, the merchant raises an eyebrow before turning back to his host.

"His choice of disciple was strange to say the least," she continued. "Not the brightest students from the *Bet Talmud*, the house of learning, but ordinary men, fishermen, even a tax collector—a collaborator with Rome."

"So, what did he teach them?"

"Jesus taught in word and deed, and he began in dramatic style! He traveled to Cana in Galilee to attend a wedding to which he had been invited. Before the end of the celebration, the wine ran out."

"Disaster!" The merchant interrupts.

The woman chuckles and says, "Yes, and deeply embarrassing for the newlyweds. Jesus' mother told Jesus the situation and Jesus replied, 'Is that any of our business, mother—yours or mine? My time has not yet come.' Jesus' mother was not convinced, however, and she told the servants to do whatever he said. Seeing the thirty-gallon waterpots used for ritual cleansing during the meal, Jesus told the servants to fill all six with water, then ladle some out and present it to the host of the wedding feast.

"When the host tasted the water—now become wine—he said to the groom, 'You've saved the best wine till last!'"

One of the newcomers asks, "Why do you think Jesus changed his mind? Deciding that his time had come?"

The woman ponders the question before answering. "I do not know. But I wonder if it was because of where he was. What better place to begin the public ministry that would lead to a new covenant than at a wedding banquet?

"From there he took his disciples to Jerusalem for the Passover. As they entered the Temple, Jesus saw the moneychangers and livestock sellers, made a whip and drove them all out of the Temple. 'Take these things away!' he shouted. 'Stop making my Father's house a den of rip-off merchants.'"

At this the merchant winces. "I imagine that did not win him many friends."

The woman sighs. "To say the least. When the religious leaders saw what Jesus was doing, they were outraged and demanded, 'What credentials can you give us to justify all this?' Jesus answered them, saying, 'Destroy this temple, and in three days I will raise it up.' The leaders said, 'It has taken forty-six years to build this Temple—and you're going to rebuild it in three days?' But, as was often his custom, Jesus did not answer them. From the very beginning of his public ministry, Jesus acted out the coming judgment on the Temple and those who put their trust in it, knowing full well that in doing so he was beginning to walk the path that would lead to his death.

The merchant's brow wrinkles. "But the Temple is still standing. What did Jesus mean?"

The woman replies, "The temple Jesus was referring to was his body. For Jesus understood where the outrage of the religious leaders would lead."

The merchant's brow wrinkles further. "But if he's talking about his body, how can he possibly, as he said, 'raise' that in three days?!"

The woman smiles and says, "Perhaps we can save that question for later as well."

The merchant laughs. "You must enjoy my company to continually invite me back to future conversations!"

"Yes," she responds, "I know. Quite honestly, so much could be said and written about Jesus that I can't imagine a world big enough to hold such a library.

"Jesus often confronted religious and social convention in such bold, though not always so combative, ways. During a trip from Jerusalem to Galilee, for example, he took the shortest route, a way spurned by the devout among my people because it requires passage through the hated land of Samaria. He stopped at Jacob's well there, where he met a Samaritan woman. When his disciples saw he was talking to a woman, they were amazed—and only more so when she left to bring back the whole village, who after hearing Jesus teach for two days declared him to be the Messiah, the Savior of the world. These 'outsiders' recognized who Jesus was, like Simeon and John before them.

"When they got to Nazareth, Jesus went to the synagogue on the Sabbath and stood up to read. When the scroll of the prophet Isaiah was handed to him, he found the place where it was written,

The spirit of the Lord is upon me,
> because God anointed me to preach the gospel to the poor.
> God has sent me to proclaim release to the captives,
> and recovery of sight to the blind,
> to set free those who are oppressed,
> to proclaim the favorable year of the Lord.

"When Jesus rolled up the scroll and gave it back to the attendant, he sat down, and every eye in the synagogue was fixed on him. This passage was speaking of Messiah—why would the son of Mary and Joseph read it? The disciples, remembering what the Samaritans had said, held their breath too. What would these people do? Then Jesus said, 'Today this scripture has been fulfilled in this place.'

"The people began talking excitedly, 'Isn't this wonderful! One of our own—listen to him.' But then Jesus cut the conversation short. 'Let me tell you something; no prophet is welcome in his hometown. There were many widows in Israel in the days of Elijah, but he was sent to none of them; instead God sent him to a gentile. And there were many lepers in Israel in Elisha's time, but he healed Naaman, the Syrian.' Jesus reminded them that the covenant that God had made with them was to bless all peoples, not just Israel.

"At these words, everyone in the synagogue was filled with rage, and they rose up to kill him. But Jesus passed through their midst and went his way. The disciples wondered at it all: the Samaritans said he was Messiah, but his own people did not.

"This was how Jesus taught his disciples—not just with words but with the things he did. After Jesus called Levi, a tax collector, to follow him, Levi gave a big reception for Jesus in his house. There was a crowd of tax gatherers and other folk who were reclining at table with him. The Pharisees and religious scholars began grumbling at the disciples, saying, 'Why do you eat and drink with the tax collectors and sinners?' Jesus intervened and said to them, 'Who needs a doctor: the healthy or the sick? I'm here inviting the sin-sick, not the spiritually fit.'

"It was one thing to call sinners to repentance out in the desert like John the baptizer; it was another thing entirely to share meals with them. But Jesus was always hanging out with the wrong people, and seemed to spend much of his time breaking bread in the wrong homes."

One of the newcomers, a tanner by trade, looks around the courtyard. "I'm sure your neighbors say the same thing about your hosting us in your home."

The host smiles wearily as she continues, "But even when Jesus was in the 'right' place, things had a habit of getting stirred up. On one occasion, a Pharisee named Simon held a special meal in Jesus' honor."

The merchant interrupts, "So these Pharisees approved of Jesus?"

"Some did, but most did not. They saw him as a peer, a teacher of Torah. But they maintained a close eye on what he was teaching. And especially on the company he kept.

"Jesus went to Simon's home, and reclined at table with him. Now there was a woman in the city who was a 'notorious sinner'; when she learned that Jesus was reclining at table in the Pharisee's house, she brought an alabaster vial of perfume, one of the tools of her trade, and began to wet his feet with her tears, and kept wiping them with her hair, and kissing his feet, and anointing them with the perfume.

"When the Pharisee saw this, he thought to himself, 'If this man really were a prophet he would know who and what sort of person this woman is who is touching him, that she is a sinner.' Jesus understood what he was thinking, and so, turning to the woman, but addressing Simon, he said, 'Do you see this woman?'"

She pauses to comment, "This was a rhetorical question, for Simon had not seen this woman. He had seen a social category: 'sinner.' The Pharisees viewed Jesus as one of their own, a teacher of Torah. Yet he would not keep Torah in the way they expected, most notably by choosing to spend so much time with those the Pharisees deemed 'unclean.' This earned him the reputation of being a 'friend of sinners.'

"Jesus said to Simon, 'I entered your home; you gave me no water for my feet, but she has wet my feet with her tears and wiped them with her hair. You gave me no kiss in greeting; but she, since she came in, has not ceased to kiss my feet. You did not anoint my head with oil in blessing, but she anointed my feet with perfume. For this reason I say to you, her sins, which are many, have been forgiven, for she loved much; but he who is forgiven little, loves little.' And he said to her, 'Your sins are forgiven.' And the others who were reclining at table began to talk among themselves, saying, 'Who does he think he is, forgiving sins?'

"Jesus had little good to say about the Pharisees, the teachers of Torah, whose attitude was revealed in incidents like this one. He believed the Pharisees laid a load on the shoulders of their people that was too heavy for them to bear, and which they were unwilling to help them with. Jesus addressed this in a parable—a teaching form he often employed. 'No one,' he said, 'puts new wine into old wineskins; for the new wine will burst the skins and it will be spilled out and the skins will be ruined. No one, after drinking old wine wishes for new, for he says, "The old is good enough."'"

"So what is the meaning of the parable?" asks the merchant.

"It depends who you ask!" she answers.

He grins and refines his question. "What do you think Jesus meant?"

The host leans forward. "I wonder if the 'old wine' in the parable is Torah, while the new wine refers to laws that the Pharisees created. Convinced that the people could not keep Torah, they built a 'fence' around it—laws that attempted to govern every detail of a person's life. This 'new wine' burst the 'wineskin' of Torah; Torah was given to liberate people from slavery and sin, and the Pharisees' additional requirements led them back into a new form of bondage. It is important to remember that Jesus said that he did not come to do away with Torah, the law of the covenant; he came to fulfill it."

As those listening to this exchange consider the host's words, the merchant interjects, "If I might return to the meal the Pharisee hosted. You said that Jesus declared the sins of this woman, this prostitute, had been forgiven. But only the gods can forgive sins! And you must go to the Temple to receive that forgiveness. Who is this man who dares to make such a claim?"

The woman smiles and says, "You are not alone in asking that question. After many months of teaching and performing miracles, the signs of God's kingdom come, Jesus went off with the disciples to a quiet place to pray. There he asked them, 'Who do the crowds say I am?'

"They answered and said, 'Some say John the baptizer,' come back to life. Others say Elijah. Still others say that one of the prophets of old has risen again.'

"Then Jesus said to them, 'And you—what are you saying about me? Who am I?'

"Peter answered, saying, 'You are the Christ, the Son of the Living God.'"

The merchant's brow wrinkles once more. "That's quite a claim for Peter to make."

"Indeed. Jesus explained to them what that meant, saying, 'It is necessary that the Messiah, the Son of Man, proceed to an ordeal of suffering, be tried and found guilty by the elders, high priests and religion scholars, be killed, and after three days be raised up alive.'

"Peter blurted out, 'God forbid it, Lord! This shall never happen to you.'"

"I can understand Peter's response," the merchant reflects. "If Jesus really is the long-awaited Messiah, why would the leaders of your people kill him?"

The woman sighs. "Because he was not the Messiah they were expecting. And they could not understand the way God would bring the salvation they were looking for. Apparently neither could Peter. Jesus responded abruptly to him. 'Get behind me, Satan. You have no idea how God works.' Then Jesus said to his disciples, 'If anyone wishes to follow me, they must deny themselves, take up their cross daily, and follow me. For whoever wishes to save their life shall lose it, but whoever loses their life for my sake, will save it.'

"His disciples struggled to understand what Jesus was saying.

However, the religious leaders of my people knew exactly what Jesus meant when he said such things, and it did not please them. They even accused Jesus of being demon-possessed on occasion. Once, when he was in the Temple, they said to him, 'We know you're crazy—demon-possessed. Abraham died. The prophets died. And you show up saying, "If you practice what I'm telling you, you'll never have to face death, not even a taste." Are you greater than Abraham, who died? Who do you think you are?'

"Jesus answered, 'If I glorified myself, it wouldn't amount to anything. But my Father put me here at this time and place of splendor, and I am doing what God says. Abraham—your "father"—with jubilant faith looked down the corridors of history and saw my day coming. He saw it and cheered.'

"The religious leaders scoffed, and said to him, 'You are not even fifty years old, and you claim to have seen Abraham?' Jesus said to them, 'Believe me, *I am who I am* long before Abraham was anything.'

"They gasped in horror at what he said, for in their eyes he had committed blasphemy by taking the sacred name of God, YHWH, and using it in reference to himself. They picked up stones to throw at him for his blasphemy but Jesus slipped away, getting out of the Temple.

"Jesus' disciples found it was no easy thing to walk in the dust of their rabbi. For one thing, it required leaving home and family, choosing homelessness, and relying on the hospitality of others for food and shelter. It meant accepting the patronage of Jesus' supporters—those who provided financial support for this wandering rabbi. Jesus' patrons were mostly women: Joanna the wife of Herod's steward, Susanna and many others. It was a humbling matter for a man to accept the patronage of a woman. Perhaps that is why the rich and powerful men who sought to become Jesus' disciples walked away.

"They encountered opposition from the religious leaders of their people. They were confronted by the demon-possessed; they were often misunderstood. Jesus' own family were concerned that he had 'lost his senses.' Sometimes it seemed even the elements were against them! More than once Jesus sent them out onto the Sea of Galilee, only for them to run into one of the storms that can so quickly blow up on that lake. On one occasion Jesus was asleep in the stern of their boat, so exhausted that the fierce gale and pounding waves did not wake him. The disciples, terrified, woke him and said, 'Rabbi, don't you care that we're going down?'

"Jesus stood, looked into the heart of the storm, and spoke to the wind and the waves, 'Hush. Be still.' The wind died down, and it became perfectly calm.

"The disciples were awestruck, and no less terrified now that the storm had gone. They said, 'Who is this, that even the chaotic sea obeys him?'"

She pauses. "Who, indeed. Throughout his public ministry, Jesus healed many people. He fed vast crowds miraculously—"

A newcomer interjects, "Manna in the wilderness."

The woman nods. "He taught vast crowds who came to him on the mountain to hear the Torah that shapes our common life. But his teaching was different than the rabbis and scribes, for he taught with authority. The rabbis commented on the teaching of other rabbis; Jesus spoke directly, daring to say such things as, 'You have heard it said, "You shall love your neighbor and hate your enemy." But I say to you, love your enemies, and pray for those who persecute you, for then you are working out of your true selves, your God-created selves.'"* As she says these words the woman sighs heavily. "My people complain that it is impossible to keep the law of the Pharisees. I say it is easier to keep their law than to keep Torah the way Jesus taught and lived it."

The merchant leans forward to take a drink. "I do not know your Torah. As your people's guiding philosophy, what does it say is most important to do in life?"

The woman smiles. "People asked Jesus that same question. On one occasion one of the experts in Torah asked Jesus, 'What commandment is foremost of all?' Jesus answered, 'The foremost is, "Hear

---

*Jesus "went up on the mountain" to teach the people kingdom living, in what is known as "the Sermon on the Mount" (Matthew 5–7). We hear echoes of Moses' story, who also "went up on the mountain" to receive Torah.

O Israel! The Lord is our God. The Lord is one. And you shall love the Lord your God with all your heart, with all your soul, with all your mind and with all your strength." The second is this, "You shall love your neighbor as yourself." There is no greater commandment than these.'"

The merchant ponders this for a moment. "Then love is the law?"

The woman replies, "Well stated! I think that, yes, according to Jesus, love is the law."

A newcomer interjects, "I have heard it said that love is the law because God is love."

The old man responds, "And we are able to love because we have first been loved by God."

"Yes," the host responds, relishing the wisdom of her friends. "Jesus taught. Jesus healed. Jesus cast out demons; he even raised people from the dead. Those with eyes to see recognized these signs of the kingdom of God, which was breaking into the brokenness of the world. And the heart of his message was the exodus all over again: freedom from bondage, whether it be the bondage of disease, the bondage of marginalization and exclusion, or the bondage of sin.

"One day Jesus was teaching in a synagogue, and there was a woman there who had suffered for eighteen years from a sickness, caused by a spirit, that left her doubled over, unable to stand up straight. When Jesus saw her he called her over and said to her, 'Woman, you're free!' Instantly she was healed, standing straight and tall, giving glory to God. But the synagogue leader was furious because Jesus had healed on the Sabbath, and he rebuked the woman. Jesus in turn rebuked the man's hypocrisy, saying, 'You frauds! Each Sabbath every one of you regularly unties your cow or donkey from its stall, leads it out for water, and thinks nothing of it.'

"And then Jesus made this amazing statement: 'So why isn't it all right for me to untie this daughter of Abraham and lead her from the stall Satan has had her tied up in these eighteen years?' He called her 'daughter of Abraham,' a statement that is unheard of among my people. Jesus made this crippled woman a full participant in the covenant.

The healing Jesus brings is more than physical. It is also restoration to community.

"Restoration to community is central to healing. It is the practice of my people to isolate those who suffer with diseases such as leprosy. We also avoid contact with 'notorious sinners,' believing that they will pollute our purity, for they are 'unclean.' To be touched by an unclean person is to become unclean yourself. Yet nearly every time Jesus healed someone, he touched them."

"But would that not make him unclean?" asks the merchant.

The woman smiles. "Jesus, if you will, 'reversed the flow.' Instead of the person's touch making Jesus unclean, Jesus' touch made the person clean. And it is a beautiful thing to be touched by someone when disease and sin has withheld that from you."

By now it has grown dark. As someone rises to light the oil lamps, the woman says to her guest, "There is one more story I would like to tell before we draw our time together to a close. It is the last encounter Jesus had with someone before he arrived in Jerusalem, seated on that donkey as I witnessed when I was just a little girl.

"As Jesus was approaching Jericho, on the very doorstep of Jerusalem, a blind man was sitting by the road, begging. Now, hearing a crowd going by, he began to ask what was going on. They told him that Jesus of Nazareth was passing by, and so he called out, 'Jesus, Son of David, have mercy on me!' Those ahead of Jesus told him to shut up, but he only yelled all the louder, 'Son of David, have mercy on me!' Jesus stopped and commanded that he be brought to him, and when he had come near, Jesus asked him, 'What do you want from me?' And he said, 'Lord, I want to see again.' Jesus said, 'Go ahead—see again! Your faith has made you whole.'

"The healing was instant: he looked up, seeing—and then followed Jesus, glorifying God. Everyone in the street joined in, shouting praise to God. This blind man could see who Jesus was! He called him 'Son of David'—Messiah—and his faith and belief in who Jesus was led to his healing."

The woman looks around the courtyard; a few of her friends doze as they recline. She turns back to the merchant and says, "We have heard just a small part of the story of Jesus of Nazareth, catching just a glimpse of the life he lived. It has been good to have you with us this evening."

"Thank you for your gracious hospitality," he replies. "And for the stories of your Jesus. He was a remarkable man."

"Yes, he is a remarkable person." She pauses. "And so much more. If I may be permitted to leave you with one more thought?" He nods, and she reaches behind her to pick up a small scroll. "We are fortunate to have copies of letters written by Paul, who has carried the gospel of Jesus throughout the empire. They have been circulating among the *ekklesias*." She finds the place in the letter she is looking for. "Hear these words Paul wrote about Jesus.

> We give thanks to the Father . . . for God delivered us from the domain of darkness and transferred us to the kingdom of God's beloved Son, in whom we have redemption, the forgiveness of sins. And Jesus is the image of the invisible God, the first-born of all creation. For by him all things were created . . . and he is before all things and in him all things hold together."

She looks intently at the merchant and says, "You were brave to dine with us tonight, for you know we are viewed with suspicion—and worse. And this is why. For we believe that Jesus was not just a remarkable man; he is God made flesh, the Creator become creature."

The merchant holds her gaze and says, "The Emperor makes a similar claim. He, like your Jesus, calls himself the 'Son of God.'"

There are a few moments of silence, and then she says, "What you say is true, my friend. But the emperor is worshiped as one god among many. The god of whom he is the son was his father. We worship the LORD God alone, the God who made covenant with Abraham, the God who delivered the children of Israel from slavery in Egypt, the God who has come to us in the person of Jesus—and who, in coming, has shown us what humanity was always intended to be."

The merchant wrestles with the enormity of her statement before saying, "If what you say is true, then it is impossible to live the life

Jesus lived—if he truly is the God of your Story become flesh. For you and I are mere mortals. What hope can we have of living Torah as he did—a God-man?"

The woman returns the scroll to its place behind her, and takes up another one. "Please indulge me this last time. Hear these words, from another of Paul's letters.

> Have this attitude in yourselves which was also in Christ Jesus, who, although he existed in the form of God, did not regard equality with God a thing to be grasped, but emptied himself, taking the form of a servant, and was made in the likeness of humanity. And being found in appearance as a man, he humbled himself by becoming obedient to the point of death, even death on a cross."

The merchant almost splutters. "Jesus died on a Roman cross?! That was the death he was walking toward? And you believe he was God?"

The woman smiles. "Yes, it is hard to believe. Yet thus we do believe. Jesus is God. Yet he laid aside his divine power, and lived life just as you and I do. But unlike us, Jesus never sinned. Everything he did was in obedience to the will of the Father, through the power of the Holy Spirit. That is what makes him the true humanity. And that is why we believe we can be like Jesus, for we also can know the will of the Father and live in the power of the Holy Spirit."

"But your Jesus died . . . how can God die?"

The woman rises, and as she does so, those assembled in her home also get to their feet, some needing to be jostled awake. She clasps the hand of the merchant and says, "If you will join us for dinner again tomorrow night, you will hear that story."

He squeezes her hand in response. "I will. Gladly."

She turns to her friends. "And so until tomorrow evening, I bid you good night. Go in peace, and may the grace of our Lord Jesus Christ be with you all." As she watches them leave, she notes that her guest looks deep in thought as he heads into the night.

10

cross

In which we hear the story of the events that

surrounded Jesus' sharing of one final Passover

with his friends . . .

Another beautiful evening, and another meal under the stars in the courtyard. As the *ekklesia* gathers in her home, the woman greets them in the portico with a kiss. She then kneels to wash their feet in the bowl of petal-strewn water she has prepared, washing away the dust of the day. She wipes them dry with the towel wrapped around her waist and sends them in to recline at table.

The merchant makes his way to the woman's house with a spring in his step. It has been a particularly good day of trade in the market-place, and a pleasant meal in good company awaits him. During the few moments when his stall was quiet today, his thoughts have gone to the remarkable story he heard the night before. He knows little of the history, culture or religion of the children of Abraham, and always enjoys learning about the people he does business with in the metro-politan centers of trade he visits. But this group, these 'Christians,' are unlike any he has encountered before. And the Jesus they serve, well, his story is truly remarkable. And if it is true . . .

When he arrives at the woman's house, he warmly greets his host and exchanges a kiss. But when she kneels at his feet and draws the bowl toward him, he steps back, shocked. "What are you doing?" he asks.

She smiles up at him. "Washing the weariness of the day from your feet, and refreshing you before dinner."

"But that is work for your servants—not their mistress!" he ex-claims.

"Permit me if you will; it is our way."

He steps forward hesitantly, sits down on a stool and removes his sandals. As she pours water over his feet and gently washes them, he feels deeply uncomfortable. As she dries them with the towel, he asks, "Why are you doing this?"

"The answer to your question lies in the story I will tell you tonight. Please—take your place at table, and I will join you when everyone has arrived."

The merchant walks into the courtyard, and as he reclines and looks around at those gathered, he finds himself wondering again, *Who are these people? And what compels them to live this way?*

◆ ◆ ◆

After dinner, his host pours him a cup of wine. "I am so glad you could join us again this evening."

He smiles and says, "You are a gracious host, and I confess I am intrigued by the life you and your friends share. But I know others are less intrigued—more disturbed by your common life. I heard talk of your *ekklesia* in the marketplace, and it was not favorable. Does that not concern you?"

The woman sighs heavily and says, "Yes. It does concern me. We have not suffered as others have, but I know our time will come."

"Then why do you choose this life?" he asks. "I heard people call you atheists—a serious charge. People fear you will bring the wrath of the gods on the city for refusing to worship in their temples. Can you not at least worship your Christ *and* the emperor?" He leans forward, genuinely concerned for his new friend. "I can tell you are good people. Be good citizens! Serve the emperor and your Christ. If you did, surely people would be more forgiving of this . . ." With a sweep of his arm he takes in the diverse group assembled in her home.

The woman is touched by his concern. "It is true that if we pledged our allegiance to Caesar by making the appropriate sacrifices in the temple of the imperial cult, we could avoid the suspicion and anger we attract. But that would be to betray Christ, whom we serve."

"But your Christ was crucified on a Roman cross! Why would you pledge allegiance to such a man?" He pauses, his face softening. "And others of your kind were crucified in Rome following the great fire.

Why do you risk incurring the wrath of Caesar, or the elders of the city, which would only lead to your sharing their fate?"

The woman's eyes become distant for a moment. For this is a question some in the *ekklesia* have been asking. And it is a good question. Why do they take such a risk? What compels her to host the assembly in her home, to teach the newcomers beliefs that some say are treasonous, to watch her business suffer as former customers take their orders elsewhere?

The answer comes as she looks around the courtyard. Warmth and peace spread through her even as tears come to her eyes. "Love," she says quietly. Then looking intently into the merchant's eyes, she repeats, "Love. Love is why we risk so much."

The merchant holds her gaze. "And this love: is it worth dying for?"

She answers, "If—or when—the time comes, I hope I will say, 'Yes.'" She pauses before saying, "More importantly, this love is worth living for."

Those reclining nearby have followed their exchange. She looks up to see her old friend smiling tenderly at her, while a newcomer blinks back tears. She turns back to the merchant. "And it was love that led Jesus to the cross. I invited you back tonight to hear that story. But as you see," she says, sweeping her arm around the room just as he had, "the story is a dangerous one. Do you still want to hear it?"

The merchant says earnestly, "If it will explain the love you share that causes you to risk so much, then I would hear it indeed."

Pouring them both another cup of wine, she says, "Then let us continue the story.

"We return to where we left the story last night, with Jesus' triumphal entry into Jerusalem for the Passover. Jesus arrived in Jerusalem, home of the Temple, and was proclaimed by the crowd as the King who comes in the name of the LORD. Yet he did not look like the king we had all been waiting for. Instead of a military leader riding a warhorse and leading an army, here was a young man, riding a donkey, weeping. He wept for his people, for he knew that in a few short days some in the crowd that hailed him as king would turn on him and demand his death. And he wept for the coming judgment his people would experience. Jesus had warned them, but they would not listen.

"As Jesus looked over Jerusalem he said, 'If you had only recognized this day, and seen the things that lead to peace. But now it's too late. In the days ahead your enemies are going to bring their military might against you and surround you, pressing in from every side. They'll smash you and your babies on the ground. Not one stone will be left intact. All this because you did not recognize and welcome God's visit among you.'

"The chief priests and scribes, the guardians of the Temple, were deeply concerned about the welcome Jesus received. Many of them were infuriated by his popularity, and so they began to put into action a plan to get rid of this upstart from Nazareth and restore the status quo.

"They were further infuriated when Jesus entered the Temple the following day and began to physically throw out the moneychangers, quoting the prophet Isaiah as he did so: 'My house is a house of prayer for the nations, but you have made it a den of thieves.' Jesus was acting out God's coming judgment on the entire, corrupt Temple system.

"However, while the Temple elite plotted against Jesus, the marginalized welcomed him, and the children continued to cry out 'Hosanna to the Son of David' wherever Jesus went. For much of the week of Passover, Jesus was in the Temple, teaching there daily."

The merchant interrupts. "Why did Jesus go to the Temple? Surely he knew that would provoke his enemies. Why not lay low, celebrate the festival and then return home safely?"

"A good question," she responds. "Perhaps as the story unfolds, you will find an answer. But you are right: his actions and his teaching did provoke his enemies. The high priests, scholars and leaders of the people were trying their best to find a way to get rid of him. But with the people hanging on Jesus' every word, they couldn't come up with anything.

"The following day he was again teaching in the Temple, and he told the people this parable. 'A man planted a vineyard and leased it to tenant farmers, and went off on a trip. He was gone a long time. In time he sent a servant to the tenants in order to collect the profits; but they beat him and sent him off empty-handed. He decided to try again and sent another servant. That one they beat black and blue and sent him off empty-handed. He tried a third time. They worked that servant over from head to foot and dumped him on the street. Then the owner of the vineyard said, "I know what I'll do: I'll send my beloved son. They're bound to respect my son."'"

Seeing the merchant's brow furrow as he tries to understand the parable, the host intervenes. "Jesus is retelling a story the prophet Isaiah told many centuries ago. This is how we understand the parable: Israel is the vineyard; God is the owner. The religious leaders are the tenant farmers who are entrusted with the land, and for the harvest that it is supposed to produce.

"Through keeping covenant with the LORD, Israel would produce a 'harvest': the people of the nations who would turn to the God of Israel. When they failed to keep covenant, God sent servants to call them back to covenant faithfulness, but the leaders of my people 'beat them and sent them away empty-handed.' These servants, the prophets of God whom God sent to Israel to call them to repentance, were abused and beaten, and ignored."

The merchant interjects, "And so God sends God's beloved son, thinking that they will listen to him. How does the parable end?"

The host continues, "'When the tenants saw the son coming,' Jesus told them, 'they quickly put their heads together. "This is our chance—this is the heir! Let's kill him and have it all to ourselves." They killed him and threw him over the fence.' Jesus then asked the crowd, 'What will the owner of the vineyard do? Right. He'll come and clean house. Then he'll assign care of the vineyard to others.'

"Those listening to the parable, understanding fully what Jesus meant, cried out, 'May it never be!' But Jesus didn't back down. 'Why do you think this was written: "The stone that the builders rejected has become the cornerstone"?'"

"They must have known Jesus told this story against them," the merchant comments.

"Yes," she replies. "The scholars and high priests wanted to drag him away right there and then, but they were intimidated by the crowds. So instead they responded by trying to reduce his standing in the eyes of the people. They sent a 'plant' to ask a politically charged question that they hoped would put Jesus between a rock and a hard place: 'Is it lawful to pay taxes to Caesar or not?'"

The merchant's eyes narrow. "A clever question. If Jesus said, 'No,' then they could have him arrested for sedition. And if he said, 'Yes,' then, well, no conquered people enjoys paying taxes to their over-lords. What was Jesus' answer?"

The host smiles. "He said, 'Show me a denarius.' One of the questioners handed him a coin. Jesus asked, 'The image engraved on this coin—who does it look like, and what does it say?'

"'Caesar,' they said.

"Jesus said, 'Then render to Caesar that which is Caesar's and to God that which is God's.'"

The merchant beamed. "A masterful response! I imagine that shut them up."

The woman smiles in return. "Yes. But Jesus was doing something beyond merely giving a clever answer." As the merchant raises an eyebrow, the woman says, "Show me a denarius." The merchant gives her one from his purse. She looks at it briefly. "The image engraved on this coin—who does it look like?"

He does not need to look. "Caesar Nero." She holds out the coin for him to examine, and suddenly he sees. "The image of a god!"

"Indeed," the woman says. "This is what Jesus was doing. He asked them for a coin because he did not have one. They were standing in the Temple, the house of the LORD who said, 'You shall have no graven images before me.' The Temple leaders were breaking the second of the Ten Words, the heart of the covenant our people have made with God, right there in the Temple."

She takes a sip of wine before continuing. "After pointing out the hypocrisy of the religious leaders, Jesus spoke to his disciples in the presence of the crowd, saying, 'Beware of the religion scholars. They love to walk around in rich garments, preening in the radiance of public flattery. All while exploiting widows, the most vulnerable among us. The longer their prayers, the worse they get. But they'll pay for it in the end.'

"Just then Jesus looked up and saw rich people putting their gifts into the treasury. They were paying the Temple tax, which was used to pay for the ongoing building project that is the center of my people's life. Then he saw a poor widow put in two small copper coins. He said, 'Here's the truth: this poor widow has put in more than all of them. All these others made offerings they will never miss; she has put in what she could not afford—all she had to live on.'

"This place—the Temple, the house of the God of Israel who cares for the orphan, the widow and the stranger—this place was in fact contributing to the devastation of the lives of the very people God is most concerned about. Jesus again points out why judgment is coming—judgment on a religious system that has betrayed the God they claim to serve.

"People were standing around talking about the Temple, remarking how beautiful it was, the splendor of its stonework and memorial gifts. Jesus said, 'All this you're admiring so much—the time is coming when every stone in that building will end up as a heap of rubble.'

"They asked him, 'Rabbi, when will this happen?'"

The merchant leans in. "How did Jesus answer that question?"

The woman replies, "He gave a long answer, which ended with these words: 'Before this happens, they'll arrest you, drag you to court and jail. You'll even be turned in by parents, relatives and friends. Some of you will be killed. There's no telling who will hate you because of me.'" Her face falls suddenly, and the merchant lays a tentative hand on her arm. She looks up, a smile shining through the tears that are falling down her face. "'Even so,' said Jesus, 'every detail of your life is in my care; nothing of you will be lost. Endurance—staying with it—that's what is required. Stay with it to the end. You won't be sorry; you'll be saved.'"

The merchant says quietly, "Those words must have come true for Jesus himself. When did his enemies come for him?"

"One of Jesus' own disciples, Judas Iscariot, betrayed him," the woman responds.

"One of his own?! Why?"

She sighs heavily. "Some believe it was because he was frustrated that Jesus did not lead the crowd against the Romans following the triumphal entry—that he was not the Son of Man people expected. Others say that the whispers of Satan, the tempter, the deceiver in the garden, caused him to betray his Lord. Whatever the reason, Judas went to the chief priests and Temple leaders and discussed how to deliver Jesus into their hands."

"When did this happen?" asks the merchant.

"During the night of the first day of the festival. While the Passover lambs were being sacrificed in the Temple, Jesus sent two of his followers, Peter and John, to prepare a place for him, their teacher and friend, to lead them in the Passover meal. In an upper room of a borrowed house, they gathered to share a meal and once more tell the story of the exodus, the story of how God delivered their people from slavery in Egypt. They had done this all their lives, but that night, it was different—so very different.

"Jesus reclined at table with them and said, 'You've no idea how much I've looked forward to eating this Passover meal with you before I enter my time of suffering. It's the last one I'll eat until we all eat it together in the kingdom of God.'" The woman leans forward and picks up her cup. "Taking the cup, he gave thanks, then said, 'Take this and pass it among you. As for me, I'll not drink wine again until the kingdom of God arrives.' She extends the cup to the merchant, who stares at it for a moment, and then lifts it to his lips. His eyes lock on hers over the rim of the cup as she continues. "As his disciples passed the cup around, I imagine they whispered to each other, saying, 'What is he talking about? These aren't the right words for the Passover. What does he mean, "Before my time of suffering"? He's beginning to scare me.'"

The woman picks up a loaf of bread from the basket before her. "Taking bread, Jesus gave thanks, broke it, and gave it to them, saying, 'This is my body broken for you. Eat it and remember me.'" She breaks the bread in two, and offers him a piece. He takes the bread and eats it, chewing thoughtfully.

"He did the same with the cup after supper, saying, 'This cup which is poured out for you is the new covenant in my blood, which is poured out for many for the forgiveness of sins.'

"Again, they must have wondered what Jesus was talking about. A new covenant? What could it mean? The old covenant involved the death of a lamb, its blood poured out over the doorway of the homes of the people in Egypt, so that death would pass over them, which ever since then had been reenacted every year at this time. As Jesus' words sunk in, I have often wondered if they remembered the words John the baptizer spoke when Jesus came to be baptized. 'Behold the Lamb of God, who takes away the sins of the world.'"

The woman turns to her old friend. "Do you hear the words of Torah in what Jesus said?"

The words come instantly to his mind. "When our people ratified the covenant at Mount Sinai, they sacrificed bulls, and as Moses sprinkled blood on the people he said, 'Behold the blood of the covenant.' The new covenant would be made not with the blood of bulls but with Jesus' own blood." Looking around the room he continues, "Another rabble of slaves have been delivered from bondage in this new covenant. And not merely from bondage to Egypt, or Babylon, or Rome, but bondage to sin and death."

The room has fallen silent as the assembled *ekklesia* have been caught up once more in the story as it is told. The merchant barely notices though, turning to the woman to ask, "This is what you believe? That this 'new covenant' can deliver your people from the power of sin and death?"

"Yes," she replies. "Thus we believe. But this new exodus is not just for my people, Israel . . ." she gestures to those gathered in the courtyard, ". . . as you can see. In the Passover meal, my people remember

Moses going to the king of Egypt and saying, 'Israel is my firstborn son. Let my son go, that he may serve me.' And through Israel, God's firstborn, God's intention was to show the other nations what God is like, inviting them into covenant relationship with God, redeeming all of humanity.

"On Passover, we remember the night when our ancestors in Egypt killed a lamb in order that the firstborn of the family might be spared. But Jesus, the firstborn over all creation, would not be spared. And the blood that he shed on the cross covered all of creation—saving everyone and everything. Jesus led all of creation out of the Egypt of violence, sin and death—the new exodus. And every time we gather to break bread and share the cup, we proclaim the Lord's death and all that he accomplished."

The merchant, struggling to comprehend what he is hearing, asks, "Did his disciples understand all this?"

The woman laughs. "Hardly. Instead, they quickly became distracted by Jesus' talk of the kingdom of God and argued amongst themselves as to which of them would be greatest in it. While they did so, Judas slipped out quietly.

"Jesus, their teacher, overheard their argument. Knowing that the Father had put him in complete charge of everything and that he came from God, and was on his way back to God, Jesus rose from supper and set aside his robe. He took a towel, wrapped it about his waist, and then poured water into a basin and began to wash his disciples' feet, and to wipe them with the towel."

The merchant comments, "And that is why you washed my feet, and the feet of all who gather here tonight."

"Yes," his host replies. "For Jesus, the Son of God, the coming King, took the role of the lowliest servant and washed his disciples' feet. And when he had finished, he put his garments back on, and reclined at the table once more. He looked each of the disciples in the eye and said, 'Do you understand what I have done to you? You address me as "Teacher" and "Lord," and rightly so. That is what I am. So if I, the Lord and Teacher, washed your feet, you must now wash each others' feet. I've laid down a pattern for you. What I've done, you do.' He continued, 'Who would you rather be: the one who eats the dinner or the one who serves the dinner? You'd rather eat and be served, right? But I've taken my place among you as the one who serves.'"

"A king who serves his people." The merchant shakes his head. "I have heard such words, but never known a king who actually does so. Yet one disciple was not there to hear those words. Where did Judas go?"

"To the Temple elite," the host replies, "to tell them where they could find Jesus." She picks up the story again as it picks up pace. "After supper, Jesus led his friends out to the Mount of Olives, to the garden of Gethsemane, just as he had done many times before. It was late, and dark, and they were tired. Jesus had one final temptation to face, and he did not want to be alone when it happened. So he asked Peter, James and John to walk a little distance away from the group and keep watch over him as he prayed.

"Then Jesus knelt to pray, and as he wrestled with the decision he faced—to embrace the death that would come on the morrow—he threw himself down, and wept, and sweated great drops of blood, saying over and over and over, 'Father, please, take this cup from me.' Finally, he lifted his face from the ground, looked upward and said quietly, 'Not my will, but yours be done.'

"And so he rose and went to his disciples, who were all asleep. He woke them, and as he started talking, a snake of fire came into view— a great crowd carrying flaming torches, led by Judas.

"Judas walked up to Jesus and kissed him, the sign that this was the one to be arrested. The Temple guards leapt forward and grabbed him while the Temple elite and the elders looked on, gloating."

The merchant interjects, "Did no one among the disciples try to stop them? To save their Lord?"

The old man answers, "Yes. Peter did. He fumbled for the sword he had brought and struck out, injuring one of the high priest's slaves. Jesus stopped him, saying, 'No more of this!' Then he healed the man Peter had wounded. Jesus did not come to deliver his people at the point of a sword. He came to bring an end to violence."

The woman takes up the story again. "Jesus looked at the religious leaders who had come to take him and said, 'What is this, jumping me with swords and clubs as if I were a dangerous criminal? Day after day I've been with you teaching the people in the Temple and you've not so much as lifted a hand against me. But this hour, and the power of darkness is yours.' And so Jesus was led away, to stand trial for daring to challenge the Temple system, for telling the Story in an unacceptable way to those who considered themselves to be the only divinely sanctioned storytellers.

"During that long night he faced four separate trials, each one a farce. The first trial was before the Sanhedrin, the ruling elders of Israel. Before Jesus was brought in to the council chambers, the Temple guards decided to have some fun with him. They blindfolded Jesus and beat him, saying, 'Prophesy! Who hit you that time?' When he was summoned, they took the blindfold off, and did their best to disguise the blood that was beginning to show through his robe. The elders had one question for Jesus: 'Are you the Messiah, the Son of God?'

"Jesus, knowing that there was no longer any danger of his being made king by force, finally answered the question that everyone had been asking. He answered them, saying, *'I am who I am.'* The high priest ripped his clothes and screamed, 'Blasphemy!' as Jesus spoke the name of God. They then took Jesus to the Roman governor, Pontius Pilate."

"Why did they take him to the governor?" the merchant asks. "Surely he would have had little interest in the people's internal religious affairs?"

The woman answers. "I'm sure Pilate did not care that Jesus was accused of blasphemy. But he knew the reason Jesus was brought before him was because only Rome can give the death sentence. That was what the elders of my people wanted."

"But Rome does not kill people for blasphemy." The merchant's statement hangs in the air for a moment before the woman responds. "Certainly not for blasphemy against the God of my people. But you are right. The Temple leaders had to make up crimes, trying to make Jesus sound like a revolutionary, a threat to the *pax Romana,* a murdering thug like Barabbas, also arrested in Jerusalem that week.

"Pilate listened to their ranting and then asked Jesus the same question, 'Are you the king of the Jews?' Jesus replied, *'I am who I am.'* Pilate gazed into Jesus' eyes and apparently saw no threat there, so he turned to the elders and said, 'I find no guilt in this man.'

"The elders exploded, insisting that he have Jesus executed, and so Pilate sent Jesus off to Herod, the self-styled king of the Jews, perhaps thinking, *Let him deal with this.*

"Now, Herod had wanted to meet Jesus for a long time, and so he asked Jesus lots of questions. But Jesus did not dignify this farce with any response. Herod wanted him to crawl, to beg for mercy, but Jesus just stood there. And so King Herod sent this one who called himself king back to Pilate. But first Herod's soldiers beat Jesus and mocked him, placing a robe of imperial purple on him, pressing a crown of thorns onto his head. The blood flowed down his face, mingling with the blood from the beating.

"So once more Jesus stood before Pilate. Pilate had had enough of this and said, 'I will let this man go. He is innocent.' But by now a crowd had been gathered outside the palace by the religious leaders, calling for Jesus' crucifixion. Pilate faced a difficult situation. This disturbance of the peace was unacceptable. He had to act to defuse the situation. But how?

"Apparently he genuinely did not want to execute Jesus. He saw the hate in the faces of the religious leaders and despised them. But he had to do something. And so, in a cowardly refusal to accept responsibility for his actions, he brought out Jesus and Barabbas, and said to the crowd, 'As is my custom, I will release one prisoner in honor of the Passover. Who shall it be? Jesus of Nazareth, one of your teachers? Or this man, Barabbas, a murderer?'

"Pilate expected the people to choose Jesus. But to his horror, they cried out with one voice, 'Kill him! Give us Barabbas!' Pilate, in utter confusion and dismay cried out, 'But for what crime?' But the crowd just screamed all the louder, 'Crucify, crucify him!' Pilate said to them, 'Shall I crucify your King?' To which the high priests replied, 'We have no king but Caesar.'"

A gasp escapes one of the newcomers. The woman turns to him, saying, "Yes. Those who accused Jesus of blasphemy committed blasphemy themselves.

"Pilate's plan had backfired, and the crowd's demands forced him into a corner. To keep his authority intact, he now had to execute Jesus. So he released Barabbas and delivered Jesus to their will. The soldiers beat Jesus one more time, until he could barely stand, and then they placed the crossbeam to which he would be nailed across his shoulders and forced him to carry it through the streets of Jerusalem, to the place of his death—Golgotha, the hill of the skull.

"With the combined power of empire and static religion arrayed against Jesus, he stumbled to his place of death. Pilate wrote an inscription to be placed on the cross. It said, 'Jesus of Nazareth, King of the Jews.' The chief priests demanded he change it to 'He said he was King of the Jews.' But Pilate replied, 'What I have written, I have written.'"

The woman sighs deeply. "And so Jesus was crucified between two bandits. As the Roman soldiers lifted the cross to drop it into the socket prepared for it, Jesus said, 'Father, forgive them—they don't know what they're doing.' One of the bandits sneered at him, saying, 'If you are the Christ, then save yourself—and us.' But the other said, 'Jesus, remember me when you come into your kingdom.'"

The merchant interjects, "But why would he say that? Jesus was dying. This is the end of Jesus' story—and his life." He looks around the room. "You are keeping the Story alive by following Jesus' teachings, and you serve Jesus as your Lord. But I'm sorry, the high priests were right: you have no king but Caesar."

The woman says, "But what if Jesus' death is not the end of his story?"

A laugh escapes the merchant. "Then that would make him truly remarkable!"

She holds his gaze until it dawns on him that she is serious. "Jesus' response to the dying man's question was this: 'I promise you, today you will be with me in Paradise.'"

The merchant's struggle to understand all this is writ large on his face. The woman says, "Let me continue the story. Storm clouds rolled in, and the sky grew dark. Jesus cried out to the heavens, '*Eloi, eloi, lama sabachthani,*' which means 'My God, my God, why have you forsaken me?'" She turns to the *ekklesia* and says, "Jesus, dying on the cross, took up the cry of all humanity, the cry of exile, the cry that escapes us, living as we do, so far east of Eden. Then he said, 'It is accomplished.' And finally, 'Father, I place my life in your hands.' And then he died.

"The centurion responsible for the executions read the plaque above his head, and these words escaped his lips: 'Surely this man was the Son of God.' Perhaps the only witness to Jesus' death who understood what it signified, and who it was who died that day, was a Roman soldier."

The merchant says, "But why did Jesus die? This kingdom of his, if he was God as you claim, why could he just not establish it with his divine power? Why did he not destroy the Romans and his enemies among his own people?"

"An important question," she responds. "The kingdom of God that Jesus proclaimed and taught about and lived would not bring liberation from the oppression of the Roman Empire. Nor would his kingdom be established as all others have been—with violent coercion. For God's power is God's love. Many of Jesus' parables indicated that his kingdom would grow up in the midst of the kingdoms of this world, like a mustard seed—tiny, yet growing into a tree; like a tiny amount of yeast that leavens an entire batch of dough; like a grain of wheat that falls into the soil and dies—only to bear much fruit. This is the mystery of the cross: in dying, Jesus brings life.

"Our apostle Paul, reflecting years later on the events of that day, wrote this:

Everything of God finds its proper place in Jesus. Not only that, all the broken and dislocated pieces of the universe—all of creation—get properly fixed and fit together in vibrant harmonies, all because of his death, his blood that poured down from the cross. You yourselves are part of that. At one time you all had your backs turned to God, thinking rebellious thoughts of him, giving God trouble every chance you got. But now, by giving himself completely at the cross, actually dying for you, Christ brought you over to God's side and put your lives together, whole and holy in God's presence."

She addresses her beloved *ekklesia*. "The Story of God has told us over and over again that we cannot save ourselves. We never get it right. We always end up making a mess of things. The catastrophe of the garden of Eden, which ruined all humanity, has led to one consistent fact: no matter what God does to meet us where we are, we turn our backs and go our own way.

"And so finally, we see why Jesus is indeed the climax of the Story—we could not do it for ourselves, and so God has to become one of us, in order to do it for us. The countless thousands of lambs, whose blood was shed in order to save the people from the death their sins deserved, are no longer necessary—because the blood of the Lamb of God has been shed on the cross, once and for all, and for all humanity.

"Jesus' death brings the new exodus—deliverance from the power of sin and death, and from the separation from God that all humanity has experienced since we were exiled from the garden of Eden. And for those of us who have felt deeply the pain that this separation has caused, who groan with all creation, who have felt the pain of the terrible injustice that exists in our world, for those of us who cry out 'Why, God, why?'—in Jesus we see how God feels about those things. Because Jesus has given God a face, and it is a face streaked with tears.

"When Jesus died, the great veil in the Temple that guarded the Holy of Holies was torn in two. We have seen in Jesus the presence of God in the midst of God's people, among those who could never enter

the inner courts of the Temple—the sick, the deformed, the ostra-
cized foreigner—now invited to see and touch God made flesh. And
with Jesus' death, the way is now clear for all humanity to return from
exile, and to come home to God."

She turns to the merchant. "Now to answer your question: is Jesus'
death the end of the story? No! Pilate received another request from a
member of the High Council. Joseph of Arimathea asked Pilate to allow him to bury the body of Jesus. Joseph was taking a huge risk—as
you know, the Romans do not bury criminals; they leave their corpses
out to rot as an example.

"Although Pilate had washed his hands of the whole affair, perhaps in
this moment he saw the opportunity to spite the Temple elite, who had
pushed him too far. Or perhaps he simply believed that Jesus deserved
better treatment in death than he gave him in life. Whatever the case, he
granted Joseph's request, and Joseph laid Jesus in a stone tomb.

"On the first day of a new week, the third day after Jesus' death,
the disciples were in hiding, for fear of the religious leaders. The council had asked Pilate to place a guard at Jesus' tomb, just in case the
disciples tried to steal the body—after all, they had heard Jesus say
something about being raised on the third day; a dead Jesus, mysteri-
ously vanished, may have been more dangerous than he was when he
was alive.

"But that morning, the faithful women set out to anoint Jesus' body
with spices, as is our custom. They were the first visitors to the tomb
in the garden, but when they arrived, they found that the stone covering the entrance to the tomb had been rolled away. They entered the
tomb, but Jesus' body was gone! In its place were two angels in white
sitting where Jesus had lain, one at the head and one at the foot."

She turns to her old friend, who smiles. "The cherubim—those
who guard the way to the presence of God. For with the veil in the
Temple ripped in two, this is now the Holy of Holies. This is the Mercy
Seat, with the cherubim present. And with the stone rolled away, the
Holy of Holies is now open, and the new creation has begun! No high
priest needed to sacrifice a bull in order for his sins to be forgiven be-

fore entering, for Jesus, the one who had no sin to be forgiven, is now our great high priest, making sacrifice on our behalf for the forgiveness of our sins. Behold the Lamb of God who takes away the sins of the world!"

The woman returns to the story. "The cherubim said to the women, 'Why are you looking for the Living One in a cemetery? He is not here; he has risen! Remember how he told you when you were still back in Galilee that he had to be handed over to sinners, be killed on a cross, and in three days rise up?'

"As they stepped out, one of the women—Mary—heard a noise. She turned around to see a man standing there, who asked her, 'Why are you weeping? Who are you looking for?'

"At first Mary thought he was the gardener, but when he spoke she recognized him and, still holding the dressings she had brought to embalm his dead body with, she cried out, 'Teacher!' Here was Jesus—alive! Jesus said, 'Go to my friends and tell them, "I ascend to my Father and your Father, to my God and your God."' She was amazed and ran to tell the disciples."

The host, her face now aglow with joy, declares, "Jesus is alive! He is risen! Death indeed is defeated! Jesus of Nazareth has been vindicated—he is indeed the Son of God, the Christ, the Messiah, the hope of Israel, and of the world! By his death, our sins have been forgiven. And by his resurrection, we have new life, eternal life, life abundant!

"And it is here, in a garden, that the new creation begins, on the first day of the week. God has been faithful to the covenant promises of Scripture, even when those who have been reading those same Scriptures have rejected the very One that the Scriptures have pointed to. For, as the prophet Isaiah saw,

He was despised and forsaken of men,
A man of sorrows, acquainted with grief;
And like one from whom men hide their face:
He was despised, and we did not esteem him.

Surely our griefs he himself bore,
  And our sorrows he carried;
  Yet we ourselves esteemed him stricken,
  Smitten of God, and afflicted.
His grave was assigned with wicked men,
  Yet he was with a rich man in his death,
  Because he had done no violence,
  Nor was there any deceit in his mouth. . . .
  My servant, will justify the many,
  As he will bear their sins. . . .
  Because he poured out himself to death,
  And was numbered among the transgressors;
  Yet he himself bore the sin of many
  And interceded for sinners."

A reverent hush has fallen over the courtyard. The woman turns to the merchant, who says, "I have never heard anything like this. That someone would be willing to die . . . How great his love must be." He shakes his head.

She says, quietly, "No greater love has anyone than this; that one lays down his life for his friends . . ."

After a moment of silence, her old friend completes Jesus' words: "And those who keep covenant with me are my friends."

The woman turns to the merchant. "That is why we risk all to serve Jesus—to keep covenant with him, to love as we have been loved. For in this new exodus, this renewal of the covenant, the forgiveness of sins, the end of exile, we remember that we have not only been freed from servitude to sin; we have also been liberated for service to God."

The oil lamps are sputtering—it is very late. The woman says, "As we draw our evening together to a close, let me read you once more the words that the apostle Paul wrote to the church in Philippi." She reaches for the scroll, and reads:

"Think of yourselves the way Christ Jesus thought of himself.

He had equal status with God but didn't think so much of himself that he had to cling to the advantages of that status no matter what. Not at all. When the time came, he set aside the privileges of deity and took on the status of a slave, became human! Having become human, he stayed human. It was an incredibly humbling process. He didn't claim special privileges. Instead, he lived a selfless, obedient life, and died a selfless, obedient death—and the worse kind of death at that—a crucifixion.

Therefore God has highly exalted him, and bestowed on him the Name which is above every name, that at the name of Jesus every knee should bow . . . and that every tongue should confess that Jesus Christ is Lord, to the glory of God the Father.

"The charge levied against Jesus by the Temple elite was blasphemy, for daring to say, '*I am who I am* before Abraham was anything'—for daring to claim the name of God. Yet God the Father has highly exalted him and has given him the name that is above every name, the very name of God: Yahweh, the LORD. Thus is Jesus' life and death vindicated. That is why we call Jesus 'Lord,' for he is indeed God."

The woman gets to her feet and offers a blessing over the *ekklesia* before they leave for home. The merchant clasps her hand in parting. "You have given me so much to think about."

She smiles and says, "I will ask the Holy Spirit to give you understanding."

His brow wrinkles. "I've heard this 'Holy Spirit' mentioned here and there throughout this story; what do you mean by it?"

Leading him to the portico, she responds, "If you will join us for dinner again tomorrow, you will hear that story." As she watches him down the street, she offers her own prayer for him, as she knows that to give yourself to the Story is no small thing. She wraps her shawl around her, and steps inside.

11

church

In which we hear the story of the earliest days of

the new community which continued Jesus' mission

in the world . . .

The merchant washes his fingers in the bowl before him, then leans back, content following another meal with his new friends. *Friends that could lose me business,* he thinks to himself. A man had approached him in the market earlier that day—but he had not come to talk trade. "I've seen you dining with my neighbor these past few nights. If you're hoping to establish yourself in our city, I suggest you choose those you recline at table with more carefully." The man had walked away without waiting for a response. A frown comes to the merchant's face at the memory, and his host asks, "Does something trouble you?"

He looks up to see her concerned expression and quickly changes the frown to a smile. "No, no. I was just thinking about some . . . unpleasantness in the market today. I ought not to dwell upon it in such pleasant company."

"Besides this unpleasantness, I trust you have had a good day of trade?" she asks.

"Business was slow today. But that gave me opportunity to think about the story you told last night." He pauses before saying, "Your Jesus truly was a remarkable man. And yet . . ." The woman tilts her head to one side, waiting for him to complete his thought. "This talk of 'resurrection.' It is difficult for me to know what to make of that. It is difficult to understand, difficult to believe. And yet you and your friends clearly do.

"So I have a question for you: If Jesus truly was raised from the dead, where is he now? You speak as if he were alive—but where? I have been thinking on this all day, and I have no answer. I would say he has taken his place among the pantheon of the gods of Rome, but I know you do not believe so—for I do not think that is what you mean by 'resurrection.'"

He shakes his head, a wry smile on his face. "There is much I do not understand." Then he looks up, intently. "But this much I do know. I know that you believe he is alive. And because you believe so, you live this life that I confess I find strangely compelling—and deeply troubling."

The woman looks into the merchant's eyes and makes the connection. "The 'unpleasantness' in the market today?" He returns her gaze and nods his head. She offers him a smile tinged with sadness and says, "So you see how it is for us—and for those who associate with us. I am truly sorry, my friend. And yet you still returned tonight."

He returns her smile. "Of course! You suggested there was still more to the story—this 'Holy Spirit'?" His face becomes serious. "And I want to know what you mean when you say that this new covenant Jesus has made can deliver a person from the power of sin and death."

"The Story raises the deepest questions of life," the woman says. "And the ones you ask get to the heart of our faith, the believing allegiance we give to Jesus as Lord and Savior. Perhaps as I tell you the story of the early days of the church, of the many *ekklesias* of which we are but one, you will find some answers." She pours them both another cup of wine and continues the story.

"After Jesus had been raised from the dead, he appeared to the disciples on several occasions over a period of forty days. At first they were terrified—they thought they were seeing a spirit. Jesus said, 'Don't be afraid, and don't let all these doubting questions take over. Look at my hands; look at my feet—it's really me! Touch me. Look me over from head to toe. A ghost doesn't have muscle and bone like this.' They still couldn't believe what they were seeing. It was too much; it seemed too good to be true. He asked, 'Do you have any food here?' They gave him a piece of fish. He took it and ate it right before their eyes."

The merchant interjects. "So Jesus has a real, physical body like us?" The woman says, "Yes. And no." She smiles as the merchant's brow wrinkles. "Yes, he has a physical body; but no, it is not like ours. This gets to your question about what Jesus has done to deliver us from sin and death. The resurrection is the very source of our hope, what enables us to keep going in the face of our difficulties. And it is what compels us to live the way we do."

The merchant frowns. "This is what I do not understand. For my people, the body is the source of weakness and sin. We believe in an immortal soul which must be liberated from its body if it is to be free. Your 'resurrection' surely enslaves the soul to a body once more?"

The woman eagerly leans forward. "That is where our story is fundamentally different from yours, my friend. We believe that the LORD God is the Creator of all that is. And God's creation is good, although it suffers under the weight of the sin of humanity. In Jesus' resurrection, we believe, the Creator has acted to usher in the new creation, which one day will see an end to sin and corruption and death. For Jesus' resurrection was to a body that will never die again—that is why I said that his body is unlike ours. And so we do not believe, as you do, that salvation means when we die our soul will be 'freed' from its body—for that would be to deny that death is our enemy, a denial of the goodness of embodied, physical life. The resurrection means that death has been defeated."

The merchant nods his understanding, so the woman continues. "As you know, for us to say 'Jesus is Lord' is to say 'Caesar is not.'"

The merchant interjects, "And that is why your people face such opposition, even persecution."

She replies, "Indeed. But it goes beyond that. The last weapon of Caesar—and any tyrant—is death." She pauses, giving him time to consider this.

His face suddenly lights up. "But if a group of people believe death has been defeated—and are not afraid to die—then where is Caesar's power then?"

"Exactly," she says. "For the overthrow of death is the overthrow of those whose power depends upon it. And it is not only Caesar who is threatened; it is all those who rely on power and violent coercion to enforce their will on others. Our brothers and sisters in Jerusalem are just as much a threat to the Sadducees as Jesus was. For the resurrection means that God is turning the world as we know it upside down, just as Mary proclaimed in her song when she was carrying Jesus in her womb:

> 'God knocked tyrants off their high horses,
> pulled victims out of the mud.
> The starving poor sat down to a banquet;
> the callous rich were left out in the cold.' "

The woman takes a sip of wine as the merchant looks deep in thought. He says, "I think I understand some of what you are saying, and you speak truly when you say it is very different from the story my people tell. But I still do not understand how Jesus' resurrection defeats death—for surely you will still die. What happens to you then?"

"As Jesus told the bandit on the cross, we will join Jesus in Paradise. And there we will wait until God ushers in the new creation in all its fullness, when we will share in the resurrection, receiving a body like Jesus, a body that will never die. And we will live in this world, in the new creation, for all eternity." She reaches behind her for a scroll. "This is what Paul wrote to the *ekklesia* in Corinth, 'For Christ has been raised from the dead, the first fruits of those who have died.' If the new creation began at the tomb of Jesus in that garden, and if our destiny is to one day share in the resurrection ourselves, then we are compelled to share in God's mission to save the world—living today in light of that coming day. For Jesus taught his disciples to pray, 'Thy Kingdom come, Thy will be done on earth, as it is in heaven.' The kingdom of heaven is where God's will is done, and God's will is for all of God's good creation to be redeemed and made whole once more. And God's work of salvation is both for and through humanity. For beginning with Abraham, God called a people through whom God will redeem the whole cosmos. That is the good news Jesus proclaimed and sent his disciples out into the world to proclaim." She laughs, "And we should probably get to that story soon, if we are going to hear it tonight!

"But before I continue the story, let me read something else Paul wrote in this letter. 'If there is no resurrection of the dead, not even Christ has been raised, and if Christ has not been raised, then our faith is in vain.' If there is no resurrection, then we are still held captive by the power of sin and death. And our suffering, such as it is, is all for nothing. That is why the resurrection is so important."

"Again, you give me much to think about." The merchant drains his cup, and pours them both some more wine. "But please, do continue the story."

The woman happily complies. "At the end of the forty days following his resurrection, Jesus gathered his disciples together and said, 'Do not leave Jerusalem, but wait for the gift my Father promised, which you have heard me speak about. For John baptized with water, but in a few days you will be baptized with the Holy Spirit.' In response, the disciples asked Jesus, 'Is this the time when God will restore the kingdom to Israel?'"

Her old friend laughs. "How often the disciples failed to understand what Jesus was saying." He turns to her and says, "This is another occasion when I picture Jesus looking at them fondly, with a look that says, 'You still don't get it, do you?'"

She chuckles, having felt the same way herself more than once. Noticing the merchant's confusion, she explains. "The disciples' understanding of 'Israel' was still limited to the descendants of Abraham. It took them a long time to understand what God's intention had been since making covenant with Abraham. But on this day, Jesus simply said, 'You don't get to know the time. Timing is the Father's business. What you'll get is the Holy Spirit. And when the Holy Spirit comes upon you, you will be my witnesses in Jerusalem, all over Judea and Samaria, even to the ends of the earth. Go into all the world and preach the gospel to all creation.' After he had said this, he was taken up before their very eyes, returning to the Father to be exalted, seated at the right hand of God the Father Almighty.

"This, then, was the mission of the disciples: to be witnesses to the coming of the kingdom of God in Jesus, to carry the good news of the new exodus—of the new creation—to the very ends of the earth, in the power of the Holy Spirit. This was the continuation of the mission of God in the world, the ongoing fulfillment of the covenant God made with Abraham, and with the people of Israel. But like those before them, the disciples were slow to understand.

"The disciples stayed in Jerusalem as Jesus had told them to. There were 120 of them—men and women—those who had followed Jesus to the end. And once more, crowds began to fill the streets as the feast of Pentecost drew near. The disciples were praying together on the day of Pentecost when suddenly a sound like a violent wind swept through the place, and in its wake flames burst in their midst, and then they divided into small tongues of fire, which came to rest on each of them."

One of the newcomers interjects, "I recognize that language. It is the description of God coming down to dwell in the tabernacle." Another adds, "And of the day when Solomon's Temple was dedicated, and God's presence came to dwell within it."

"Indeed," the woman responds. "This was why Jesus said to his disciples, 'It's better for you that I leave. If I don't leave, the Holy Spirit will not come. But if I go, I will send the Spirit to you.' The Holy Spirit is the very presence of God among us, no longer 'restrained' by a building. The living church has now replaced the tabernacle and Temple of old." She picks up the scroll again, and unrolling it reads, "'You realize, don't you, that you all—the body of Christ—are the Temple of the Holy Spirit.'"

The merchant, very much confused, asks, "So you have three gods? The Father, Jesus and the Holy Spirit?"

"No," the woman says, "we serve the LORD God who is one. Yet God exists as a community of relationships, Father, Son and Holy Spirit." The merchant shakes his head, and the woman laughs. "I know. It is difficult to grasp. I do not know if I can explain it to you beyond what I have spoken."

Her friend interjects, "Perhaps I may add something?"

"Please do!" she replies.

"At the very beginning of our story, after God makes the very first human, *ha-adam*, God declares, 'It is not good for *ha-adam* to be alone.' Our story tells us that *ha-adam* was created in the image of God. And so we understand that part of what it means to be made in the image of God is 'to not be alone.'

"What might it mean for God to not be alone? For us, it means that the one Creator God exists as this community of relationships: Father, Son and Holy Spirit."

Once more the merchant shakes his head. Nothing has prepared him for the Story he is hearing among these people. The woman leans across and lays her hand on his arm. "Trust me—there are many gathered here who have felt the way you do. Let me continue.

"As God's presence came down in their midst, they were all filled with the Holy Spirit and began to speak in languages they did not know or recognize. But there were people around them who did, and a crowd quickly gathered in amazement at what was happening. They could see these people were all native Galileans, yet they heard them speak in their languages, singing the praises of God. The disciples did not know what they were saying until they were told. People began to wonder aloud what this meant. Some said that they must be drunk."

The woman's friend leans forward and says, "If I may speak again?"

"Of course," she replies.

He turns to the merchant. "Very early on in our Story, the people of the world spoke only one language. In their arrogance they built a great tower to try and reach into the heavens and to make a name for themselves."

"The tower of Babel," the merchant says. "I am familiar with this story."

The old man nods and says, "Then you know that God came down to confuse their language, which resulted in their being scattered to the ends of the earth, each family with their own language. On the day of Pentecost, God came down once more—not to confuse their language this time but to give them language, so that all the nations present in Jerusalem on that day would hear the Story in their native tongue. And that Story was to be taken from Jerusalem to the ends of the earth, as Jesus instructed his disciples."

The woman thanks her friend and continues. "Peter stood to address the crowd that had gathered. He told them that they were not drunk but that what they were seeing fulfilled a vision that the prophet Joel had been given: in the last days God would pour out God's Spirit on every kind of people, that men and women would prophesy.

"He told them that Jesus of Nazareth, put to death by their people so recently, was the long-awaited Messiah. He told them they had been blind to all the ways God confirmed Jesus' identity as Messiah. He told them that Jesus, now raised from the dead, sits at the right hand of God, and that God's Spirit was now being poured out on those who had followed Jesus. When he finished, he may well have anticipated stones to come flying out of the crowd, but to his amazement, the whole crowd fell to their knees weeping, calling out to God for forgiveness. The disciples baptized about three thousand people in the name of Jesus, and they too received the gift of the Holy Spirit.

"From that day on, every day more people came to believe that Jesus was the Messiah, and they were baptized, and they too received the Holy Spirit. The church, the people of God, the *ekklesia*, had been born!"

The old man interrupts once again. Apologizing to his friend and host, this time he turns to the newcomers. "When our people Israel made covenant with the LORD God at Sinai, you remember that very soon afterward they broke covenant by worshiping the idol they had made, an Egyptian golden calf. God's judgment on their breaking covenant was swift and tragic—about three thousand died that day. And now here, on the day that the first people are drawn into the new covenant, about three thousand are added to the disciples' number. Sinai has not been forgotten; God is faithful to God's covenant. What was lost was being reclaimed."

The woman thanks her old friend once more and continues the story. "As the weeks went by, the disciples continued to see the power of the Holy Spirit at work in and through them. The very things they had seen Jesus do, they did. One day, Peter and John were approaching the Temple and noticed a man who had been lame from birth. He was calling out for alms but didn't bother asking them; he could see that they had no money by the way they were dressed. But he didn't need money; he needed to be able to walk, and to work, to be a full member of the community. So Peter walked up to him and reached down his hand, saying, 'I don't have any money, but what I do have I can give you: in the name of Jesus of Nazareth, rise up and walk.'

"Perhaps he looked at Peter for a long moment, and then grabbed his hand and pulled himself up. Instantly he was healed, and he began leaping around for joy. And then, for the first time in his life, he entered the Temple with them to give thanks to God. Once more, the disciples saw how Jesus not only physically heals people, but through them he restores them to community.

"God healed many others through the disciples. They cast out demons from some people. On one occasion God raised someone from the dead through Peter—a woman named Dorcas. She was one of the disciples, renowned for caring for the poor.

"The disciples were amazed that God was performing signs of the kingdom through people like them, just as he had through Jesus. They remembered Jesus' words when he told them, 'The person who trusts me will not only do what I'm doing but even greater things, because I, on my way to the Father, am giving you the same work to do that I've been doing. You can count on it. From now on, whatever you request along the lines of who I am and what I'm doing, I'll do it.'

"Just as the disciples were amazed at what God was doing through them, the people around them were delighted with what was happening."

"Surely not everyone was delighted?" interjects a member of the *ekklesia*.

"Indeed," replies the woman. "Just as with Jesus, the religious leaders of my people were not pleased with what was happening. John and Peter were arrested more than once for telling the Story to the crowds in the Temple. On one occasion they would have been killed on the spot if Gamaliel, one of our most respected rabbis, hadn't spoken up."

She turns to the newcomers, saying, "So my friends, it should not surprise us that others treat us harshly for telling the Story, and for giving our allegiance to the One whose Story this is. As our apostle Peter has written to us, 'To the degree that you share the sufferings of Christ, keep on rejoicing: for if you are despised for the name of Christ, you are blessed, for the Spirit of glory and of God rests on you.'"

She turns back to the merchant. "Jesus had told his disciples that they would be his witnesses in Jerusalem, Judea, Samaria and to the ends of the earth. God's plan from the beginning was for the world to know who God is. They were simply continuing the mission of God's people that began with Abraham—to bless all the families of the earth. But the disciples were slow to understand this in the beginning. Even after Pentecost, after being filled with the Holy Spirit, they still did not get it at first.

"In the beginning, instead of leaving Jerusalem as Jesus had said, they stayed put, and people had to come to them to be healed. After the murder of Stephen, however, a great persecution arose against the church in Jerusalem; and all the people—apart from the apostles— were scattered throughout the regions of Judea and Samaria.*

"The apostles still thought the gentiles† were 'outsiders' to the kingdom. Even though the disciples had watched Jesus draw all kinds of people to him throughout his life, God had to speak to Peter directly in a dream before he understood. While praying on a rooftop, he saw a great sheet lowered from the sky before him, and in it were many of the creatures Torah declares to be unclean. Peter heard a voice say, 'Go to it, Peter—kill and eat.' But Peter said, 'Oh no, Lord, I've never

---

Apostles refers to Jesus' disciples, and those who follow in their footsteps. It means "sent ones."
†*Gentile* refers to anyone who is not a descendant of Abraham.

so much as tasted food that was unclean.'

"The voice came a second time: 'What God has cleansed do not consider unclean.' This happened three times, and then the sheet was taken up into the sky. As he was trying to figure out what the vision meant, strangers came to take him to a Roman centurion, who had also had a vision that he was to meet with Peter.

"When Peter arrived, the centurion, whose name was Cornelius, and all his family and friends were waiting to hear what Peter had to say. Then Peter understood the vision God had given him, and so he told them, 'You know it is unlawful for my people to associate with a foreigner or to visit his home; yet God has shown me that I should call no one unholy or unclean.'

"After Cornelius explained his own vision, Peter fairly exploded with his good news: 'It's God's own truth, nothing could be plainer: God plays no favorites! It makes no difference who you are or where you're from—if you want God and are ready to do as God says, the door is open. The message is sent to the children of Israel—that through Jesus Christ everything is being put together again—well, he's doing it everywhere, among everyone.'

"They invited Peter to tell them the Story, and while he was doing just that, the Holy Spirit fell upon them all, and they began speaking in other languages, praising God, just as the disciples had on the day of Pentecost. Peter turned to those looking on in amazement, and said, 'Surely no one can refuse the water for these to be baptized, can they? For they have received the Holy Spirit just as we did.' And so they baptized them in the name of Jesus Christ.

"After that, Peter returned to the church in Judea, excited to tell them that the gentiles were no longer outsiders. But some gathered there were angry with him, and said, 'What do you think you're doing rubbing shoulders with that crowd, eating what is prohibited and ruining our good name?' How many times had the disciples heard such words as these coming out of the mouths of the Pharisees when they criticized Jesus for his choice of dining companion?" She sighs as she looks at the merchant. "How often have some of us? Peter told them all that had happened, and then they understood and glorified God for bringing outsiders, gentiles, into the family.

"But there were still those who were unhappy about this, and they began to tell the gentile believers that they had to receive the mark of the old covenant, circumcision, in order to be saved. Circumcision had been replaced by baptism, the sign of the new covenant, but some among my people would not accept that. Others, including our apostle Paul, argued that circumcision was not necessary for gentiles, and they believed that the unity of the followers of Jesus was deeply threatened by this.

"So Paul came to Jerusalem to report to the elders what God was doing among the gentiles. But even then, instead of rejoicing with him, they began arguing. Finally Peter stood up and challenged the council, saying, 'Friends, you well know that from early on it was made quite plain that God wanted the pagans to hear the message of this good news and embrace it. And God, who can't be fooled by any pretense on our part, gave them the Holy Spirit exactly as God did for us. God treated the outsiders exactly as God treated us, beginning at the very center of who they were and working from that center outward, cleaning up their lives as they trusted and gave their allegiance to God. So why are you now trying to out-god God, loading these new believers down with something that neither we nor our ancestors could bear? Don't we believe that we are saved because the Lord Jesus amazingly and out of sheer generosity moved to save us just as he did those beyond our nation? So what are we arguing about?'

"After more debate, James, the half-brother of Jesus, stood up and declared that the gentiles did not need to be circumcised, and that they were an equal part of the church. He spoke up because he saw that what was happening was that of which the prophet Amos had spoken centuries before. He understood that the building up of the community of Jesus' followers with gentiles alongside children of Abraham was indeed the restoration of the house of David. Together they formed the people of the new covenant.

"Paul commented on this in a letter to the *ekklesia* in Galatia: 'In

Christ's family there can be no division into Jew and non-Jew, slave
and free, male and female. Since you are Christ's family, then you are
all children of Abraham, heirs according to the covenant promises.'
Still, the elders in Jerusalem did not accept this for a long time. Later
on they even made Paul perform one of my people's religious rites in
order to prove himself to them—and to those who were accusing Paul
of teaching those like us, who live among gentiles, not to circumcise
our children. Instead of refusing to listen to gossip and standing by
Paul and his work among the gentiles, they asked him to make this
concession to his accusers." She shakes her head, saying, "Still so slow
to believe."

The merchant asks, "But Jesus' disciples—they understood, surely?"

The woman replies, "Not for a long time I am afraid. The disciples,
including Peter, revealed early on that they still had not understood
all that Jesus had tried to teach them. As the church grew in numbers,
they were serving a daily meal for many of the widows among them—
that at least they had learned from Jesus. After a while, some of the
Greek-speaking widows complained that they were being discrimi-
nated against.

"The twelve disciples called everyone together and said, 'It wouldn't
be right for us to neglect preaching the word of God in order to serve at
table. So choose seven men from among you whom everyone trusts, men
full of the Holy Spirit and good sense, and we'll assign them to the task.
But we will devote ourselves to prayer, and to speaking God's word.'

"Perhaps the twelve thought that waiting at tables was somehow
beneath them, or that preaching was more important. How quickly
they had forgotten what Jesus had said to them at that last meal they
shared together,

> Kings like to throw their weight around and people in authority
> like to give themselves fancy titles. It's not going to be that way
> with you. Let the senior among you become like the junior; let
> the leader act the part of the servant.
>
> For who is greater, the one who reclines at the table or the

one who serves at table? Is it not the one who reclines at the table? But I am among you as the one who serves.

"And yet, there they were saying, 'It wouldn't be right for us to neglect preaching in order to serve at table.' They had not listened to Jesus.

"But others understood. Among the seven people chosen to serve the widows were Stephen and Philip. Stephen later stood before the Sanhedrin and told the Story, and was stoned to death for it, becoming the first martyr of the church. And Philip took the good news to Samaria, even telling the Story to a man from Ethiopia—someone from the ends of the earth—baptizing him before he returned to Africa. These men who waited at table acted as apostles, doing just what Jesus had told the disciples to; whereas the disciples stayed in Jerusalem and argued about who was truly welcome in the kingdom.

"But they did finally learn, and went their separate ways, taking the good news of the kingdom, the Story of God, wherever the Spirit led them." The host's body slumps forward. "For many of them, telling the Story has cost them their life. Peter was killed in Rome after the Great Fire,* crucified just as his Lord was. Paul was beheaded; being a Roman citizen spared him from crucifixion.'"

The *ekklesia* still feels these losses deeply, and tears come to the eyes of those listening to the story. The merchant is surprised to find himself wiping tears from his own eyes. "Yet you still choose to give your allegiance to Christ. I think you are as remarkable as your Jesus."

The woman shakes her head and says with a sad smile, "We do not think so. We have found a way of living, a common life that is beautiful and, yes, costly at times. We share a deep hope and a joy from being a small part of the work of new creation that God is doing. We experience the same sense of *koinonia*† that those first *ekklesias* did." She perks up. "Let me tell you of life in the early days of the church.

"Those first believers committed themselves to the teaching of the

---

*The 'Great Fire' was the burning of Rome (during which "Nero fiddled"), in C.E. 64.
†*Koinonia* is a Greek word meaning "communion," or fellowship created by intimate participation in each others' lives.

apostles, to fellowship, sharing a common meal and praying. Everyone around was in awe—all those wonders and signs done through
the apostles! And all the believers lived in a wonderful harmony, holding everything in common. They sold whatever they owned and
pooled their resources so that each person's need was met. They followed a daily discipline of worship in the Temple followed by meals at
home, every meal a celebration, exuberant and joyful, as they praised
God. People looked on and liked what they saw. Every day their number grew as God added those who were being saved.

"As they shared what they had with each other, so that there was
not a needy person among them, they recalled the stories of their ancestors in the wilderness, and God's provision of manna, so everyone
always had enough—God continued to give them daily bread.

"As time went on they embraced the mission of God, telling the
Story wherever they went, finally living life together in the way that
God had always intended, as God had given in Torah. They saw before
their very eyes the words of Deuteronomy become reality: 'There will
be no poor among you, since the LORD will surely bless you in the land
which the LORD your God is giving you . . . if only you listen obediently
to the voice of the LORD your God, and carefully keep Torah.'

"Other people looked on at their common life and were amazed:
there was nothing in their culture that could explain what they were
seeing. And the same is true for many of us." She turns to the newcomers. "We were drawn to the *ekklesia* because of the life we saw our
friends living. For in the *ekklesias*, people who should not be friends
become friends, breaking bread together, sharing all they have with
each other, unashamed to call each other sister and brother."

The merchant says, "The philosophers of my people write of the
friendship you describe—and which I see you all share—as the
highest ideal of human love, which few if any could ever achieve. Yet
here you are, fishermen and businesswomen, slaves and masters,
young and old, sitting at the same table together, sharing the same
bread, and drinking the same cup. You are . . . not the kind of people
the philosophers thought could live this way."

The woman laughs. "It's no wonder that Paul wrote, 'Take a good look friends, at who you were when you got called into this life. I don't see many of "the brightest and the best" among you, not many influential, not many from high-society families. Isn't it obvious that God deliberately chose men and women that the culture overlooks and exploits and abuses, chose these "nobodies" to expose the hollow pretensions of the "somebodies"? That makes it quite clear that none of you can get by with blowing your own horn before God. Everything that we have—right thinking and right living, a clean slate and a fresh start—comes from God by way of Christ Jesus.'

"The early churches certainly were communities of ragamuffins, but people kept joining them, drawn by what God was doing in their midst. They found themselves standing square in the middle of God's covenant promises to Abraham, God blessing the nations of the world through God's people. They may have been a bunch of ragamuffins, but there were some remarkable men and women in the church."

"Especially women," her old friend says, lifting his cup to toast her. He turns to the merchant. "Besides Dorcas, who our host briefly mentioned, there was also Lydia, who was head of her household. When Paul told the Story in Philippi, Lydia heard him and gave her allegiance to Jesus. When she returned to her hometown, Thyatira, she told the Story there, and the whole community became believers. As head of the household, she became the leader of the church that met in her home—like my dear friend here.

"In Thessalonica there were some prominent Greek women who studied the Scriptures with Paul and became believers. And Priscilla and her husband Aquila taught Apollos, a man well-versed in the Scriptures. Priscilla corrected his misunderstanding of the Story before he went to Corinth to lead the church there. Since the beginning, God has used both men and women to lead the *ekklesias*."

The woman smiles and raises her cup to her old friend, and then addresses the *ekklesia*. "My friends, as always it has been a joy to share this meal with you. But now it is getting late. Before we depart for our homes, I would like to read from one more letter." She reaches behind her for one of her precious scrolls. "This is a letter Peter wrote to circulate among the *ekklesias*, to encourage and exhort us in our allegiance to Jesus—the allegiance which cost him his life. Let us listen and take his words to heart." She unrolls the scroll, and reads.

"So clean house! Make a clean sweep of malice and pretense, envy and hurtful talk. You've had a taste of God. Now, like infants at the breast, drink deep of God's pure kindness. Then you'll grow up mature and whole in God.

Welcome to the living Stone, the source of life. The workmen took one look and threw it out; God set it in the place of honor. Present yourselves as building stones for the construction of a sanctuary vibrant with life, in which you'll serve as holy priests offering Christ-approved lives up to God. The Scriptures provide precedent:

Look! I'm setting a stone in Zion,
    a cornerstone in the place of honor.
Whoever trusts in this stone as a foundation
    will never have cause to regret it.
To you who trust him, he's a Stone to be proud of, but to those
        who refuse to trust him,

The stone the workmen threw out
    is now the chief foundation stone.
For the untrusting it's

. . . a stone to trip over,
    a boulder blocking the way.
They trip and fall because they refuse to obey,
        just as predicted.

But you are the ones chosen by God, chosen for the high calling of priestly work, chosen to be a holy people, God's instruments to do God's work and speak out for God, to tell others of the night-and-day difference God made for you—from nothing to something, from rejected to accepted."

The woman returns the scroll to its place, and then offers some parting words to her friends. "Let us remember who we are—and whose we are. And let us go to tell the Story, to be God's priests in the world, to bring others into an experience of the new exodus, the return from exile—no longer estranged from God and from each other—and to partner in the work of new creation!"

As the *ekklesia* makes their way into the night, the merchant lingers. He takes the arm of the old man as he passes, and then turns to the woman. Looking them both in the eye he says, "I have one more question to ask you."

The three talk late into the night in hushed, sober tones. One question turns into two and then three as the merchant continues to wrestle with the Story and the implications of accepting the invitation he hears to find his place in it.

12

consummation

In which we hear what it means to embrace the

Story as it moves toward the end . . .

It is the first day of the week. As his friends arrive to break bread together, the old man looks around the group assembling in his house. As he does, his mind goes back to a setting very similar to this one, to the time when he first heard the Story of God.

That group met in an open courtyard, sharing their meals together publicly. This group dares not meet so openly, instead gathering in an interior room of his home, after dark. The face of his gracious host from those long years ago comes to mind, and he smiles fondly. Who would have thought that almost three decades later he would be hosting an *ekklesia* in his home? That now he would be the one to tell the Story to newcomers?

He had stayed in that city for several months, learning the Story of God from the woman and her friend. Everything was so new to him, and he continued to have many questions. As he shared life with them he realized that he was beginning to give believing allegiance to their Jesus. Was there a particular day when he decided to abandon his gods and serve Christ instead? He does not remember. He simply stopped going to the temples and shrines of those other gods.

If there was a day, it was probably when he approached a customer in the market—a good customer who no longer placed orders with him. *Why was this so?* he wanted to know. The man replied, "I do not do business with 'Christians.'" He remembers standing there stunned, unable to respond as his former customer turned on his heel and walked away. He closed up shop and walked down to the river to think. And to pray—to Jesus.

That night he told the woman that he wished to receive the sign of the covenant; he wished to be baptized in gratitude for the forgiveness of his sins, to formally declare his allegiance to Jesus and to be anointed for service of God's kingdom in the new creation. And so he had been. A month or so later, as business continued to decline, he met with the woman and her friend and told them he intended to return to his home city to carry the message of Jesus—to tell the Story of God to his family and friends.

His shoulders sag as he remembers the cold reception he received. They would not listen, accusing him of bringing shame upon the family. Some never spoke to him again. Nevertheless, he spent many hours telling the Story to customers in his shop, and a few of them began to meet with him in his home to break bread and hear more. Those few were the beginnings of the *ekklesia* he has hosted and led all these years.

Many of those who fled in the diaspora that followed the destruction of Jerusalem* had made their way to his city. He had welcomed those refugees, helping them to become established here. He chuckles as he remembers their amazement that he knew so much of their people's story, and as he looks around the room he sees the faces of those who chose to embrace Jesus as Messiah.

They had told horror stories of the Roman siege of Jerusalem and the destruction of the Temple—all of which, he recalls, Jesus had foreseen and tried to forewarn his people. In response to an uprising of zealots, Titus Flavius's legions had besieged and finally utterly laid waste to the city, even digging up the foundations of the city walls, so that not one stone remained upon another—except for one section of wall, left intact to demonstrate how great a city had once stood in that spot, and to bear witness to the penalty for defying the Empire.

But you do not have to take up arms against Rome to threaten the power of Empire, he thinks. He looks around him at the small group of men and women huddled together, some with anxious expressions

---

*Jerusalem was sacked and destroyed by the Romans during Vespasian's rule in C.E. 70.

on their faces revealed in the light of oil lamps, whose smoke coils and writhes upward to blacken the low ceiling of the room. He wipes the back of his hand across his eyes as he thinks of Tychicus, one of their number, who was executed today. Their community is growing ever smaller, as some are killed while others slip away, unable to endure the persecution they are undergoing.

He sighs deeply. Those left need a word of hope, a reason to keep going; they need to hear from God, to hear that God has not forgotten them, and that their suffering is not in vain.

He smiles wearily to himself, for he too needs a word of hope. And so the old man once more reaches for the letter that has been circulating among the churches. As his brothers and sisters share a meal together, he says, "My friends, hear again the message of God to the churches.

"'The revelation of Jesus Christ, which God gave to make plain to God's servants what is about to happen. God delivered it by angel to God's servant John. And John told everything he saw: God's word—the witness of Jesus Christ! How blessed the reader! How blessed the hearers and keepers of these prophetic words, and all the words written in it.

"'Time is just about up—'"

A knock at the door! Some of his guests jump to their feet in alarm. But a few moments later a familiar face appears. "I'm sorry I'm late, but I was delayed." They breathe a collective sigh of relief and settle down. He then turns and beckons toward a couple standing behind him. The group casts wary glances at the strangers but makes room for them in the circle, offering them bread and wine, as the late arrival addresses his friends. "I went to the executions today."

Before the group can protest, he continues. "I know, I know. Foolishness. But I had to. I watched as they strung up some bandits. And then they brought Tychicus out. He had been beaten and was struggling to stand. He was no more than a stone's throw away from where I stood, but he never looked in my direction. One eye was closed, anyway. As they drew their swords, he squared his shoulders, and lifted his face to heaven. I could see he was praying. They hit him from behind, and he fell to his knees."

A pause. Tears roll gently down the man's cheeks. "As they read out the charges against him—'blasphemy against the divinity of the emperor'—he looked them in the eye, and I could hear him clearly as he said, 'Father, forgive them, they don't know what they're doing.' The sword swung, and our brother gave his life for our Lord.

"I could not hold back the tears, and knew I was in danger, so I left quickly and made my way across town to be here tonight. But I was followed—by them." He gestures toward the two women. "As I ducked down an alley, they called out, asking me to stop. I was afraid and almost ran, but something prevented me from doing so.

"They approached me and looked around before asking, 'Are you one of the "Christians"?' I wanted to say 'No!' But how could I, having just witnessed what I did? So I said, 'Yes, I am.'" He turns to one of the women, "Tell them what you told me."

The woman looks at the faces gazing at her with keen interest. "My friend and I have witnessed many public executions. You Christians do not die like the others, begging for mercy. You do not kiss the image of the emperor and save yourselves. We know some of you have lost your homes; we are not permitted to trade with you. How can you live? They say you are idolaters, atheists, even cannibals! But we watch how you die. And we see how you live. And we cannot explain it. So we wish to know more of this Jesus, this Christ that you claim as Lord, and for whom you are willing to die. Will you tell us?"

The group looks to the old man, who finds himself smiling unexpectedly. "I was just about to do that. Please, stay, share our meal and listen." They smile in return, and the leader picks up the scroll again to continue.

"'I John am writing this to the seven churches in Asia province: grace to you and peace, from the God who is, who was and who is to come; and from the Seven Spirits assembled before God's throne, and from Jesus Christ—Loyal Witness, Firstborn from the dead, Ruler of all earthly kings.'"

He looks around the circle of expectant faces. "These are dark days for us. We have lost family and friends, and their fate may await some of us. Others among us have left, unable to endure what we are suffering. Perhaps some of us are thinking of doing the same. We are all asking the same question: Why does God not deliver us from evil? How long will God allow the wicked to prosper? Why does God stand far off, hiding in times of trouble?" He looks around the circle; many are nodding their heads. He lifts his head and declares, "Yet God is where God has always been: on God's throne, as the psalmist also says, 'The LORD's throne is in heaven, the LORD sees. God tests the sons of men. The LORD tests the righteous and the wicked, and God hates the one who loves violence.' Throughout the Revelation the LORD is on the throne, sovereign, no matter what humanity does. We may think that Rome is in charge—after all, who can challenge its military and economic power? But empires rise, and empires fall, and God is still Ruler of all.

"The persecution we are undergoing has given us tunnel vision. We must lift our eyes to the throne, where the Alpha and the Omega sits, the One who is, who was and who is to come, Almighty God."

He returns to the letter. "John received the Revelation of Jesus Christ when he was in the Spirit on the Lord's Day. And he has sent it to us, to seven churches: Ephesus, Smyrna, Pergamum, Thyatira, Sardis, Philadelphia and Laodicea."

"There are Christians in only these seven cities?"

The leader looks at the questioner, one of the newcomers. "What is your name?"

"Hera," the woman replies.

"An auspicious name! The wife of Zeus, and queen of the gods, no?"

The woman says shyly, "Yes. But you Christians say there is only one God, is that not so?"

The leader looks around the circle. "Yes, we believe in the One God, the Alpha and the Omega. And so do the people of Israel, but they have permission from the emperor for their belief in the One God, although they are taxed for it; we do not, and so we are charged with blasphemy for refusing to embrace the official religion of the empire.

"Which brings me back to your question. There are Christians throughout the empire, in many, many cities. But the imperial cult, the worship of the emperor, has important centers in these seven cities. So these seven churches represent all those Christians who are facing persecution because of their allegiance to Jesus, the Christ, and their rejection of the cult of empire."

The leader returns once again to the text, reading each of the messages that Jesus gave John to give to the seven churches before commenting, "Each message has a similar structure to it. First, Jesus is identified in ways that echo the beginning of the Revelation: 'The First and the Last'; 'The Son of God'; 'The Holy One, the True One'; 'The Amen, the faithful and true Witness.' Then Jesus tells each church that he knows their situation. Some are commended, while others are chastised. Then Jesus gives an exhortation and a promise to each church, ending each message with the same phrase: 'Are your ears awake? Listen. Listen to the words of the Spirit blowing through the churches.'"

"Wait!" Hera says. "I thought Jesus was talking. What is this Spirit?"

The leader laughs. "Yes, it is confusing the first time you hear it, as I well remember. We believe that Jesus is present to us in the Spirit, even as he is seated at the right hand of God the Father." And the leader once more finds himself with the difficult task of explaining to someone who serves many gods the concept of one God who exists as a community of relationships.

The group returns to discussing the messages to the churches. The descendants of Abraham comment once more on similarities they hear in the prophet Daniel's message. "As we have listened to the letter," the old man says, "it seems that the message of Revelation is directed at four groups: to those wavering in their conviction, the Revelation counsels faithfulness; to those holding firm in their obedience to God, it encourages endurance; to those who are losing their life through martyrdom, it promises reward; and to those persecuting the faithful, it pronounces judgment."

Hera, looking at her friend, speaks up again. "Is your God going to judge us? After all, till now we have obeyed the emperor and have had nothing to do with you Christians. Are we included in those who are persecuting you?"

The leader leans forward, for this is an important question. "Hera, remember that we have just read the messages to the *churches*. God will judge us *all*, pagan and Christian alike. As we hear the rest of the Revelation, you will see that there is really just one central question that Jesus poses to us: 'Where does your allegiance lie?'

"As we listen to Jesus' words in this letter, some of us in the church will be surprised to discover that we are not, in fact, on God's side after all. As we continue, you will see that the kingdoms of this world often stand in opposition to the kingdom of God, and anyone who is more invested in the systems of empire than in God's kingdom is standing in a very precarious place, even if they are part of the church."

Hera throws up her arms and exclaims, "Then who can be saved?"

The leader picks up the scroll once more, rolling ahead to find the place he is looking for. "Let us see if this is helpful. 'Then I heard a loud voice in heaven say, "Salvation and power are established! Kingdom of our God, authority of God's messiah! The accuser of our brothers and sisters thrown out, the one who accused them day and night before God. They defeated him through the blood of the Lamb and the bold word of their witness. Their love was not for themselves but for Jesus and they were willing to die for Christ."'

"Hera, the Revelation of Jesus is a call for us to overcome, as we heard in each of the messages to the seven churches. We are called to overcome all those powers that stand in opposition to God's reign, however seductive they may be. Rome is the most powerful empire this world has ever seen. But its glory and wealth have come through its military and economic oppression of all those it has conquered. The Revelation of Jesus gives us a view from the 'underside of history,' from the perspective of the victims of Rome's power and glory. God invites us to seek and enter God's kingdom, which means we must refuse to bow to any other gods—including any empire, nation or state that demands our allegiance and which uses economic and military power to further its own interests at the expense of others. And if we do that, if we refuse to bow down to such idols, then we will be maligned and mistreated; and as you—and we—know all too well, we may lose our lives for remaining faithful to God.

"But our death is not defeat! This is the hope of the Revelation. For this letter challenges our imagination. It lifts the veil from our eyes and allows us to see our situation—and indeed, all of history—from God's perspective.

"To those of us who look at our situation and see things as basically all right, it challenges us to see things as they really are. And for those of us who see things as being terrible, it offers encouragement. Seeing things from God's eternal perspective calls us to respond, calls us to overcome, to take up the weapons of overcoming that God has provided us: not the sword and the spear but patient endurance and faithfulness, knowing that the battle has already been won, even if it seems we are losing it. Remember, God is seated on the throne."

The woman's brow wrinkles. "So are you saying that by focusing on a reward in 'heaven' you will be able to escape what's going on all around you?"

"No!" The old man says earnestly. "I'm not saying that the here-and-now gets left behind by a belief in mystical future events; rather, the here-and-now looks quite different when it is open to the perspective of eternity that calls us to faithful living today."

There is silence for a while as the people reflect on what has just been said and what it might mean for each of them. Hera once more breaks the silence. "What you just read, the part about the blood of the lamb? What does that mean? How does that help anyone overcome, as you said?"

A member of the *ekklesia* speaks up. "That sounds like the part of the letter that talks about the scroll in heaven, the one that no one was worthy to open—when John wept."

"That's right," the leader says. "Let me read that part to you." He finds the place and reads, "'One of the Elders said to me, "Don't weep. Look—the Lion from Tribe Judah, the Root of David's Tree, has conquered. He can open the scroll, can rip through the seven seals."'"

"Who is this Lion?" asks Hera.

He reads further. "'So I looked and there, surrounded by Throne, Animals and Elders was a Lamb slaughtered, but standing tall. Seven horns he had, and seven eyes, the Seven Spirits of God sent into all the earth.'" The old man looks up at Hera. "The Lion is Jesus."

"Wait a minute, I thought we were hearing about a Lion. Now it's a Lamb? I am completely lost!"

The leader looks at Hera with compassion, remembering the time, long ago, when a woman invited him into the *ekklesia* that met in her home and first told him the Story. "It will be hard for you to understand much of the rest of the Revelation, Hera, because you do not know the story of God's people, nor our Scriptures. The Revelation comes to us in the form of 'apocalypse,' something that few people can understand outside those deeply steeped in its style. Some believe the images in this apocalypse are timeless symbols, which each generation must reinterpret for itself. Others believe that the images can be decoded to predict future events. But in reality the strange and wonderful images of the Revelation are full of allusions from our Scriptures, and also full of contemporary allusions from our culture."

"Give me an example. That would help."

"Well, an easy one is the numbers found in the Revelation." Someone pipes up, "Yes, it's full of numbers: three, six, seven—lots of sevens!—twelve, even 144,000."

Hera looks in the direction of the voice. "What's the point of them all?"

The old man answers her. "I wonder if the point of all the numbers is that there *is* no point to them; they are not precise calculations that somehow need to be decoded to be understood. The *importance* of the numbers is that they lend a sacred character to what is being described. The frequent repetition of the patterns of numbers remind us that we do not live in a world of chaos but that we inhabit a God-ordered cosmos unfolding in a God-ordained way, just as we have seen from the very beginning of the Story. That is why, even in terrible times such as these, we can continue to trust that God is working God's purposes out, and will continue to do so until God brings all things to an end."

Hera speaks up. "Well, if I don't understand your numbers, what about the contemporary allusions you were talking about? Perhaps I can understand some of those."

"Yes, I think you will be able to, Hera. Most of the 'secrets' of the Revelation are actually revealed in other places. For the last few weeks we have been talking about a 'Beast' described in the scroll; perhaps you can discover its identity. Let me begin, though, with 'the Dragon.'"

He rolls the scroll to the place he's thinking of and reads, "'When the Dragon saw he'd been thrown to earth he persecuted the Woman who had given birth to the Man-Child and then went off to make war with the rest of her children, who keep God's commands, and hold firm to the witness of Jesus. And the Dragon stood on the sand of the seashore. I saw a Beast coming out of the sea. And the Dragon turned over its power to the Beast, its throne and great authority.'

"Now, Hera, you probably won't see who this Dragon is as quickly as we who know our Scriptures do. But this Dragon is Satan, the devil, the one who opposes God's purposes in the world, and the one who stands behind all nations and empires that act in opposition to God."

Hera's face begins to show the light of comprehension. "But if the Dragon is standing on the seashore, that is at the margins of evil, correct? Because the sea represents chaos, the evil powers loose in the world."

"That's right, Hera. Our Story tells us the same thing that yours does. But if the Dragon stands on the margins of evil and welcomes a Beast coming out of the sea, and gives him power and his throne and great authority . . ."

"Then that must be Rome!" she exclaims. "Who else came across the sea and conquered us, and has great power and authority?"

"That is what we think also, Hera. Listen, as the Revelation continues, 'I saw another Beast rising out of the ground. It had two horns like a lamb but sounded like a dragon when he spoke. It was a puppet of the first Beast, and made earth and everyone in it worship the first Beast.'"

"He's talking about the imperial cult—worshiping the emperor. And even though he's a dragon, he looks like a lamb . . . We're being deceived!" Her brow wrinkles again. "But we keep talking about 'lambs'—is this the same one?"

"No, Hera. Remember, this is really a beast that looks like a lamb. The true Lamb is the One standing in the midst of the throne of God, of whom the elders in heaven sing, 'Worthy is the Lamb that was slain! Take the power, the riches, the wisdom, the strength! Take the honor, the glory, the blessing!' The One before whom the elders fall down and worship: this is Jesus. You came here to learn more about him, and now seems like a good time to introduce you to his Story."

The old man starts at the beginning, with Torah, and continues through all the Prophets, pointing out everything in the Scriptures that referred to Jesus. When he finishes telling them the Story, there are tears in their eyes. "We have been deceived! The emperor is not divine. And all our other gods, they have no real power. And we have been killing you Christians, just as Jesus was killed. We are guilty of their blood! God will surely judge us!"

"No, Hera, you will not be judged for ignorance. You will be judged, as we all will, for those ways in which you willingly participated in the imperial system that stands opposed to God's purposes in the world. For Rome is just the latest in a long line of powerful nations that oppose God's will. And many more will rise up after Rome falls.

"The Revelation describes Rome thus: 'Babylon the great,' the city 'built on seven hills,' who causes the nations to drink the wild wine of her whoring, and the kings of the earth to go off whoring with her, and the merchants of the earth to become rich by partnering with her.' We must choose whether we will be part of 'Babylon' or refuse its

ways. And those who will come after us will face the same choice that
we do, because any society for whom Babylon's cap will fit must wear
it. Any society which absolutizes its own economic prosperity at the
expense of others, will come under Babylon's condemnation. And
those of us in the church who choose to willingly benefit from such
oppressive economic practices backed by military might—those who
bear what the letter describes as 'the mark of the beast'—will fall
under the same condemnation as Babylon.

"This mark is symbolized by the number 666—a way of saying
that somebody has so profoundly lost their way that they are acting in
opposition to God." He pauses. "And those of us who choose to oppose Babylon's practices, to disassociate from Rome's oppressive system and instead adopt the practices God has given God's people since
the very beginning of our Story, will pay the price."

At this the leader's head droops as he, like the others, brings to
mind the faces of their friends for whom this has been true, those who
have paid the ultimate price for their believing allegiance to Jesus. But
then he lifts his head once more, and his voice gains strength as he
continues.

"But is this not what we should expect? Did not the powers-that-be
kill Jesus for challenging their authority? And yet, his death was not
the end! No, it was the beginning, for the Lamb that was slain is alive,
and those of us who remain faithful to the end will share in his victory
over death, and over the Dragon." Once more he takes up the scroll,
and reads.

"'I looked again. I saw a huge crowd, too huge to count. Everyone
was there—all nations and tribes, all peoples and languages. And
they were dressed in white robes and waving palm branches, standing
before the Throne and the Lamb and heartily singing: "Salvation to
our God on the Throne. Salvation to the Lamb!" All who were standing around the Throne—Angels, Elders, Animals—fell on their faces
before the Throne and worshiped God.

"'Just then one of the elders addressed me: "Who are these dressed
in white robes, and where did they come from?" Taken aback, I said,

"O Sir, I have no idea—but you must know." Then he told me, "These are those who come from the great tribulation, and they've washed their robes, scrubbed them clean in the blood of the Lamb. That's why they're standing before God's Throne. They serve God day and night in God's Temple. The One on the Throne will pitch his tabernacle there with them: no more hunger, no more thirst, no more scorching heat. The Lamb on the Throne will shepherd them, will lead them to spring waters of life. And God will wipe away every last tear from their eyes.""

As the leader finishes reading, tears freely flow down the cheeks of this tired group, this weary band of brothers and sisters. But they are not merely tears of pain; these are tears mixed with joy and hope, for their friends who have paid the price of martyrdom are now experiencing the truth of these words.

Hera's eyes too glisten with tears. "Beautiful. But is all you can hope for the promise of peace in heaven? Will this Dragon always be at war with God, deceiving the nations, killing God's people? Is this devil equal in power to your God?"

Once more the leader picks up the scroll, rolling it toward the end. "No, Hera, that is not how it will always be. Indeed, the victory has already been won. For Jesus defeated the power of sin and death—and all powers opposed to God—through the cross and his resurrection, and by his ascension to the right hand of God. We are called to resist the violence of empire through faithful worship of God and patient endurance. In the Revelation, Jesus' followers never take up arms themselves; they never embrace the myth of redemptive violence that empire relies upon. When Rome brings 'peace,' it creates a wasteland. But the Prince of Peace, Jesus, will one day bring an end to violence.

"In the Revelation, Jesus is primarily portrayed as a victim, as the slaughtered Lamb. The empire demands our worship, our unquestioning allegiance. But the one truly worthy of our worship and our allegiance is the Lamb who suffers violence and apparent defeat at the hands of empire. God's vindication of the Lamb is an indictment of the violence that has plagued humanity since the earliest days of our Story.

"And so in the Revelation's vision of the end of empires, the weapons of the Lamb are his own blood, and the sword of his mouth, the word of God—the proclamation of the kingdom of God. As our prophet Isaiah saw, there will be no end to his ever-expanding, peaceful kingdom.

"Hear now how the Revelation ends. 'I saw heaven and earth new-created. Gone the first heaven, gone the first earth, gone the sea.' At the end of history, the sea of chaos, which represents all that is evil, will be done away with."

"Then the earth," interjects Hera, "it will be destroyed also, and a new one replace it?"

"No," replies the old man. "The Creator God made a covenant with Noah, and all creation, that never again would God destroy creation. God is faithful to the covenant with creation. Thus God will finally abolish the sea of chaos and remove the threat of another flood. The 'new earth' is the first creation, finally restored to its original state."

The old man picks up where he left off. "'I saw Holy Jerusalem, new-created descending resplendent out of heaven, as ready for God as a bride for her husband.'" He looks up. "We, the church, will be the city of God, and as it has been throughout the Story, God will dwell in the midst of God's people.

"We are the bride of Christ. In the Revelation we read of 'the Marriage of the Lamb,' and we are told that 'his Bride has made herself ready.' An Angel declares, 'Blessed are those invited to the Wedding Feast of the Lamb.' The Story began with a marriage in the Garden of Eden. God made a marriage covenant with God's people Israel at Sinai. And when Jesus began his mission, it was at a wedding feast. So here, the Story ends with a marriage. The Story begins and ends with covenant love, and has been a story of love throughout."

The old man continues to read. "'I heard a voice thunder from the throne: "Behold, the tabernacle of God is among all people. God is making God's home with men and women. They're God's people. God will wipe away every tear from their eyes. Death is gone for good—tears gone, crying gone, pain gone—all the first order of things gone." And the One who sits on the Throne said, "Behold—I am making all things new." Then he said to me, "It is accomplished. I am the Alpha and Omega, the beginning and the end. The one who overcomes shall inherit these things.""""

The old man declares aloud, "The church, the New Jerusalem, will see the covenant God made with Abraham finally come to pass in all its fullness. For, as Jesus says, 'There is no Temple in the New Jerusalem, for the Lord God, the Almighty, and the Lamb are the Temple. The City doesn't need sun or moon for light. God's Glory is its light, the Lamb its lamp! The nations will walk in its light and earth's kings will bring in their splendor.'

"And just as the Story began with creation, it will end with the fullness of the new creation, humanity gathered around the Tree of Life in the Garden once more. 'The Tree of Life, which bears twelve kinds of fruit, a ripe fruit each month. The Tree of Life, whose leaves are for healing the nations. Never again will anything be cursed.' This is the full and final return from exile."

A reverent awe fills the room. Hera's trembling voice speaks once more. "When will this come to pass?"

The leader moves to the final words of the Revelation of Jesus.

"Behold, I am coming quickly, and I will render to everyone my reward according to how they have lived. I am the Alpha and the Omega, the first and the last, the beginning and the end. How blessed are those who wash their robes! The Tree of Life is theirs for good, and they'll walk through the gates into the City.

Yes, I'm on my way! I'll be there soon!

Amen. Come Lord Jesus."

The old man sets down the scroll and turns to the newcomers. "Hera, you and your friend have heard just some of the Story of God that has laid claim to our lives. No doubt you have many questions, as we all do. But the message of the Revelation of Jesus Christ leaves us all facing the same choice: to whom will we give our believing allegiance? Which Story will we choose to live by?

"My prayer is that you will choose the Story of God, and that you will come to experience the fullness of life in the new creation—the forgiveness of sins, a return from the alienation of exile, and the vocation of partnering in the mission of God to heal and restore shalom to all that is broken in God's beautiful world."

The old man rises to his feet and invites those gathered to do the same. He reads the final words of the Revelation as a parting benediction.

"The grace of the Lord Jesus be with all. Amen."

Postscript to the Reader

"Remember . . . remember . . . remember." That is God's constant refrain to God's people—because we are so quick to forget! But also remember that this telling of the Story of God is not *the* metanarrative of Scripture; it is *our* understanding of the metanarrative, which continues to deepen each time Rebecca and I walk through the Story with others.

May this book draw you deep into the grand Story of Scripture, as you read it with others and discuss the difficult question of what it means to be faithful to the God who makes covenant with us. Whether this is your first time to hear the Story, or the hundred and first time, may you hear the voice of God's *hesed*, God's lovingkindness, gently inviting you to step into the narrative and partner with God in the work of new creation.

Shalom.

Sources and References

Scripture references and external sources are listed in order of their first occurrence in each chapter. For the larger context of each chapter, see the "Suggested Scripture Readings" (p. 244). Scripture quotations in chapters 1-8, unless otherwise indicated, are taken from the New American Standard Bible. Scripture quotations in chapters 9-12, unless otherwise indicated, are taken from *The Message*. In both cases the translations have been adapted for minor matters of style and word choice.

CHAPTER 1: CREATION

Psalm 137.

Isaiah 49:15-16.

Genesis 1.

Deuteronomy 6:4.

Colossians 1:15.

Philippians 2:6-7.

Walter Brueggemann, *Genesis,* Interpretation (Atlanta: John Knox Press, 1982), pp. 35, 46. I am grateful to Brueggemann for his insights, particularly regarding "what it means to be human: vocation, permission and prohibition."

Genesis 2.

CHAPTER 2: CATASTROPHE

Psalm 121.

Genesis 3.

Dennis Kinlaw, *Let's Start with Jesus: A New Way of Doing Theology* (Grand Rapids: Zondervan, 2005). Some material in this chapter ("When she was tempted . . ."; "they died as one being . . ."; "This catastrophe began . . .") is quoted directly or paraphrased from pages 119 and 128.

Walter Brueggemann, *Genesis,* Interpretation (Louisville, Ky.: John Knox Press, 1982). The description of how "the impact of their actions touched every part of what it means to be human" is adapted from this source.

CHAPTER 3: COVENANT

Psalm 105.

Genesis 12; 15–18; 21–22.

Paul Borgman, *Genesis: The Story We Haven't Heard* (Downers Grove, Ill.: InterVarsity Press, 2001), pp. 41, 92, 96-97.

Isaiah 48.

Psalm 41:13; cf. Psalm 106:48; 136; Isaiah 40:28.

Walter Brueggemann, *The Prophetic Imagination,* 2nd ed. (Minneapolis: Augsburg Fortress, 2001).

Jeremiah 29:7.

Psalm 105.

CHAPTER 4: COMMUNITY (PART ONE): EXODUS

Exodus 1–14.

Rob Bell and Don Golden, *Jesus Wants to Save Christians* (Grand Rapids: Zondervan, 2008), esp. pp. 35, 144.

Exodus 15.

Desmond Tutu, quoted in Shane Claiborne and Chris Haw, *Jesus for President* (Grand Rapids: Zondervan, 2008), p. 46.

CHAPTER 5: COMMUNITY (PART TWO): SINAI

Psalm 119:41-48 *The Message.*

Sandra Richter, *The Epic of Eden* (Downers Grove, Ill.: InterVarsity Press, 2009).

Deuteronomy 5.

Deuteronomy 28.

CHAPTER 6: CONQUEST

Judges 4–5.

Joshua 1–5.

Job 30:16-20.

Psalm 137.

Job 31:29-30.

Lawston Stone, "The Role and Status of Women in the People of God: An Old Testament Perspective," seminar, Asbury Theological Seminary, November 2, 2001.

CHAPTER 7: CROWN

Jeremiah 7:4.

Rob Bell and Don Golden, *Jesus Wants to Save Christians* (Grand Rapids: Zondervan, 2008), esp. pp. 40, 43.

Walter Brueggemann, *The Prophetic Imagination,* 2nd ed. (Minneapolis: Augsburg Fortress, 2001), esp. p. 36.

Psalm 51.

CHAPTER 8: CONCEIT

Psalm 74 NIV.

Ezekiel 10.

Ecclesiastes 12.

Isaiah 36–37.

Isaiah 39.

Jeremiah 7.

Ezekiel 36.

Isaiah 54.

Isaiah 58.

Isaiah 40.

Micah 6:8.

Jeremiah 29.

Jeremiah 16.

Isaiah 19:25.

Isaiah 65.

Rob Bell and Don Golden, *Jesus Wants to Save Christians* (Grand Rapids: Zondervan, 2008), esp. chap. 2.

Isaiah 9.

Daniel 7.

CHAPTER 9: CHRIST

Psalm 118:20-24, 26 NASB.

Matthew 1:1-17.

Luke 1:26-56.

Luke 2:25-32.

Malachi 3:1 NASB.

Micah 5:2 NASB.

Luke 3. The text of the "voice from heaven" is adapted from the NIV.

Isaiah 61:1-2.

Joel B. Green, *The Gospel of Luke*, New International Commentary on the New Testament (Grand Rapids: Eerdmans, 1997), pp. 728-29.

Class notes from Joel Green, "Exegesis of Luke, Asbury" Seminary, fall 2001.

Luke 9:18-24 NASB.

Colossians 1:13-17 NASB.

Philippians 2:5-8 NASB.

CHAPTER 10: CROSS

Luke 19:41.

Sandra Richter, *The Epic of Eden* (Downers Grove, Ill.: InterVarsity Press, 2009), p. 89.

Rob Bell and Don Golden, *Jesus Wants to Save Christians* (Grand Rapids: Zondervan, 2008), esp. pp. 144-47.

Colossians 1:18-23.

Philip Yancey, *Grace Notes* (Grand Rapids: Zondervan, 2009), entry for December 14.

Walter Wangerin, *Reliving the Passion* (Grand Rapids: Zondervan, 1992), pp. 145-46.

James Alison, "Thoughts on the Atonement," paper presented in Brisbane, Australia, August 2004 <www.jamesalison.co.uk/pdf/eng11.pdf>.

Isaiah 53 NASB.

"God's power is God's love" is a concept articulated by the late Ray Anderson, and shared repeatedly with me by my friend Matt Russell.

John 15:13-14. While most of this chapter is drawn from the Synoptic Gospels (Matthew, Mark and Luke), I have taken some creative license by including a few stories from John's Gospel—which was written two to three decades after this conversation would have taken place.

Philippians 2:5-8 *The Message*; 2:9-11 NIV.

CHAPTER 11: CHURCH

N. T. Wright, *Surprised by Hope* (San Francisco: HarperOne, 2008).

Luke 1:52-53 *The Message*.

1 Corinthians 15:20 NASB.

Matthew 6:10 KJV.

1 Corinthians 15:13-14 NASB.

Mark 16:15.

1 Corinthians 6:19, paraphrased.

Genesis 2:18.

Genesis 11.

Rob Bell and Don Golden, *Jesus Wants to Save Christians* (Grand Rapids: Zondervan, 2008).

John 14:11.

1 Peter 4:13.

Galatians 3:28.

Luke 22:24-26 *The Message;* 22:27 NASB.

Deuteronomy 15:4-5 NASB.

1 Corinthians 1:26.

1 Peter 2:1-10.

CHAPTER 12: CONSUMMATION

Psalm 11:4-5 NASB.

Luke Timothy Johnson, *The Writings of the New Testament* (Minneapolis: Fortress, 2002), pp. 575-76.

Richard Bauckham, *The Theology of the Book of Revelation* (Cambridge: Cambridge University Press, 1993), pp. 8, 20, 39 et passim.

Isaiah 9:7.

Rob Bell and Don Golden, *Jesus Wants to Save Christians* (Grand Rapids: Zondervan, 2008), p. 130.

SUGGESTED SCRIPTURE READINGS

When we have told the Story in a group setting, we have assigned Scripture readings—parts of the Bible from which the story being told is drawn—as "homework" for the following week. Reading the relevant Scriptures ahead of time helps people prepare for hearing the Story with others, and also raises questions for people to listen particularly for when the Story is told.

Now, we don't ask people to read all of the Old and New Testaments in the course of the study (although one gentleman did read the entire Bible in twelve weeks when he walked through the Story with us!). Instead, we offer two paths for the reading: the "sprint" and the "marathon." The sprint includes Scriptures that are directly referenced in the Story or that provide important background. The marathon entails reading much more widely outside the particular narrative being focused on each week.

So, here are the two paths. The numbers refer to the chapters to be read in each book of the Bible mentioned. Note that the amount of reading varies from week to week: some weeks the sprint has just a few chapters, while other weeks it has a marathon feel to it! We encourage you to read what you can ahead of time; you can always go back and read what you missed later.

Week	SPRINT	MARATHON
Creation	Genesis 1–2	Genesis 1–2
Catastrophe	Genesis 3–11	Genesis 3–11
Covenant	Genesis 12–22	Genesis 12–50
Community 1: Exodus	Exodus 1–15	Exodus 1–15
Community 2: Sinai	Exodus 16–24; 32–34; 40; Numbers 9–14; Deuteronomy 26–34	Exodus 16–40; Leviticus 1–5; 8–10; 16–19; 25–26; Numbers 9–14; 20–24; Deuteronomy 4–11; 15–18; 28–34
Conquest	Joshua 1–8; 22–24; Judges 1–8; 19–21	Joshua 1–24; Judges 1–8; 13–16; 19–21; Ruth 1–4
Crown	1 Samuel 1–3; 7–20; 24–31; 2 Samuel 1–2; 5–7; 11–12; 1 Kings 1–3; 6–11	1 Samuel 1–31; 2 Samuel 1–12; 22–24; 1 Kings 1–11; Proverbs 1–3; Ecclesiastes 1–6; 11–12
Conceit	1 Kings 12–19; 2 Kings 2–5; 17–25; Isaiah 1; 5–7; 38–43; 51–53; 64; Jeremiah 1–8; 11; 24–33; 52; Ezekiel 4–11; 34–37; Daniel 1–6; Ezra 1; 3–6; 9–10; Nehemiah 1–13; Malachi 1–4	All the sprint reading plus Jonah 1–4; Hosea 1–14; Micah 1–7
Christ	Luke 1:1–19:27	All the sprint reading plus Matthew 1–20; Mark 1–10; John 1:1–12:11
Cross	Luke 19:28–24:53	All the sprint reading plus Matthew 21–28; Mark 11:1–16:8; John 12:12–21:25
Church	Acts 1–15; 1 Peter 2	Acts 1–28; 1 Peter 1–5; 1 Corinthians 1–16; Philippians 1–4
Consummation	Revelation 1–5; 12–13; 19–22	Psalms 95–100; Daniel 7–12; Revelation 1–22

Select Bibliography

Bible versions used in *The Story of God, the Story of Us:*
The New American Standard Bible. La Habra, Calif.: Lockman Foundation, 1995.
Peterson, Eugene H. *The Message.* Colorado Springs: NavPress, 1993.

The soil from which *The Story of God, the Story of Us* sprang:
Wright, N. T. *The Challenge of Jesus.* Downers Grove, Ill.: InterVarsity Press, 1999.

Two excellent introductions to the Story of God:
Erlander, Daniel. *Manna and Mercy.* Freeland, Wa.: self-published, 1992.
Richter, Sandra L. *The Epic of Eden.* Downers Grove, Ill.: InterVarsity Press, 2008.

Books that significantly shaped my reading of the Story of God:
Bauckham, Richard. *The Theology of the Book of Revelation.* Cambridge: Cambridge University Press, 1993.
Borgman, Paul. *Genesis: The Story We Haven't Heard.* Downers Grove, Ill.: InterVarsity Press, 2001.
Brueggemann, Walter. *Genesis.* Interpretation series. Atlanta: John Knox Press, 1982.

————. *The Prophetic Imagination.* Minneapolis: Augsburg Fortress, 2001.

Green, Joel B. *Luke.* New International Commentary on the New Testament. Grand Rapids: Eerdmans, 1997.

Myers, Ched. *Binding the Strong Man.* Maryknoll, N.Y.: Orbis, 1988.

Wright, N. T. *The New Testament and the People of God.* Minneapolis: Fortress Press, 1992.

Books that were very helpful during the rewriting process:

Bauckham, Richard. *Bible and Mission.* Grand Rapids: Baker, 2003.

Bell, Rob, and Don Golden. *Jesus Wants to Save Christians.* Grand Rapids: Zondervan, 2008.

Hirsch, Alan. *The Forgotten Ways.* Grand Rapids: Brazos, 2006.

Kinlaw, Dennis F. *Let's Start with Jesus.* Grand Rapids: Zondervan, 2005.

Roberts, Vaughan. *God's Big Picture.* Downers Grove, Ill.: InterVarsity Press, 2002.

Sleeth, J. Matthew. *Serve God, Save the Planet.* Grand Rapids: Zondervan, 2006.

Wright, N. T. *Surprised by Hope.* New York: HarperCollins, 2008.

Books that introduced me to narrative theology:

McLaren, Brian D. *The Story We Find Ourselves In.* San Francisco: Jossey-Bass, 2003.

Theissen, Gerd. *The Shadow of the Galilean.* Minneapolis: Fortress Press, 1987.

Walsh, Brian J., and Sylvia Keesmaat. *Colossians Remixed.* Downers Grove, Ill.: InterVarsity Press, 2004.

One of my favorite books on reading the Bible:

Peterson, Eugene H. *Eat This Book.* Grand Rapids: Eerdmans, 2006.

A beautiful version of the Story for the whole family:

Lloyd-Jones, Sally and Jago. *The Jesus Storybook Bible.* Grand Rapids: Zondervan, 2007.

User's Guide

If you choose to read the book aloud with others, here are some suggestions for ways to interact with the Story together.

SETTING THE SCENE

When we first read the Story aloud with Communality in Lexington, Kentucky, we wanted to find a way to place ourselves in the setting in which the people of God found themselves during exile in Babylon. We met indoors instead of around a campfire under the stars, so we put a bunch of candles in the middle of the room and strung Christmas lights across the ceiling. As we listened to "On the Willows" from the musical *Godspell,* we dimmed the lights, lit the candles, and plugged in the Christmas lights, and prepared ourselves to hear the Story of God with the exiles. That ritual has been our pattern for reading the Story with others ever since.

INTERACTING WITH THE STORY

After completing each week's story, we would extinguish the candles. Everyone would be given a 3x5 card and a pen, and we would sit in silence for a few minutes, writing down our answers to two questions:

What was something that struck me as I heard the Story?

What question(s) came up for me as I heard the Story?

When the size of the group or the space where we were gathered allowed for it, we would break into groups of three or four. Using various media (markers, paint, modeling clay, pipe cleaners, etc.), each person would create a piece of artwork inspired by the Story, and then share it (along with their responses to the questions) with the other members of their group. Each group would then choose one piece of art and one question or observation to share with the wider group. As ostensibly simple as these interactions are, we find that each gathering invariably yields new insights for the whole group.

After we've completed all twelve chapters, we gather for a final time together to talk about our experience of the Story. We place multiple copies of the following questions in a hat:

- Which was your favorite chapter? Why?

- Which was your least favorite chapter? Why?

- Describe an "Aha!" moment you had from hearing the Story.

- What really challenged you from hearing the Story?

- What surprised you in the Story?

- Describe something that is really sticking with you from the Story.

The hat is passed around the room; each person draws a question, and then the group takes turns answering the question they drew out. The hat is passed again, and each person answers a question until it's time to end. (If someone draws the same question more than once, simply return it to the hat and draw again.)

Specific Ideas for Each Chapter

The following are ways we have interacted with the Story using various artistic media. We offer them here as a springboard for your own creativity.

Creation. Draw a picture of something that struck you from hearing the Story.

Catastrophe. Think of five or six words, phrases or pictures that describe the movement from the man and the woman being "naked and unashamed" to life lived outside the garden. Paint a picture to illustrate what you come up with.

Covenant. Build an "altar" (we used Styrofoam "stones") in a separate space from where the Story is being told. After hearing the Story, draw pictures to illustrate how God blessed Abraham and how God has blessed you. On a separate card, write down what you are relying on to secure your future. Then take a prayerful walk to the "altar" to lay down the card and what it names.

Community (Part One): Exodus. Using modeling clay, sculpt a response to one of these questions:

- Where have I experienced God's liberating power in my own life?

- Where have I seen God's liberating power at work in the world?

- Where do I still see the need for God's liberation in my life?

- Where do I still see the need for God's liberation in the world?

Community (Part Two): Sinai. Make a collage from magazine pictures that depicts the ways in which the world has shaped your identity. Discuss with the group how the Story of God is shaping your identity.

Conquest. Draw a picture of something that struck you from the Story.

Crown. As a group, discuss each of the three kings' stories; try to find a phrase, theme or event that sums up their individual reigns. Then draw three pictures that illustrate those phrases, themes or events.

Conceit. If the group is large enough, divide into eight smaller groups (of three or more people) and assign one chapter to each group. Groups have fifteen minutes to come up with a two-minute skit that portrays the major themes or highlights of their chapter. (We had a basket of props groups could use, including one prop that was mandatory for all eight groups to incorporate—in our case, a piñata sun.)

Christ. Using pipe cleaners, sculpt something that represents one of the major themes from the Story thus far that shows up in the life of Jesus.

Cross. This is a special week for us. We tell the Story in the context of a three-course meal, the Story punctuated by each of the three courses. We also watch the crucifixion scene from Franco Zeffirelli's *Jesus of Nazareth* (www.imdb.com/title/tt0075520/)—beginning from his carrying the cross through the streets of Jerusalem and ending with the silence after Jesus says, "It is accomplished." When we read about the meal on pages 185-86, we pass the cup and the bread in communion with Jesus and each other.

Church. As a small group, discuss the mission of the church, and then draw a picture of it together. Then describe where you see yourself participating in that mission (or where you would like to see yourself doing so).

Consummation. As a small group, create two collages from magazine pictures that depict the following:

• What "Babylon" looks like in our culture.

• What the kingdom of God "on earth as it is in heaven" looks like.

OTHER PEOPLE'S STORIES

Over the years the Story has been shared by all kinds of groups, in all kinds of places and in all kinds of ways. We have been inspired by people's creativity. One group hiked part of the Appalachian Trail together, pausing in various places to read the Story aloud. They began at a beautiful scenic overlook and heard the story of creation. They stopped at the top of a cliff to hear the catastrophe of the choices made by the first humans. After dinner they lay on their backs under the stars to hear the story of the covenant God made with Abraham. The next morning they crammed into a concrete outhouse to hear the story of oppression in Egypt. And so on.

Something to consider. What might an urban version of this kind of journey look like?

Another group, who met on a college campus, used 8' x 4' cardboard boxes as vessels for art for each week of the Story. As they heard the story of community, suspended from the ceiling above them was a box, a pillar of fire and a pillar of cloud painted on opposite sides. Each person was given a small box, on which they painted those things that they were tempted to make an idol in their life. Those small boxes were used to create a 10' tall "golden calf." When the group arrived at week ten, using several of the boxes they had painted during the weeks before, they built a 20' tall cross on the university quad.

Something to consider. How can you incorporate your group's unique talents and creative interests into your experience of the Story?

We've created a Facebook page where we hope you will share your experience of hearing the Story with others, along with creative ideas for telling the Story. Stop by www.facebook.com/storyofgod to interact with others about *The Story of God, the Story of Us.*

THE STORY OF GOD, THE STORY OF US

A Video Curriculum by

Sean Gladding explores the core themes of the Bible's story in six brief videos designed to stimulate conversation about who God is, who we are, and how the two intersect. Designed to enhance a group reading of *The Story of God, the Story of Us,* but equally valuable as a thematic survey of the Scriptures, this video will be your group's next great resource. Go to www.twotp.com and search for "Sean Gladding."

INDIVIDUAL VIDEOS: $15

SET OF SIX VIDEOS: $30

Interact with others about the Story on Facebook: www.facebook.com/storyofgod

LIKEWISE. *Go and do.*

A man comes across an ancient enemy, beaten and left for dead. He lifts the wounded man onto the back of a donkey and takes him to an inn to tend to the man's recovery. Jesus tells this story and instructs those who are listening to "go and do likewise."

Likewise books explore a compassionate, active faith lived out in real time. When we're skeptical about the status quo, Likewise books challenge us to create culture responsibly. When we're confused about who we are and what we're supposed to be doing, Likewise books help us listen for God's voice. When we're discouraged by the troubled world we've inherited, Likewise books encourage us to hold onto hope.

In this life we will face challenges that demand our response. Likewise books face those challenges with us so we can act on faith.

likewisebooks.com